OECD Urban Policy Reviews: Viet Nam

OECD
BETTER POLICIES FOR BETTER LIVES

This work is published under the responsibility of the Secretary-General of the OECD. The opinions expressed and arguments employed herein do not necessarily reflect the official views of OECD member countries.

This document, as well as any data and any map included herein, are without prejudice to the status of or sovereignty over any territory, to the delimitation of international frontiers and boundaries and to the name of any territory, city or area.

Please cite this publication as:
OECD (2018), *OECD Urban Policy Reviews: Viet Nam*, OECD Publishing, Paris.
http://dx.doi.org/10.1787/9789264286191-en

ISBN 978-92-64-28609-2 (print)
ISBN 978-92-64-28619-1 (PDF)

Series: OECD Urban Policy Reviews
ISSN 2306-9333 (print)
ISSN 2306-9341 (online)

The statistical data for Israel are supplied by and under the responsibility of the relevant Israeli authorities. The use of such data by the OECD is without prejudice to the status of the Golan Heights, East Jerusalem and Israeli settlements in the West Bank under the terms of international law.

Photo credits: Cover © Jeffrey Fisher

Corrigenda to OECD publications may be found on line at: *www.oecd.org/about/publishing/corrigenda.htm*.

Preface

Urbanisation will be one of the most important transformations of the 21st century. Already today, more than 50% of the world's population lives in cities. This figure is projected to reach 85% by 2100. Within 150 years, the urban population will have increased from less than 1 billion in 1950 to 9 billion by 2100. This highlights the need for better public policy to support quality urbanization, which is a shared responsibility across levels of government.

Southeast Asia is in the midst of the global urbanisation trend. Since 1990, Viet Nam's urban population has almost doubled, and since 2010 it is growing by 3% per year, which is even faster than the average of Southeast Asian countries (2.5%). Rapid urbanisation taking place in countries like Viet Nam can offer strong opportunities for economic growth. Indeed, cities have enormous potential for job creation, innovation and overall economic growth. The importance of cities to their wider metropolitan regions and the national economy makes them critical players in the international marketplace.

However, urbanisation *per se* cannot automatically bring such economic growth. To maximise the benefits of urbanisation, cities need to address a number of urban challenges, from traditional problems such as urban sprawl, traffic congestion, air and water pollution, abandoned districts and poverty, to newer issues such as competitiveness, innovation, city marketing, climate change and resilience. Effective urban governance is another critical factor for "getting cities right".

The OECD's urban programme has been set up as a forum for enhancing the evidence base, sharing experience, and tailoring policy responses through place-based solutions to common problems. The programme also aims to help countries implement global agendas, including the New Urban Agenda adopted at the Habitat III Conference in October 2016.

This is the first time an OECD Urban Policy Review has addressed a country in Southeast Asia. This report on Viet Nam provides a broad-based understanding of the country's urbanisation and related policy challenges, and suggests concrete policy options for the short, medium and long term. Implementation of these recommendations will help guide Viet Nam's decision-making towards better urban policies for better lives in this highly urbanised 21st century.

Lamia Kamal-Chaoui, Director
Centre for Entrepreneurship, SMEs, Regions and Cities
OECD

Foreword

Viet Nam has experienced rapid urbanisation. This urbanisation has contributed to the process of the *Doi Moi* reform since 1986 and the subsequent economic and social transformation of the country with a high economic growth of 7% on average in recent decades. However, Viet Nam is also faced with acute urban challenges including an unskilled labour force, an unstable job market in cities, a lack of urban infrastructure, serious flood risks, and weak institutional capacity. These challenges require that policies across a range of sectors be aligned. While many national policies affect urban development, they are rarely looked at through an "urban lens".

The OECD Urban Policy Review of Viet Nam provides a comprehensive assessment of Viet Nam's urban policies and analyses how national spatial planning for urban areas, along with specific sectoral policies, directly and indirectly affect Viet Nam's urban development. It points to a number of policy areas which Viet Nam can tap into, in order to fully capitalise on the unique opportunities that its urbanisation process may bring about, including urban transport, housing, land, the quality of urban environment, and urban green growth. The review also assesses the efficiency and effectiveness of current urban governance arrangements, and makes recommendations for Viet Nam to develop an attractive and well-managed system of large and medium-sized cities, thereby contributing to achieving its sustainable development objectives.

OECD Urban Policy Reviews are conducted by the OECD Regional Development Policy Committee through its Working Party on Urban Policy, a unique forum for international exchange and debate. The OECD reviews follow a consistent methodology that features cross-national comparisons and recommendations on the integration of sectoral policies into urban development policy, planning and programmes. The OECD has previously carried out six Urban Policy Reviews: Poland (2011), Korea (2012), Chile (2013), People's Republic of China (2015), Mexico (2015) and Kazakhstan (2017).

Acknowledgements

This review of Viet Nam is part of a series of Urban Policy Reviews produced by the OECD Centre for Entrepreneurship, SMEs, Regions and Cities under the leadership of Lamia Kamal-Chaoui within the Programme of Work of the Regional Development Policy Committee and its Working Party on Urban Policy. This report was made possible through the contribution of the Japanese Ministry of Finance, the French Development Agency, the United Nations Human Settlement Programme (UN-Habitat), the Global Green Growth Institute (GGGI) and the Ministry of Construction of Viet Nam.

The OECD Secretariat is grateful for the co-operation and support of several officials and experts in Viet Nam who responded to the OECD questionnaire and prepared the background report to this study, and who organised the field trips and interviews of the OECD team. Special thanks are herein conveyed to H.E. Pham Hong Ha, Minister of Construction of Viet Nam, H.E. Phan Thi My Linh, Vice Minister of Construction, Dr. Nguyen Tuong Van, Director General of Urban Development Agency, Dr. Tran Quoc Thai, Deputy Director General, Dr. Hoang Vinh Hung, Dr. Tran Ngoc Linh and Tran Lam Ha. In addition, Dr. Duong Quoc Nghi, seconded to the Ministry of Construction under the framework of Technical Supporting Unit project (Ministry of Planning and Investment of Viet Nam) provided additional data and policy information during and after the field trips. The Secretariat is also grateful to the two country peer reviewers: Rupert Kawka (Germany) and Hitoshi Sawada (Japan) for sharing their experience throughout the policy dialogue and interviews with the stakeholders in Viet Nam. Rick Roelofs and Sjors Hoetink (Netherlands), Keith Thorpe (UK) and Lewis Dijkstra (European Commission) are also acknowledged for providing valuable comments to the draft report and for having shared their experience throughout the process.

The review was managed by Tadashi Matsumoto, Co-ordinator for National Urban Policy, Climate Change and Green Growth, under the supervision of Rudiger Ahrend, Head of Economic Analysis, Statistics and Multi-Level Governance Section, and Joaquim Oliveira Martins, Special Advisor to Director of CFE. The report was drafted by a core team comprised of Andres Sanabria (Chapter 1), Jane Reid (UN-Habitat) (Chapter 2), Nguyet Pham (GGGI) (Chapter 3), Adam Ward (GGGI) (Chapter 3), and Oscar Huerta Melchor (Chapter 4). Valuable comments were provided by Karen Maguire, Baku Kawai, Tamara Krawchenko, Paolo Veneri and Aziza Akhmouch, OECD Secretariat. Viet Tran provided assistance with data and the preparation of the graphics. Kate Lancaster provided editorial assistance. Pilar Philip and Joanne Dundon prepared the review for publication.

Tables of contents

Figures

Acronyms and abbreviations

AFINUA	Action Framework for the Implementation of the New Urban Agenda
ADB	Asian Development Bank
AFD	Agence Française de Développement
AOMP	Adjustment Orientation Master Plan for Urban Development, until 2025 with a vision to 2050
ARUAM	Approved Regulations on Urban Architecture Management
BOLUC	Building Ownership and Land Use Certificates
BRS	Business Rates Supplement
BRT	Bus Rapid Transit
BTC	Belgian Technical Cooperation
CCAP	Climate Change Action Plans
CFLs	Compact Fluorescent Lamps
CIEM	Central Institute for Economic Management
CTTPP	Centre for Technology Transfer of Physical Planning
DEWATS	Decentralised Wastewater Treatment System
DFID	Department for International Development
DOC	Department of Construction
DOIT	Department of Industry and Trade
DONRE	Department of Natural Resources and Environment
DOT	Department of Transport
DPI	Department of Planning and Investment
EE	Energy Efficiency
EP	Environmental Protection
ESMAP	Energy Sector Management Assistance Program
FDI	Foreign Direct Investment
FIAS	Facility for Investment Climate Advisory Services
FUA	Functional Urban Area
GDP	Gross Domestic Product

GGAP	Green Growth Action Plans
GGGI	Global Green Growth Institute
GHG	Greenhouse Gas
GIZ	Deutsche Gesellschaft für Internationale Zusammenarbeit
GSO	General Statistics Office
ICB	Inter-ministerial Coordination Board
ICCT	International Council on Clean Transport
IUDF	Integrated Urban Development Framework
LPF	Land Price Framework
LURC	Land Use Rights Certification
MACC	Marginal Abatement Cost Curve
MARD	Ministry of Agriculture and Rural Development
MDC	Mayoral Development Corporation
MOC	Ministry of Construction
MOIT	Ministry of Industry and Trade
MONRE	Ministry of Natural Resources and the Environment
MOT	Ministry of Transport
MoUD	Ministry of Urban Development
MPI	Ministry of Planning and Investment
MPLIS	Multipurpose Land Information System
NAPCC	National Action Plan on Climate Change
NCCC	National Commission on Climate Change
NCCS	National Climate Change Strategy
NDC	Nationally Determined Contribution
NESC	National Economic and Social Council
NHDS	National Housing Development Strategy to 2020, with a vision to 2030
NHF	National Housing Federation
NTDC	New Town Development Corporation
NTP-RCC	National Target Program to Respond to Climate Change
NUA	New Urban Agenda
NUDP	National Urban Development Programme, 2012-2020
NUP	National Urban Policy
NUUP	National Urban Upgrading Programme
ODA	Official Development Assistance

PAYT	Pay As You Throw
PDP 7	Power Development Plan VII
PGGAP	Provincial Green Growth Action Plan
PPC	Provincial People's Committee
PPP	Public-Private Partnership
PV	Photovoltaic
RE	Renewable Energy
SEDP	Socio-Economic Development Plan
SEDS	Socio-Economic Development Strategy
SDGs	Sustainable Development Goals
SMEs	Small and Medium Enterprises
TfL	Transport for London
TIF	Tax Increment Financing
TOD	Transit-Oriented Development
UDC	Urban Development Corporation
UNDP	United Nations Development Programme
UNFPA	United Nations Population Fund
USAID	United States Agency for International Development
VGGAP	Viet Nam Green Growth Action Plan
VGGS	Viet Nam Green Growth Strategy
VILG	Vietnam Improved Land Governance and Database Project
VNEEP	Viet Nam National Target Program on Energy Efficiency and Conservation
VUF	Viet Nam Urban Forum
WHO	World Health Organisation

Executive summary

The context

- With 91.7 million people in 2016, Viet Nam is the third most populated country in Southeast Asia. Since the *Doi Moi* reform started in 1986, Viet Nam has been transforming from an agriculture-based economy into a rapidly urbanising industrial economy. The country has boosted income per capita fourfold since 1990 and sustained a remarkable economic growth rate, 7% per year, thanks to the thriving manufacturing and construction sectors, robust exports and growing foreign direct investment (FDI).
- Since 1990, Viet Nam's urban population has almost doubled, and has been growing much faster (3% per year since 2010) than the average of Southeast Asian countries (2.5%). The urbanisation has been accompanied by strong economic growth and higher quality of life. In 2015, the two largest metropolitan areas of Ha Noi and Ho Chi Minh City produced more than one-third of the national GDP and hosted more than 25% of national employment. The average labour productivity of the two cities is three times that of the rest of the country.
- The planning and management of urban areas in Viet Nam depends on a complex network of policies and plans. The current policy model, led by the 2009 Adjustment of Orientation Master Plan (AOMP), does not provide many tools and incentives to co-ordinate across other urban-related policies and their supporting programmes to ensure coherence. At present, the focus is largely on local infrastructure development and supply management to accommodate population growth, rather than on residents' well-being and sustainability.
- The country is divided into 58 provinces and five centrally-administered cities. They are subdivided into district-level administrative units, and further into 11 162 municipalities. Poor multi-sectoral co-operation and co-ordination at central and lower levels of government, together with an unclear demarcation of the mandates of various agencies in charge of urban policies, is posing particular difficulties for Viet Nam.

Key urban challenges

- The educational attainment of the economically-active population is low. In 2015, 80% of the labour force in Viet Nam did not have any type of technical or professional qualification (college, university or higher). The large unskilled labour force is associated with a high degree of insecure and temporary jobs as well as significant disparities in wages across urban areas. For example, in 2014, the wage per capita in Ha Noi and Ho Chi Minh City was almost three times higher than the country's average, while the wage per capita in Lau Chau province was just 40% of the national average.

- Boosted by a growing middle class, Viet Nam registers the fastest growth in car sales in Southeast Asia, with an average annual growth of 39% since 2012, demonstrating a clear shift from motorcycles. The level of traffic accidents is a very serious concern for the country. Viet Nam recorded 25 road traffic deaths per 100 000 people in 2014, which is far above OECD countries such as Australia (5) and Spain (4).
- Viet Nam's rapid urbanisation has also been accompanied by serious environmental challenges in urban areas, putting at risk the health of its population. For example, the annual average PM_{10} level in Ho Chi Minh City (96 $\mu g/m^3$) is far above the level recommended by the World Health Organisation (20 ug/m^3). The increasing urban population puts further pressure on the already weak solid waste and wastewater management systems.

Key policy recommendations

- Develop a more explicit urban policy, which can coordinate across sectoral policies and address urban challenges in a more systematic and holistic way. Use the window of opportunity provided by the ongoing development of the Urban Development Management Law to implement the to-be-developed national urban policy.
- Tackle the rapid shift from motorbikes to cars and ensure a smooth transition to public transport, through better regulated motorcycle traffic, promotion of e-bikes and e-scooters, as well as congestion and parking charges, while accelerating public transport investment.
- Increase the supply of affordable housing in the formal housing market, while addressing the growing low-quality informal housing stocks.
- Review existing land legislation and regulations to streamline the regulatory framework and reduce the administrative burden that hampers developments and land regularisation.
- Mainstream green growth into key urban development policy frameworks, while including it as one of the objectives in the Law on Urban Planning so as to incentivise smart, resilient and compact cities in the city classification system.
- Foster collaboration mechanisms and "metropolitan thinking" for local governments, by adopting a functional urban area (FUA) approach to urban development management and by allowing municipalities to conduct investment jointly.
- Enhance collaboration and co-ordination among central ministries and agencies through strengthening the existing inter-ministerial committees to supervise co-ordination of urban policy more comprehensively.
- Establish a more transparent mechanism to determine tax sharing ratios and a more strategic use of earmarked transfers, for example to foster metropolitan co-ordination.
- Attract and retain highly trained staff in the public sector, by reviewing the public sector salary system and introducing strategic workforce planning.

Assessment and recommendations

Viet Nam: a rapidly growing and urbanising economy

With 91.7 million people in 2016, Viet Nam is the third-most populated country in Southeast Asia, after Indonesia and the Philippines. The *Doi Moi* reform, started in 1986, has led its transformation process from an agriculture-based economy into a rapidly urbanising industrial economy. Since 1990, the country has boosted income per capita fourfold and sustained a remarkable economic growth rate, 7% per year, thanks to the thriving manufacturing and construction sectors, robust exports and growing foreign investment. Since 2003, the country has ranked, on average, as the third destination of foreign direct investment in the Asia-Pacific region after China and India. Recently, the service sector has also experienced strong growth and now represents more than 40% of Viet Nam's GDP.

Viet Nam's rapid economic growth has also raised people's living standards and dramatically reduced poverty rates. While its economy is forecasted to keep growing over 6% in the coming years, some challenges to improve competiveness and quality of life for all persist. In particular, the rapid urbanisation has raised serious concerns about the sustainable development of the country and people's well-being. This report *OECD Urban Policy Review of Viet Nam* analyses Viet Nam's urban development and related challenges, policy and governance practices. It begins by analysing and comparing internationally Viet Nam's urban system, urbanisation process and economic, social and environmental performance in its urban areas. Chapter 2 then focuses on the national urban policy frameworks supporting urban development at the local and regional levels. Chapter 3 focuses on Viet Nam's endeavour to foster green growth in urban areas. Chapter 4 evaluates Viet Nam's urban governance architecture and institutions.

The Vietnamese urban system and its challenges

Redefining Viet Nam's urban areas may help to better understand the urbanisation level

The current territorial structure in Viet Nam, updated in 2013, divides the country into 58 provinces and five centrally-administered cities: Ha Noi, Ho Chi Minh City, Hai Phong, Da Nang and Can Tho. They are subdivided into district-level administrative units, and further into municipalities. All 11 162 municipalities in Viet Nam are classified as either "urban" municipalities (wards and townships) or "rural" municipalities (communes). By the end of 2015, 2 184 municipalities (1 581 wards and 603 townships) were classified as urban, which accounts for 20% of all municipalities. The current definition examines each municipality and gives urban or rural status individually, instead of looking at functional boundaries and connections among these municipalities.

In order to provide a meaningful comparison of Viet Nam's urbanisation level with other countries and to address some of the drawbacks of the current methodology, this report proposes and applies the OECD-EU methodology to define Functional Urban Areas (FUAs) in Viet Nam. FUAs define urban areas as functional socio-economic units, rather than using official administrative boundaries. As a result, 63 FUAs are identified in Viet Nam which cover 7% of the national territory and host 41% (37.1 million people) of the population in 2013. Out of the 63 FUAs, 12 are classified as metropolitan areas (with a population of 500 000 or more). Using a residential population grid (or a grid based on higher resolution population data) is likely to show even higher levels of urbanisation. The FUA analysis shows that Viet Nam's urbanisation level may be in fact much higher than currently defined by the national statistics (32% in 2013).

Viet Nam's urbanisation is among the fastest in Southeast Asia, boosted by young migrants

Since 1990, Viet Nam's urban population has almost doubled, and has been growing much faster (3% per year since 2010) than the average of Southeast Asian countries (2.5%). Upon closer look, this rapid urbanisation was mainly driven by rural-urban migration. Just between 2004 and 2009, 4.3% of the total population moved to a province (or centrally-administered city) different from their native one. More than 40% of those moved to the two largest cities: Ho Chi Minh City (30%) and Ha Noi (11%). Importantly, almost half of the inter-provincial migrants during this period were between 20 and 29 years old.

The FUA analysis provides an international perspective to Viet Nam's urbanisation. Between 2004 and 2013, all the 63 FUAs of different sizes in Viet Nam grew much faster (at an average annual rate of 4.3%) than the FUAs in OECD countries on average (0.8%). While in OECD countries larger FUAs grew faster than smaller FUAs, Viet Nam showed a different pattern: both the three largest FUAs (Ho Chi Minh City, Ha Noi and Hai Phong, with a population of 1.5 million or more) and smaller FUAs (with a population of less than 200 000) grew faster (5.5% and 4.3%, respectively), compared to medium-sized FUAs.

The urbanisation has been accompanied by strong economic growth and higher quality of life

Urbanisation per se is an opportunity, not a guarantee, for economic development to occur. In the case of Viet Nam, it appears the country has seized the opportunity – as its urbanisation process has come together with strong increases in income levels. Also, the analysis of disaggregated GDP shows that economic growth has been led by large urban agglomerations. Between 2010 and 2015, the average GDP growth of the five centrally-administered cities (11%) has been four percentage points higher than the rest of the country. In 2015, the two largest metropolitan areas of Ha Noi and Ho Chi Minh City produced more than one-third of the national GDP and hosted more than 25% of national employment. The average labour productivity of the two cities is three times that of the rest of the country. This clearly follows a trend of OECD countries: city size is positively related with labour productivity.

The strong economic growth, in turn, has resulted in poverty reduction and higher quality of life. The share of people living in extreme poverty has fallen drastically from about 50% in 1990 to 3% in 2014. By 2015, almost all households had access to electricity and water, which is a major achievement given that related coverage was less than half in 1990. Viet Nam also stands out for its high educational performance. In 2015, Viet Nam ranked among the top ten countries in sciences, according to the PISA results for high school students.

Low-skilled labour, poor living and mobility conditions, and pollution challenge Vietnamese cities

Even though all these facts underscore Viet Nam's current success, several challenges are also identified. First is the low educational attainment of the economically-active population. In 2015, 80% of the labour force in Viet Nam did not have any type of technical or professional qualification (college, university or higher), a share which represented almost two thirds of the labour force within urban areas. The large unskilled labour force in Viet Nam is associated with a high degree of insecure and temporary jobs and serious disparity in wages across urban areas. In 2014, the wage per capita in Ha Noi and Ho Chi Minh City was almost three times higher than the country's average, while the wage per capita in Lau Chau province was just 40% of the national average. International comparison also illustrates that the regional income disparity in Vietnam is among the highest in the world.

Poor housing and living standards, as well as mobility and safety in urban areas, with large disparities across cities, are also serious concerns. For example, in 2014, 25% of urban households still sourced their water from hand-dug wells or rain water. Only 21% of households have access to the internet. In urban areas, the proportion is higher (42%) but still far below the average of all households in OECD countries (78%). Boosted by a growing middle-class, Viet Nam registers the fastest growth in car sales in Southeast Asia, with an average annual growth of 39% since 2012, demonstrating a clear shift from motorcycles. The increasing car usage, coupled with the lack efficient public transport alternatives, poses one of the most critical policy challenges for urban areas in Viet Nam. Besides traffic congestion, the level of traffic accidents is a very serious concern for the country. In 2014, traffic accidents were the second cause of death in Viet Nam, accounting for 5% of the total deaths. The country recorded 25 road traffic deaths per 100 000 people in 2014, which is far above OECD countries such as Australia (5) and Spain (4).

Viet Nam's rapid urbanisation has also been accompanied by serious environmental challenges in urban areas, putting at risk the health of its population. Air pollution and poor solid waste and wastewater management are among the most critical issues in Viet Nam. The annual average PM10 level in Ho Chi Minh City (96 $\mu g/m^3$) is far above the level recommended by the World Health Organisation (20 ug/m3). Ha Noi generates almost 800 kg of waste per capita every year, much more than an average OECD city does (516 kg). The increasing urban population puts further pressure on the already weak solid waste and wastewater management system. The performance in solid waste and wastewater management is poorer in smaller cities. For example, only 5% of Class IV and V cities meet the national wastewater treatment criteria.

Vietnam's urban policy framework

While the strong focus on economic development objectives is understandable, approaches which better address goals of green and inclusive growth should offer the surest paths to equitable and sustainable development. Addressing this challenge necessitates the timely application of a clear and workable urban policy framework. A key to "getting cities right" is a holistic and integrated approach to urban challenges and policies. This report applies such an approach to the current national-level policy frameworks in Viet Nam.

The national-level urban policy framework lacks a long-term vision for urbanisation and co-ordination mechanisms

The planning and management of urban areas in Viet Nam depend on a complex network of policies and plans. The foundational element of the Vietnamese spatial policy framework is the 2009 Adjustment of Orientation Master Plan to Develop Viet Nam's Urban System until 2025 with a Vision to 2050 (AOMP) that provides – as stated in its name – the goals for urban development until 2025 and the vision for a further quarter-century. A challenge is that the current policy model led by AOMP does not provide many tools and incentives to co-ordinate across other urban-related policies and their supporting programmes to ensure coherence. While the social and economic prerogatives of the Socio-Economic Development Strategy (SEDS) and the spatial focus of the AOMP should work in tandem, in reality, spatial master plans frequently lack considerations for social and economic questions, and investment plans based on SEDS typically do not consider their spatial implications. This lack of co-ordination between sectoral policies manifests itself even simply in the duration of the respective plans. For example, some sectoral master plans and transport plans have a longer duration than the SEDS, and therefore frequently are not reflecting the up-to-date socio-economic policy objectives of the country.

Stronger legislative frameworks can help policy orientation and hierarchical alignment

The urban legislative framework in Viet Nam will play a key role in addressing the above-mentioned problem. The current framework, despite its considerable scope (*e.g.*, laws, plans, strategies and programmes), is not performing as effectively as it should, due to a lack of clear hierarchical alignment among the networks of laws, government decrees and other policy documents. This problem, and the resulting complexity for compliance and enforcement, has gone beyond being an inconvenience to become a contributing factor to the ad hoc urban development that so frequently occurs at the local level. A key opportunity for Viet Nam is to strengthen the framework by specifying government's policy position to guide the future growth and management of urban areas, in addition to serving as a guide on process and procedures. The expected new legislative framework on urban development management, which is currently under discussion led by the Ministry of Construction, will be a good window of opportunity for the whole government to address this challenge together and develop a legislative framework which supports implementing Viet Nam's long-term vision for urbanisation and a clearer demarcation of responsibilities among the existing laws, government decrees and other policy documents across relevant ministries.

The development of a more explicit urban policy can provide more concrete policy direction

The experience of some OECD and non-OECD countries shows that a well-designed National Urban Policy (NUP) can promote linkages between sectoral policies, provide a basis for co-ordination within and amongst ministries responsible, and thus address urban challenges in a more comprehensive way. A NUP can also strengthen urban, peri-urban, and rural links through more integrated national level territorial development, and support a stronger connection between national, regional and local governments, while defining closely the roles and responsibilities of each. A more clearly formulated NUP would be expected to induce a larger degree of coherence between different urban policies undertaken at the national level. It would also help provide the Vietnamese legislative framework with a stronger hierarchical delineation and policy direction. It is timely to use the window of opportunity provided by the ongoing development of the Urban Development Management Law, to implement the to-be-developed NUP. A NUP could also be a key tool to support the implementation of global frameworks in Viet Nam, such as the New Urban Agenda and urban-oriented SDGs.

City classification system: ensuring coherence with the AOMP and other urban strategies

Viet Nam ranks "urban areas" by a government decree. Centrally-administered cities, provincial cities, towns and townships are all considered within the classification and therefore defined as "urban areas" (for readability, this report uses "cities" hereafter). They are classified hierarchically into six classes – Special and Class One (I) to Five (V) – based on a threshold of infrastructure development, population size and socio-economic characteristics. In 2016, Viet Nam had 799 cities, with two cities with Special Class (Ha Noi and Ho Chi Minh City) and 17 cities with Class I.

This classification system has been, since its initiation in an early form in 1990, a key tool for urban management. The system has profound implications for administrative functions, tax collection and funding decisions. Indeed, the entire system is characterised by an ascending degree of autonomy and, accordingly, of financial transfers from the national government. The greater autonomy and increased financial flexibility that comes with the higher classifications creates an incentive for attaining upward mobility within the scale. This may be seen as a positive factor, in encouraging urban administrators to be ambitious on behalf of their cities and the provinces they serve, but it also carries certain disadvantages. For example, as the scoring system emphasises infrastructure development and population growth, local infrastructure development is prioritised above adherence to the 2009 Adjustment of Orientation Master Plan to Develop Viet Nam's Urban System until 2025 with a Vision to 2050 (AOMP) and other urban strategies which place a stronger focus on sustainability. Emphasis on population growth has resulted in municipalities expanding their existing administrative boundaries in order to "catch" neighbouring rural areas and convert them to urban land, so as to add to their population figures. Monitoring and evaluation, along with the incentive mechanism coherent with the AOMP and other urban strategies, holds the key to ensuring that the classification system can emerge as a flexible and dynamic tool for urban management. Another possible improvement to the classification system is that it could also value interconnections between cities within a metropolitan area, fostering a stronger metropolitan approach to development.

Urban transport policies: tackling the shift from motorbikes to cars and ensuring a smooth transition to public transport

The current major transport-related investment in urban areas in Viet Nam has a heavy focus on road and street construction. Although such an approach may be justified in the short term, the most urgent policy agenda for Viet Nam is to tackle the rapid shift from motorbikes to cars and ensure a smooth transition to public transport. The current national policy framework for urban transport, the 2013 Adjusted Strategy for Development of Vietnam's Transport through 2020, with a vision toward 2030, follows this direction, as it gives priority to the development of mass transit systems in Ha Noi and Ho Chi Minh City. All the related policies, in particular road development policies and land use policies, need to be consistent with this direction. Immediate action is needed to make Vietnamese roads safer through better regulated motorcycle traffic, address noise and air pollution through promoting the use of e-bikes and e-scooters, and allocate a greater proportion of the real cost of car usage to the owners of the vehicles themselves, particularly through fiscal measures such as congestion and parking charges. Longer-term transport investments should explore such financing means as public-private partnerships and value capture mechanisms. Bus Rapid Transit (BRT) initiatives in Ha Noi and elsewhere require specific efforts to harmonise with the principles of Transit-Oriented Development (TOD) and intermodal connectivity to ensure ridership and maximise the investment benefit.

Housing policies: addressing the growing informal housing market

The 1986 reforms and subsequent policy development on land and housing resulted in an influx of investment in housing and created favourable conditions for construction activities. Nonetheless, under the unprecedented urbanisation process, access to affordable and high-quality housing is one of the foremost challenges for Viet Nam's urban areas. Formal housing in Viet Nam today is out of reach for large segments of the population, while the informal housing market is expanding rapidly. Catering to the urban poor and unregistered rural migrants, the informal sector indeed embodies an estimated 75% of housing production, and 75 to 80% of housing finance, leaving only about 20% of actual urban housing to the modern and formal production mechanisms. The informal housing market creates under-quality housing stocks in cities, some of which are even in unsafe conditions. It may also hinder the development of a skilled and competitive construction sector. Moreover, informal housing development tends to occur in areas with concentrated poverty or with high risks of floods and other natural disasters. These areas are also often spatially segregated from other urban neighbourhoods, which is associated with other social problems.

In order to address these problems, it is urgent to consider policy options for increasing the supply of affordable housing for middle- and low-income households in the formal housing market. At the same time, the government may need to address the growing low-quality informal housing stocks. The current national strategy for housing, the National Housing Development Strategy to 2020, with a vision to 2030 (NHDS), established in 2011, and the Housing Law, established in 2006 and substantially revised in 2015, may need to face this problem and provide an explicit strategy for the informal housing sector. Options to be considered include strengthening inspection and guidance to improve the housing quality and developing financing mechanisms such as micro-credit for low-income home owners to fix their housing problems.

Land policies: streamlined regulations for efficient urban development

The primary law overseeing land use and management issues in Viet Nam is the Land Law, updated every ten years since the first Land Law of 1993, which had recognised land rights for private persons and established their trade and pricing mechanisms. In addition, land usage and management is determined by the multiple requirements and regulations of plans from different sectors: the land use plans under the responsibility of the Ministry of Natural Resources and the Environment (MONRE) and the spatial plans of the Ministry of Construction (MOC) which themselves have to reflect the orientations of the socio-economic plans of the Ministry of Planning and Investment (MPI) and of sectoral plans for housing or transport and infrastructure. In addition, a large number of other sectoral laws and institutions still impact the sector of land use and management.

This complexity of laws, regulations, plans and institutions on land in Viet Nam reveals an inherent need for co-ordination or consistency across relevant actors. It also means likely delays for project development, including of urban infrastructure. Importantly, given the pressing needs for development under urbanisation, the complexity and opaqueness of the system also open the door to corruption.

Since the state is responsible for the allocation of land to institutions, organisations, individuals and households for long-term use, and it grants and limits the rights of land use and exchange, the role of the state is crucial for ensuring efficient operation of the land system and addressing the increasing development needs in cities. An immediate policy action should be to review existing legislation and regulations in order to streamline the regulatory framework and reduce the administrative burden that hampers developments and land regularisation. In the longer term, the land use planning system under the Land Law could explore a more dynamic and flexible approach, rather than one that is definitive and prescriptive, in order to better adapt to the dynamic circumstances of urban development that directly answer to socio-economic needs.

Policies for the quality of the urban environment: key to a city's prosperity

The rapidity of Vietnamese urbanisation has posed challenges for government in terms of its ability to ensure a quality environment for urban residents. For example, there remains a struggle for the provision of open space in the dense inner-city centres. In Ha Noi, between 2000 and 2010, the area devoted to parks and public gardens per capita went from $2.17m^2$ to $1.58m^2$. In Hoan Kiem district, Ha Noi's old quarter, the area was only $0.14m^2$ per person in comparison to the national average ($1.7m^2$) and the target set in the 2008 Viet Nam Building Code ($7m^2$). A high quality urban environment, such as streets and public open spaces, is essential not only for people to gather and interact, but also for urban eco-systems and for cultural heritage in cities. National level urban policy frameworks should actively safeguard the quality of the urban environment, and each city needs to plan and invest in its urban environment based on the city's long-term vision. A successful practice, such as a weekend pedestrian zone within Hoan Kiem district, can be replicated in many other cities and districts, inspired by many OECD cities' experiences and lessons. Viet Nam should also consider setting up a dedicated development agency for inner city revitalisation which can comprehensively address inner city problems.

Making Vietnamese cities sustainable and productive through green growth policies

Viet Nam's greenhouse gas (GHG) emission has remarkably increased six-fold since 1990. The country emits much more CO_2 per GDP than OECD countries and worryingly the figure is still increasing. Since most of Vietnam's population and economic activity are located in the Mekong and Red River Deltas and other coastal areas, they are vulnerable to sea-level rise which may be accelerated by climate change. Viet Nam urgently needs to address these global climate challenges and other increasing environmental concerns, while continuing its economic growth and social progress. Green growth has been recognised as a key growth policy in Viet Nam. This report argues the need for strengthening urban green growth policies, given the increasing role of cities in national green growth performance.

Green growth is yet to be incorporated into key urban development policy frameworks

Viet Nam has put green economic development at the core of its socio-economic agenda, and laid a solid foundation for the implementation of urban green growth. The National Green Growth Strategy (VGGS) in 2012 and the National Green Growth Action Plan (VGGAP) in 2014 are two milestones for the national level strategies. Urban green growth cuts across a number of policy solutions in the VGGS and is given prominence, for example within "sustainable urbanisation", one of the 17 solutions in the VGGS. However, these strategic orientations towards urban green growth in the VGGS and VGGAP are yet to be incorporated into key urban development policy frameworks. The first step would be to include green growth as one of the objectives in the Law on Urban Planning, as the current law does not refer to green growth and the only links to the concept are through policy targets on green spaces, number of trees and environmental impact assessments. The city classification system could also incentivise smart, resilient and compact cities. Such actions would give strong incentives to city leaders who currently tend to consider urban green growth as just another sectoral policy and prioritise other policy objectives.

While VGGS and VGGAP frameworks count on subnational actions, most subnational governments face capacity challenges. While the VGGAP requires all the provinces to develop a Provincial Green Growth Action Plan (PGGAP), only 23 provinces out of 63 have completed their PGGAPs. Significant variations are observed among the completed PGGAPs in scope and levels of analysis. The Ministry of Planning and Investment (MPI) and other relevant ministries could expand their support towards provinces, for example by making their guideline document more articulated, establishing a knowledge sharing platform, providing technical assistance and trainings, and finally, by providing financial support for provinces with limited resource.

Cities present opportunities for renewable energy and energy efficiency

Urban areas present a strong opportunity for renewable energy (RE) investment in Viet Nam, especially for solar energy. An important policy action is to develop a local strategy for RE, which can help mobilise private investment. OECD cities' successful practices, such as solar thermal ordinances in Spanish cities, can inspire Vietnamese cities. Ho Chi Minh City's pilot programme promoting the grid-connected PV system could be supported and replicated countrywide. Energy efficiency (EE) is another opportunity area to drive urban green growth with strong potential of subnational action. Potential policy options include: developing a local strategy for EE; allowing subnational governments' discretion to set more stringent EE standards; setting up an EE central fund to leverage public and private investment in EE; and establishing a platform for multi-level, multi-stakeholder knowledge sharing.

Accelerating wastewater treatment and solid waste management

Wastewater collection and treatment is a fundamental public service to sustain economic activities and quality of life. The current system has caused serious health problems for Vietnamese urban residents. The costs of pollution from untreated wastewater were estimated as equivalent to 5% of Viet Nam's GDP. While the main constraint is insufficient resource to build adequate levels of wastewater management systems, a challenge may also lie in public awareness and consensus building. For example, many urban households are reluctant to be connected to sewerage systems and to pay for municipally-managed wastewater treatment. It is critical for Viet Nam to allocate more resources for safeguarding the country's urban eco-systems and people's health. Illegal wastewater discharge in residential or industrial zones must be more strictly controlled. Wastewater tariffs should also be revised so as to reflect the operation and management cost. Proper data collection is key for such policies.

Solid waste management is another untapped green growth opportunity for Viet Nam. Despite the ambitious national targets to reduce municipal waste, effective policies have not been introduced to promote waste separation at source or waste-to-energy incinerators, which has significant growth potential by recycling and generating energy. As a result, governments continue to suffer from the problems of existing sub-quality landfills and illegal damping. Green growth policies and effective governance of the circular economy in cities can shift the paradigm to regard solid waste as a source of revenue rather than as a source of problems. Among many policy options to be considered, Viet Nam could consider retrofitting the existing landfills to minimise the environmental impacts and generate energy. With relatively small investment, some of them could be much more effectively managed. Another key is effective waste pricing reflecting the volume and the environmental cost.

More effective horizontal co-ordination, legal frameworks and reporting mechanisms can help deliver urban green growth

Improving the governance structure may drastically improve the performance of green growth policies in urban areas in Viet Nam. The unclear allocation of responsibility in urban green growth has resulted in co-ordination challenges at the national and local levels. For example, air pollution monitoring in urban areas has created some confusion across the relevant agencies, because it is not clearly defined who should monitor air pollution from transport in cities. The proposed Inter-ministerial Coordination Board (ICB) for green growth could help address these problems, by placing stronger focus on policy co-ordination in urban areas. At the subnational level, a similar co-ordination structure could be developed to avoid duplications and strengthen each department's actions.

Stronger urban legal frameworks can also effectively support green growth implementation at subnational level. Currently, national green growth policies and strategies are neither legally founded nor mainstreamed into sectoral legal frameworks such as the Law on Urban Development. This has kept subnational green growth actions "optional" for some subnational governments. Providing clearer legal mandates and incentives for subnational governments to support green growth will actively steer subnational governments toward allocating their manpower and budget on green growth actions.

Improving data and reporting mechanisms for green growth at the city level is another key strategy Viet Nam could consider. While several sets of green growth indicators for cities have been proposed by international partners, none of these indicators has been officially recognised or enforced by the central government, leaving cities few incentives to invest resources to achieve these goals. The Ministry of Construction's current effort to make a circular and guideline on this issue will be an important step to engage cities. It is also an urgent task to improve the reporting system to monitor the progress of the National Green Growth Strategy.

Governing urbanisation in Viet Nam

Fostering collaboration mechanisms and "metropolitan thinking" for local governments

Viet Nam's local government system comprises three levels of government: provincial; district; and communal. A key feature of the Vietnamese system of local government is the subordination of lower levels of government to the level immediately above. Local authorities can only carry out administrative functions that are assigned by national legislation. As a consequence, Viet Nam does not appear to have effective co-ordination mechanisms that facilitate and encourage a more integrated approach among subnational governments at district and communal levels. Importantly, this reflects the absence of metropolitan thinking; district level governments plan without reference to the functional urban area, and no master plan per region or metropolitan area has been developed. OECD studies have shown that metropolitan areas with fragmented governance tend to have lower levels of productivity.

By adopting a functional approach to urban areas, Viet Nam could benefit from the effectiveness and efficiency of pooling resources, and make better use of the available structure and capacity within provinces. For instance, this could imply allowing municipalities to conduct investment jointly, rather than relying on upper levels of government, when they are better placed to do so to improve capacity and spur public sector innovation in lower levels of government. Upper level governments could, in turn, focus on facilitating this collaboration and act merely as arbiters in cases of disagreements or conflict. Contractual arrangements or financial transfers such as "metropolitan funds" may also provide tools for co-operation and co-ordination. The city reclassification system could also be used to facilitate such multi-level collaboration. The Association of Cities of Viet Nam (ACVN) can be used as a platform for the exchange of information and best practices on urban development.

Urban development management must overcome silo approaches and requires pragmatism and mechanisms for co-ordination at the central level

The experience of OECD countries has shown that urban management requires the interaction of several domains and the seamless co-ordination across ministries and levels of government to build up synergies. However, multi-sectoral co-operation and co-ordination at central and lower levels of government is posing particular difficulties to Viet Nam. The following barriers for co-operation and co-ordination are identified: i) restrictions on sharing information across ministries; ii) organisational cultures under which co-operative work across ministries is not encouraged; iii) the division of the whole-of-government budget into separate ministerial allocations; iv) public managers who only have experience within a single ministry; and v) accountability structures that focus mainly on ministry-specific issues.

Collaboration and co-ordination among central ministries and agencies could be strengthened through the systematic sharing of data, joint analysis and collaborative use of a variety of levers to enable government-wide implementation of urban policy. Encouraging working level contacts among ministries in urban-related issues would be a pragmatic way to unleash collaboration. Streamlining bureaucratic formalities for exchanging information should be part of these efforts. Viet Nam should also consider strengthening existing inter-ministerial committees to supervise co-ordination of urban policy more comprehensively. The Urban Development Agency could be given the responsibility of co-ordinating urban development across ministries and levels of government, drawing inspiration from the experience of Sweden, for example. In addition, such committees could be complemented by inter-ministerial conferences as in Belgium where national and subnational level authorities discuss and agree on national urban priorities and strategies and, more importantly, assess the results of policy implementation. The central government could also take advantage of the Viet Nam Urban Forum (VUF) to enhance collaboration across governments.

Fiscal decentralisation and a clearer distribution of responsibilities will increase effectiveness of subnational investment

The expenditure structure in Viet Nam is highly decentralised. In 2013, around 54% of public spending was carried out at the subnational level. However, unclear demarcation of the mandates of various agencies in charge of urban policies continues to leave room for discretion in interpretation of responsibility and accountability. Vietnamese authorities could consider promoting fiscal decentralisation for a more dynamic urban management and sharpening the distinction between central and subnational governments' responsibilities. Viet Nam could also consider increasing the capacity for subnational governments to adjust revenue or spending (i.e. taxing autonomy, mandatory spending). An asymmetric decentralisation of responsibilities can be an interesting way forward in devolving expenditure responsibilities to subnational governments, as is the case in Colombia. Following the *OECD Principles for Effective Public Investment across Levels of Government*, Viet Nam may wish to employ a fiscal framework adapted to the different investment policy objectives pursued.

A more transparent and predictable transfer system can improve incentives for local government

The main sources of income for Vietnamese subnational governments are taxes, followed by grants and subsidies. Tax rates and bases are determined by the National Assembly, and subnational governments only have limited independence for setting fees. Allowing local governments to set tax fees and user charge rates so that the costs of local services are better covered is an efficient strategy that increases local resources available for investment. In the current system, poorer provinces keep 100% of the shared taxes collected, while richer provinces keep a lower portion (between 15% and 60%). In the period 2011-2015, 50 of the 63 provinces retained 100% of the shared taxes collected within their jurisdiction, while 13 kept only a portion. A problem is that the actual "sharing rates" are often reached by negotiation as there is no specific objective formula for determining them. To improve this, Vietnamese authorities may consider establishing a more transparent mechanism to determine tax sharing ratios. The central government also could consider a more strategic use of earmarked transfers, for example to foster metropolitan co-ordination for certain projects.

Unleashing subnational governments' potential by making better use of borrowing

Local governments are legally allowed to mobilise capital from issuing local government bonds and from other legal borrowing, but in practice this is very limited. Viet Nam may consider easing the limits for issuing bonds and borrowing from capital markets for those subnational governments that have a strong base of own-source financing, under continuous monitoring of central government. Providing loans to local governments for the renewal of urban infrastructure through central government programmes is a viable way to overcome the lack of funding. As the experiences of Mexico and Turkey suggest, it may require a specific institution providing technical and financial support to subnational governments.

Improving the efficiency of Official Development Assistance

Viet Nam is the biggest recipient of Official Development Assistance (ODA) in Southeast Asia, receiving more than half of the total ODA for infrastructure in the region (almost 2% of Viet Nam's GDP). As the country is reaching middle income levels, Viet Nam will need to develop ODA projects in policy areas that are more strategically urgent, such as in urban rail transport and flood protection. The Vietnamese government may also wish to work together with subnational governments to channel ODA not only to large cities but also to small and medium-sized cities that are rapidly growing and struggling to finance their public service infrastructure.

Improving capacity of the public sector

The Vietnamese public service faces a fundamental challenge: how to attract, retain and motivate high performing people into the civil service. Many attractive opportunities outside the public service may lure qualified and talented people away from the public administration. This situation creates the risk of leaving the civil service, particularly at subnational levels, under-qualified and under-motivated. For cities, the lack of technical knowledge and experience of public servants to implement urban policies undermines the level of quality and coverage of public services and the effective and efficient use of resources. Public sector salaries, in general, need to be more competitive to attract and retain highly trained staff. Allowing higher salaries for competitive or highly specialised staff, and making salaries commensurate with risks and with market alternatives, can mitigate one factor that contributes to corruption. Making salary increases selective, and matching them to improved qualifications, skills or responsibilities rather than length of service, could have a more positive effect to improve motivation and recognition.

Strategic workforce planning is an essential tool. The Vietnamese public service could invest to anticipate possible future developments and to maintain a well-structured workforce of an appropriate size. Training courses for civil servants on issues such as municipal governance, local budgets, inter-budgetary relations, personnel management, tax collection and tax administration could help bridge the gap between existing skills and the competencies needed to implement urban policies and programmes. Finally, citizen participation, transparency and control of corruption are key challenges faced by the Vietnamese public administration. Ensuring sustained political commitment to ethical behaviour, establishing workable codes of conduct, setting an ethics co-ordinating body, and introducing accountability mechanisms should be considered to enhance trust in the Vietnamese public service.

Conclusions

As Viet Nam's urbanisation continues, the role of cities in overall national economic, social and performance is growing more rapidly than ever. Therefore, making well-functioning urban areas is crucial for the country's sustainable future development. This report points to a number of policy areas which Viet Nam can tap into, in order to fully capitalise on the unique opportunities that its urbanisation process may bring about. An immediate opportunity lies in the formulation of a more explicit urban policy that can demonstrate a clear vision for Viet Nam's sustainable urbanisation. Legal frameworks can play a key role in defining clear mandates and responsibilities of all urban actors to achieve such a vision. Policy experience and lessons from urbanised OECD countries and cities in transport, housing, land use, solid waste and wastewater management, and the quality of the urban environment, as illustrated in this report, are instrumental for Vietnamese policy makers to develop their own tailored approach. Redefining Viet Nam's urban areas with more reliable data can help Viet Nam advance evidence-based policy making. Finally, institutional and financial capacities both at the national and subnational levels remain key challenges requiring immediate action.

Chapter 1

Viet Nam's urban structure and development trends

This chapter provides an overview of the urban structure, development trends and challenges of urban areas in Viet Nam. It first analyses Viet Nam's urban structure in an internationally comparative context. Then it presents the urbanisation process in the country and analyses its economic drivers and impacts. It also covers the challenges for Viet Nam's sustainable urban development. While most of the analysis is based on official data according to the administrative definition of urban areas in Viet Nam, it also introduces the Functional Urban Areas, providing a new picture of urban agglomerations in the country, grounded on settlement patterns.

Viet Nam: a country with a rapidly growing economy

With 91.7 million people in 2016, Viet Nam is the third-most populated country in Southeast Asia (after Indonesia and Philippines) and the thirteenth in the world. The country covers half the land area of France and one similar to Finland. It is the country with the third highest population density in the region (after Singapore and Philippines) and the fifth among OECD countries. The Doi Moi reform in Viet Nam, started in 1986, has led the process of transformation from an agriculture-based country into a rapidly urbanising industrial economy.[1] Since 1990, the country has boosted income per capita fourfold by sustaining a remarkable economic growth rate, 7% per year, which has placed Viet Nam as the fourth fastest growing economy in the world since 1990 (World Bank, 2016).

The economic structure has been characterised by an increasing participation of the industry and construction sectors that have almost doubled their share in the economy since 1990. The fast growing service sector represents more than 40% of Vietnamese GDP with average growth rates of 7% in the last two decades. Robust exports and growing foreign investment have underpinned the positive economic performance in Viet Nam. Since 2003, the country has ranked, in average, as the third destination of foreign direct investment in the Asia-Pacific region, surpassed only by China and India, and the fifth among all developing countries (UNCTAD, 2017). Viet Nam's economy is forecasted to keep growing over 6% in the next four years between 2017 and 2021 (OECD, 2017a). Such growth has also raised people's living standards and dramatically reduced poverty rates.

Despite the remarkable economic performance, challenges to improve competiveness persist. According to the global competitiveness Index 2015-2016 prepared by the World

Economic Forum, Viet Nam is ranked at 60th out of 138 countries (Sala-i-Martin and Swab, 2014). Although it is well positioned among middle-income countries, it is in the bottom three among the East Asia and Pacific economies, behind five other Southeast Asian economies. Low innovation capacity and poor quality on roads and railroads infrastructure are some of the lowest indicators in the index. Furthermore, the lower educated labour force is highlighted as one of the most problematic factors for doing business.

In 2015, according to official data, one third of Viet Nam's population lived in urban areas, significantly below the average urbanisation rate of Southeast Asia (48%) and low middle-income countries (40%) (UNDESA, 2014). This is partly due to the fact that Vietnamese method to classify urban population might not be reflecting the economic relation among urban centres and their neighbouring communities. According to the functional urban area analysis developed in this chapter, the urbanisation rate in Viet Nam may have already reached more than 40%.

This chapter first analyses Viet Nam's urban structure in an internationally comparative context. Then it presents an overview of the urbanisation process in the country and analyses its economic drivers and impacts. It also covers the challenges for Viet Nam's sustainable urban development. While most of the analysis is based on official data according to the administrative definition of urban areas in Viet Nam, this chapter introduces the Functional Urban Areas (thereafter, FUAs), providing a new picture of urban agglomerations grounded on settlement patterns.

Viet Nam's urban structure

Definition of "urban"

The current territorial structure in Viet Nam, updated in 2013, divides the country in 58 provinces and 5 centrally-administered cities; Ha Noi, Ho Chi Minh City, Hai Phong, Da Nang and Can Tho. Each province is further divided into "provincial cities", "towns" and "rural districts", whereas each centrally-administered city is divided into "urban districts", "rural districts" and "towns". These administrative units, collectively called "district level administrative units", are subdivided into municipalities (communes, wards and townships) (Figure 1.1). The OECD follows a territorial classification which categorises administrative units into tiers (Box 1.1). Applying the classification to the territorial structure in Viet Nam makes international comparison feasible and meaningful.

All 11 162 municipalities in Viet Nam are classified as either "urban" municipalities (wards and townships) or "rural" municipalities (communes). Urban municipalities are defined administratively based on complex criteria, including thresholds of population density (at least 10 000 people/km^2 for wards within urban districts, or 4 000 people/km^2 for wards within towns), levels of agricultural labour force (less than 30% for wards within towns) among others.[2] Urban population is therefore defined as the people living in urban municipalities, regardless whether they are within a rural district or provincial city at the district level. By the end of 2015, 2 184 municipalities (1 581 wards and 603 townships) were classified urban, which accounts for 20% of the total municipalities. Municipal fragmentation is not significantly higher than the OECD average. Viet Nam has an average of 12 municipalities per 100 000 inhabitants, just slightly higher than OECD average (10.5 municipalities per 100 000 inhabitants).

Figure 1.1. Administrative structure of Viet Nam

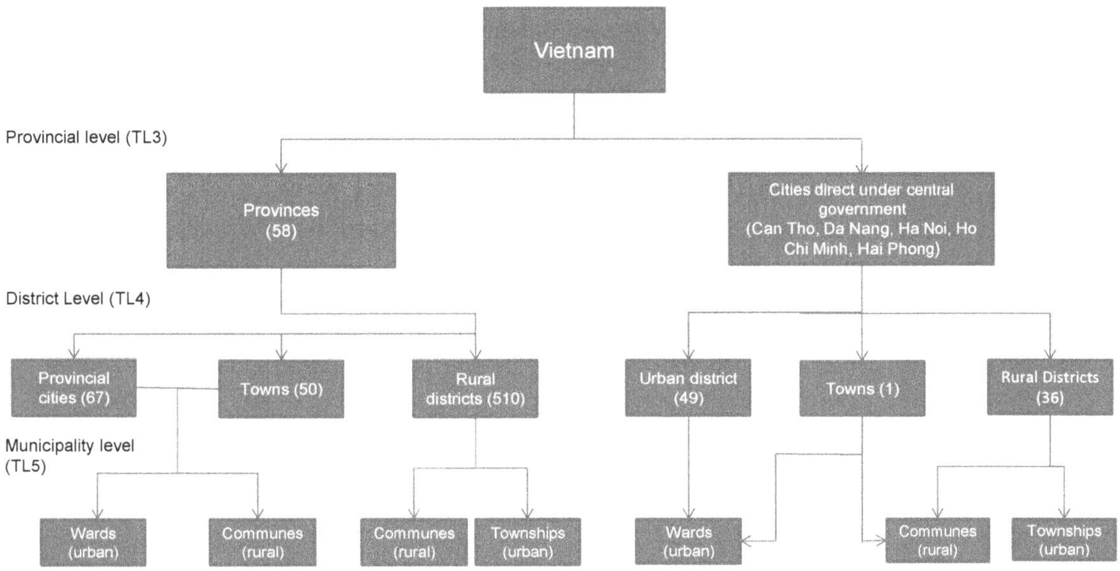

Source: Ministry of Construction of Viet Nam (2017), Answers to the OECD questionnaire, May 2017, unpublished; and General Statistics Office (2015), Database of administrative units, www.gso.gov.vn/default_en.aspx?tabid=773.

Box 1.1. The OECD territorial classification

Regions within the 35 OECD countries are classified on two territorial levels reflecting the administrative organisation of countries. The 398 OECD large (Territorial Level 2, or TL2) regions represent the first administrative tier of subnational government, for example, *the Ontario Province* in Canada. The 2 241 OECD small (TL3) regions are contained in a TL2 region. For example, the TL2 *Capital Region* in Korea encompasses three TL3 regions: *Seoul, Incheon* and *Gyeonggi-do*. TL3 regions correspond to administrative entities, with the exception of Australia, Canada, Germany and the United States. All the regions are defined within national borders. This classification facilitates greater comparability of geographic units at the same territorial level. Indeed, these two levels (TL2 and TL3), which are officially established and relatively stable in all member countries, are used as a framework for implementing regional policies in most countries.

When applying this classification to Viet Nam, TL2 regions correspond to the six territorial regions (Northern Midlands and Mountains, Red River Delta, North and South Central Coast, Central Highlands, Southeast and Mekong River Delta). These TL2 regions in Viet Nam are not administrative units. TL3 regions correspond to the 58 provinces and 5 centrally-administered cities.

We can extend the former classification to the smaller administrative units of Viet Nam. The 646 district level administrative units (546 rural districts, 49 urban districts and 51 towns) are therefore categorised as TL4 regions and the 11 162 municipalities (communes, wards and townships) are categorised as TL5 regions.

Source: OECD (2017b), "OECD Territorial Grids", *Better Policies for Better Lives*, OECD Centre for Entrepreneurship, SMEs, Regions and Cities, Paris, www.oecd.org/regional/regional-policy/territorial-grids-2017.pdf; OECD (2016a), *OECD Regions at a Glance 2016*, OECD Publishing, Paris, http://dx.doi.org/10.1787/reg_glance-2016-en; Data of Viet Nam comes from General Statistics Office of Viet Nam, database of administrative unites as of 31 December 2015, www.gso.gov.vn/default_en.aspx?tabid=773 (accessed 27 July 2017).

Definition of "cities" and the city classification system

In parallel to the definition of "urban" at the municipality level or TL5, Viet Nam also ranks "cities" through a National Assembly Resolution. Centrally-administered cities (TL3), provincial cities (TL4), towns (TL4) and townships (TL5) are all considered within the classification and therefore defined as "cities". They are classified hierarchically into six classes, mainly based on a threshold of infrastructure development, population size and socio-economic characteristics (Table 1.1).[3] "Special" is the highest Class, followed by a classification from Class one (I) to Class five (V), where Class V refers to the smallest cities (townships). According to the criteria, the five centrally-administered cities can be classified either as special class or Class I, while the 50 towns under provinces can only belong to Class III or IV. In 2016, Viet Nam had 799 cities, with two cities with special class (Ha Noi and Ho Chi Minh City) and 17 cities (including three centrally-administered cities) with Class I. Since 1999, the number of cities has increased by 195 (30%).

Table 1.1. Criteria of "city" classification system

City Class	Type of City/Urban Centres	Population (million)	Population Density (Population/ km²)	Share of non-agricultural labour (% of total labour force)
Special Class	Centrally-administered cities	≥ 5 (inner city ≥ 3)	Whole urban centre ≥ 3 000 (Inner area: ≥12 000)	Whole urban centre ≥ 70 (Inner area: ≥ 90)
Class I	Centrally-administrated cities Provincial cities Towns within centrally administered cities	Centrally administrated cities: ≥ 1 (inner area ≥ 0.5) Provincial city: ≥ 0.5 (inner area ≥ 0.2)	Whole urban centre ≥2 000 (Inner area: ≥10 000)	Whole urban centre ≥ 65 (Inner area: ≥ 85)
Class II	Provincial cities. Towns within centrally administered cities	≥ 0.2 (Inner area: ≥ 0.1)	Whole urban centre ≥1 800 (Inner area: ≥8 000)	Whole urban centre ≥ 65% (Inner area: ≥ 80)
Class III	Provincial cities Towns within centrally administered cities Provincial towns	≥ 0.1 (Inner area: ≥ 0.05)	Whole urban centre ≥1 400 (Inner area: ≥7 000)	Whole urban centre ≥ 60 (Inner area: ≥ 75)
Class IV	Provincial towns Townships	≥ 0.05(Inner area: ≥ 0.02)	Whole urban centre ≥1 200 (Inner area: ≥6 000)	Whole urban centre ≥ 55 (Inner area: ≥ 70)
Class V	Townships	≥ 0.04	≥ 1 000/km2	≥ 55

Notes: The classification of urban centres was updated at the end of 2016, modifying some of the criteria established in the resolution of 2009. The new resolution includes towns under centrally administrated cities as part of the classification. Currently, the only town of this kind is Soy Tay (class III), which was absorbed by Hanoi during its expansion process of 2008.

Source: Resolution 1210/2016/UBTVQH13.

The classification system has profound implications for administrative functions, tax collection and funding decisions. It determines, for example, the level of infrastructure investment and incentives from the central or provincial government. Chapter 2 will further examine the classification system's impact.

In Viet Nam, data below the provincial or centrally-administered city (TL3) level are extremely limited. For example, demographic (age structure or labour force) and economic (employment and income) data at the district level (TL4) and at the municipality level (TL5) is not available at the General Statistics Office but only found partially at each local government. As the urbanisation rate in Viet Nam depends on characteristics at the municipality level, more statistical information at this level is crucial for both national and local governments to structure effective urban policies. It could also allow for better international benchmarking, which could be useful for policymaking.

Redefining Viet Nam's urban areas

The current definition of urban population in Viet Nam examines each municipality and gives urban or rural status individually, instead of looking at functional boundaries and connection of these municipalities. In addition, the legal criterion to define urban status of a municipality (population density, infrastructure and share of non-agricultural labour) is not easily measured due to the lack of homogeneous data at the district and municipal levels. As a result, in many cases, the urban status reflects rather political motives than current demographic realities in a given municipality. For instance, some municipalities within Ha Noi but being located at fringes are classified as rural, although the non-agriculture labour rates may be higher than 50%, whereas Class II provincial cities such as Tra Vinh or Ninh Binh classify more than 82% of its population as urban.

Globally, defining geographical extension of urban areas has never been an easy task, and each country has developed its own methodology for determining which areas are considered urban. In order to provide a meaningful comparison of Viet Nam's urbanisation level with other countries and to correct for some of the drawbacks of the current methodology, this review applies for the first time the OECD-EU methodology to define Functional Urban Areas (FUAs) in Viet Nam. This methodology identifies urban areas as functional economic units, with densely inhabited urban cores and commuting zones whose labour market is highly integrated with the cores (Box 1.2). FUAs define urban areas as functional economic units, rather than using official administrative boundaries which can guide Viet Nam's national authorities and city administrations to better design and implement infrastructure, transport, housing and schools, as well as space for culture and recreation in a more integrated and co-ordinated manner. FUAs are the adequate level to provide public services at the scale of the entire urban agglomeration (OECD, 2014).

Box 1.2. The OECD-EU definition of functional urban areas

The OECD-EU definition of functional urban areas (FUAs) consists of highly densely populated urban cores and adjacent municipalities ("commuting zones") with high levels of commuting (travel-to-work flows) towards the cores. This definition overcomes previous limitations for international comparability linked to administrative boundaries. This methodology is a clear example of how geographic/morphological information from geographic sources and census data can be used together to get a better understanding of how urbanisation develops.

As the first step, the distribution of the population at a fine level of spatial disaggregation – 1 km^2 – is used to identify the urban cores which are constituted by aggregations of contiguous municipalities that have more than 50% of their population living in high-density clusters. These clusters are made of contiguous 1 km^2 grid cells with a population density of at least 1 500 inhabitants per km^2 and a total population of at least 50 000 people.

As the second step, two urban cores are considered part of the same (polycentric) FUA if more than 15% of the population of any of the cores commutes to work to the other core.

The third step defines commuting zones using information on travel-to-work commuting flows from surrounding municipalities to the urban core. Municipalities sending 15% of its resident employed population or more to the urban core are included in the commuting zones, which thus can be defined as the "worker catchment area" of the urban labor market, outside the densely inhabited urban core.

The methodology makes it possible to compare FUAs of similar size across countries, proposing four types of FUAs according to population size:

- Small urban areas, with population between 50 000 and 200 000
- Medium-size urban areas, with population between 200 000 and 500 000
- Metropolitan areas, with population between 500 000 and 1.5 million
- Large metropolitan areas, with a population of 1.5 million or more.

The definition is applied to 30 OECD countries (among 35 OECD countries, it is not available for Iceland, Israel, New Zealand, Latvia and Turkey), and it identifies 1 197 FUAs of different sizes. Among them, 281 metropolitan areas (including 81 large metropolitan areas) have a population higher than 500 000 and are included in the OECD Metropolitan database.

Box 1.2. The OECD-EU definition of functional urban areas (*cont.*)

As of 2014, they account for 49% of the OECD overall population, 57% of gross domestic product and 51% of employment. Other FUAs include 411 medium-sized urban areas and 506 small urban areas. Besides, the definition has been applied to Colombia, where 54 FUAs have been identified (Sanchez-Serra, 2016).

Source: OECD (2016a), *OECD Regions at a Glance 2016*, OECD Publishing, Paris, http://dx.doi.org/10.1787/reg_glance-2016-en; Sanchez-Serra, D. (2016), "Functional Urban Areas in Colombia", *OECD Regional Development Working Papers*, No. 2016/08, OECD Publishing, Paris, http://dx.doi.org/10.1787/5jln4pn1zqq5-en; OECD (2012), *Redefining "Urban": A New Way to Measure Metropolitan Areas*, OECD Publishing, http://dx.doi.org/10.1787/9789264174108-en; Gridded population data comes from the *Landscan project* developed by Oak Ridge National Laboratory (United States).

Figure 1.2. Location of FUAs in Vietnam

Names of FUAs depict the twelve metropolitan areas

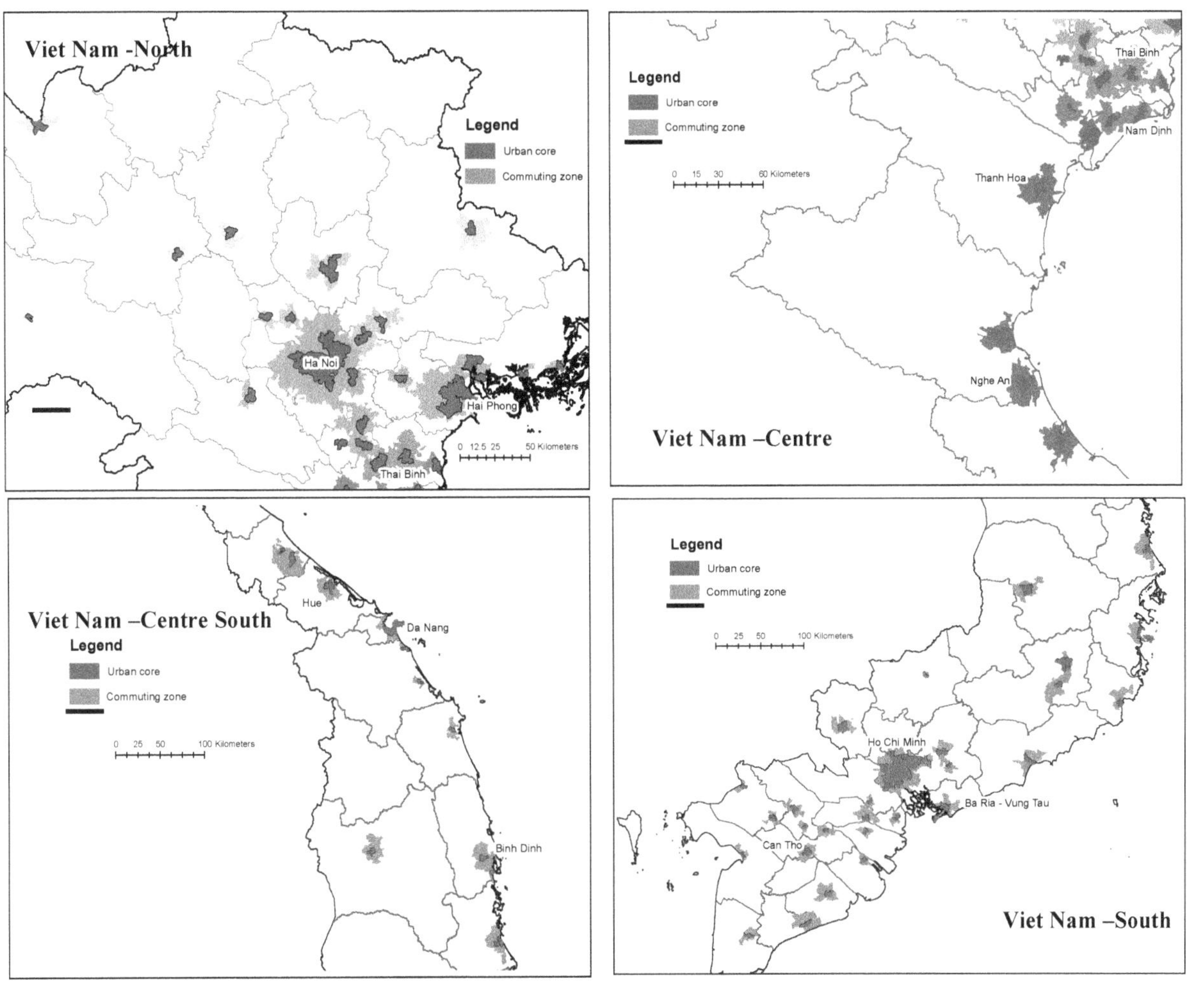

Note: This document and any map included herein are without prejudice to the status of or sovereignty over any territory, to the delimitation of international frontiers and boundaries and to the name of any territory, city or area.

Source: OECD elaboration based on data from LandScan Global Population Database (http://web.ornl.gov/sci/landscan/index.shtml), General Statistics Office (2017a) and Ministry of Construction of Viet Nam (2017).

In the case of Viet Nam, the OECD-EU methodology required an adaptation to overcome the lack of commuting data by using driving time patterns to identify the commuting zones (Annex 1.A1). This exercise identifies 63 FUAs in Viet Nam which cover 7% of national territory, and host 41% (37.1 million people) of overall population in 2013 (Figure 1.2 above). Using a residential population grid or a grid based on higher resolution population data is likely to show even higher levels of urbanisation.[4] The FUA analysis shows that Viet Nam's urbanisation level may be in fact much higher than currently defined by the national statistics (32% in 2013) and suggests revisiting the current definition. The urbanisation rate based on the OECD-EU methodology (41%) is still below the OECD average (56%), although higher than that of two OECD countries (Slovenia and Slovak Republic). The result also indicates that around 1 718 municipalities classified officially as rural are within the FUAs, while 631 municipalities (mainly in the north-western part of the country) officially classified as urban are not part of any FUA, as they form urban centres with either less than 50 000 inhabitant or a population density inferior to 1 500 persons per km^2.

Out of the 63 FUAs, there are 20 small urban areas, 31 medium-size urban areas, 9 metropolitan areas and 3 large metropolitan areas (Table 1.2). Viet Nam's functional urban system is characterised by a high proportion of small and medium size FUAs (81% of all FUAs) in comparison to OECD countries (75%). Overall, the population living in the 12 metropolitan areas of Viet Nam (9 metropolitan areas and 3 large metropolitan areas) corresponds to 28% of the national population. In fact, one-fifth of national population lives in the three large metropolitan areas: Ho Chi Minh City, Ha Noi and Hai Phong (Table 1.3).

Benchmarking the metropolitan areas in Viet Nam with those of OECD countries provide useful information. The national population share of metropolitan areas (28%) is relatively low in comparison to OECD countries (44%) and other countries such as China (59% in 2010) (Figure 1.3). Viet Nam's 12 metropolitan areas are highly dense, the second densest among OECD countries, just surpassed by South Korea (Figure 1.4). Regarding the degree of spatial concentration within the metropolitan areas, 70% of the population concentrates in the urban core municipalities. This is slightly higher than the OECD average (68%). Dense and concentrated urban agglomerations are more attractive to both individuals and firms and can create productivity increases (Dobbs et al., 2012), if well planned and managed.

Table 1.2. Functional urban areas in Viet Nam by size

	Number of FUAs	Population 2013 (thousands)	Urban core population share (%)	Commuting zone population share (%)
Large metropolitan areas (>1.5m)	3 (Ha Noi, Ho Chi Minh and Hai Phong)	18 325	77%	23%
Metropolitan areas (0.5m-1.5m)	9	6 386	51%	49%
Medium-size urban areas (0.2m-0.5m)	31	9 659	50%	50%
Small urban areas (<0.2m)	20	2 714	65%	35%
Total FUAs	63	37 084	64%	36%

Source: OECD elaboration based on data from LandScan Global Population Database (http://web.ornl.gov/sci/landscan/index.shtml), General Statistics Office (2017a) and Ministry of Construction of Viet Nam (2017).

Table 1.3. FUAs and official urban population, 2013

FUAs		Population FUA 2013 (thousand)	Share urban core population in FUA (%)	Official Urban Population 2013 (thousand)
Metro areas	Ho Chi Minh city	9 764	91	6 479
	Ha Noi[1]	6 743	61	2 827
	Hai Phong	1 818	61	897
	Thai Binh	1 158	42	179
	Da Nang	792	82	861
	Thanh Hoa	739	29	492
	Binh D□nh	664	42	465
	Can Tho	649	57	818
	Hue	617	60	543
	Ba R□a – Vung Tau	611	57	524
	Nghe An	588	56	454
	Nam D□nh	568	29	333
Total metro areas		**24 711**	**70**	**14 871**
Viet Nam's urban population		**37 084**	**64**	**28 875**
Total municipalities		**2 860**		**1 773**

1. Size of Hanoi's FUA coincides with the size projected in the *Hanoi Capital Region* plan determined under Decision No. 490/QD-TTg of 2008. It forecasts the development of Hanoi into a multi-polar urban region consisting of the Hanoi province as the core city and satellite towns in the vicinity as suburban areas within a pervasive radius of 25-30 km.

Source: OECD elaboration based on data from "LandScan Global Population Database", http://web.ornl.gov/sci/landscan/index.shtml (accessed July 2017) and the General Statistics Office of Viet Nam (2017a) and the Ministry of Construction of Viet Nam (2017).

Figure 1.3. Share of metropolitan areas in overall population (2013)

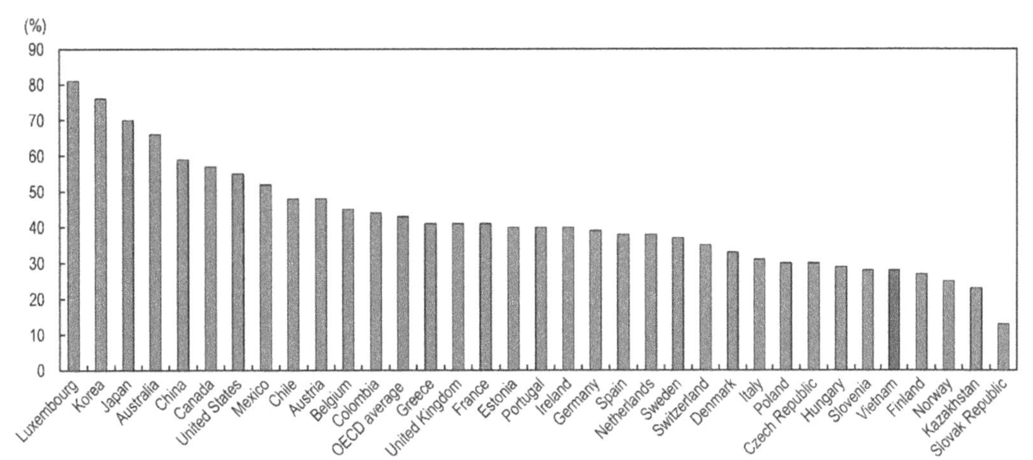

Source: OECD (2017b), "Metropolitan areas", OECD Regional Statistics (database), http://dx.doi.org/10.1787/data-00531-en; For Kazakhstan: OECD (2017c), *OECD Urban Policy Reviews: Kazakhstan*, OECD Publishing, Paris, http://dx.doi.org/10.1787/9789264268852-en; For China: OECD (2015a), *OECD Urban Policy Reviews: China* 2015, OECD Publishing, Paris, http://dx.doi.org/10.1787/9789264230040-en; For Viet Nam: OECD elaboration based on data from LandScan Global Population Database (http://web.ornl.gov/sci/landscan/index.shtml), General Statistics Office (2017a) and Ministry of Construction of Viet Nam (2017).

Figure 1.4. Density of metropolitan areas in Viet Nam and selected OECD countries (2013)

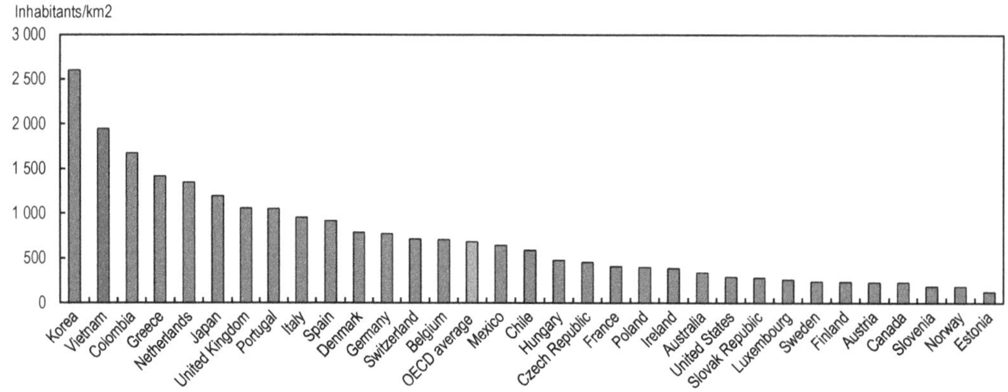

Source: OECD (2017b), "Metropolitan areas", OECD Regional Statistics (database), http://dx.doi.org/10.1787/data-00531-en; For Kazakhstan: OECD (2017c), *OECD Urban Policy Reviews: Kazakhstan*, OECD Publishing, Paris. http://dx.doi.org/10.1787/9789264268852-en; For China: OECD (2015a), *OECD Urban Policy Reviews: China* 2015, OECD Publishing, Paris, http://dx.doi.org/10.1787/9789264230040-en; For Viet Nam: OECD elaboration based on data from LandScan Global Population Database (http://web.ornl.gov/sci/landscan/index.shtml), General Statistics Office (2017a) and Ministry of Construction of Viet Nam (2017).

The three largest FUAs are driving urban population growth in Viet Nam

Between 2004 and 2013,[5] population of FUAs in Viet Nam grew much faster (4.3% annual average) than the average of the OECD countries (0.8% annual average). This rapid growth in Viet Nam's urban areas is being led by the three large metropolitan areas (Ho Chi Minh City, Ha Noi and Hai Phong). They grew at an annual average rate of 5.5% (Figure 1.5), much faster than the average growth in large metropolitan areas of OECD (1.1%) and in other countries like China (1.4%, between 2000 and 2010). The growth rates in the 9 metropolitan areas and 31 medium-size urban areas in Viet Nam were 2.4% and 3.6% annually, respectively, but still above the average growth of the equivalent FUAs in OECD countries (less than 1% annually). The FUA analysis also shows that the population of the 20 small urban areas in Viet Nam grew at a faster pace than medium size cities with an average annual rate above 4%. This rapid growth might in part reflect the effect of the continuous administrative reclassification in the country and the incentives created by the city classification system to expand urban land area.

Figure 1.5. Population growth of FUAs by city size, 2004-2013

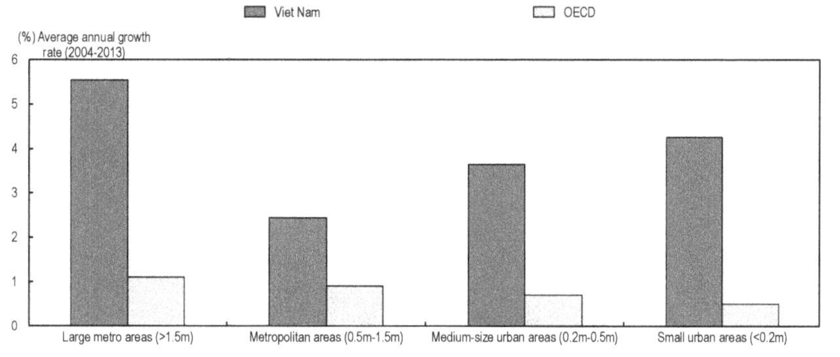

Source: OECD (2017b), "Metropolitan areas", OECD Regional Statistics (database), http://dx.doi.org/10.1787/data-00531-en; For Viet Nam: OECD elaboration based on data from LandScan Global Population Database (http://web.ornl.gov/sci/landscan/index.shtml), General Statistics Office (2017a) and Ministry of Construction of Viet Nam (2017).

Urbanisation and economic development in Viet Nam

The rapid urbanisation and economic growth in Viet Nam during the last decades have occurred in parallel, with high inflows of people migrating to urban areas attracted by high income and quality of life. This section will overview the urbanisation process in Viet Nam and analyse its economic drivers and impacts. Due to the limited data availability, the information presented in this section is based on official urbanisation figures, not based on the FUA.

Viet Nam's urbanisation is among the fastest in Southeast Asia

The urbanisation pace in Viet Nam has been accelerating since the economic opening. Between 1970 and 1990 the urban growth in the country stagnated, with urban population growing at just half the rate as between 1950 and 1970 (Figure 1.6). Since 1990, Viet Nam's urban population has almost doubled, and since 2010 the average urban growth (3% annual) surpassed the average of Southeast Asian countries (2.5%) and achieved similar rates as China (3.1%). During the last five years, population growth in rural areas has been close to zero and it is expected to turn negative in the coming years (UNDESA, 2014).

Figure 1.6. Urbanisation rate, Viet Nam and selected countries (1950-2015)

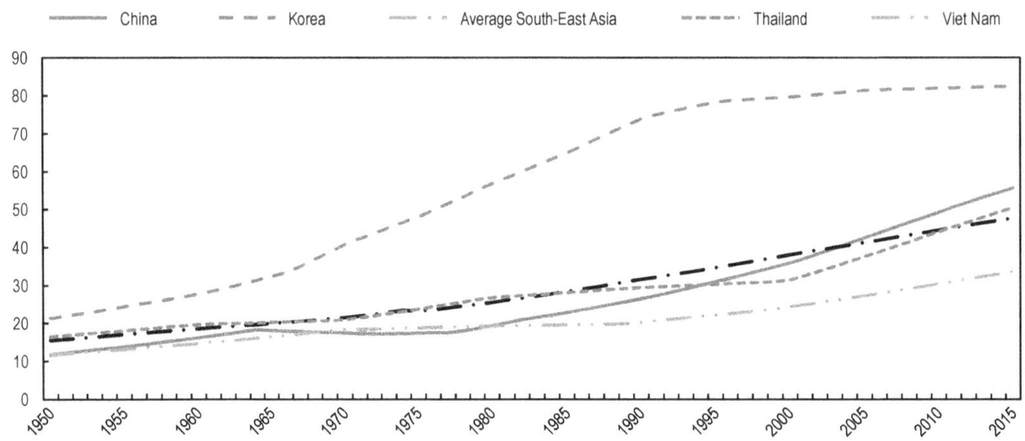

Source: UNDESA (2014), "World Urbanisation Prospects: The 2014 Revision", United Nations Department of Economic and Social Affairs, https://esa.un.org/unpd/wup/ (accessed June 2017).

The increase of population in urban areas since the 1990s has been boosted by high rural-urban migration. After a period of strong registration policies that discouraged regional mobility through a household registration system *Hộ khẩu*,[6] liberalisation movement laws during the 2000s made it easier for people to migrate within the country.[7] In particular, migration across different provinces in the country increased substantially after 2000 in response to the opportunities created by the industrialisation process. Just between 2004 and 2009, 4.3% of the total population moved to live in a province or centrally administrated city (TL3) different from their place of birth, almost half of which were between 20 and 29 years old. A big proportion of this movement (3% out of the 4.3%) occurred between regions (TL2), which is much higher than the average in TL2 OECD regions during the same period (2.1%) (OECD, 2016a). More than 40% of the Viet Nam's inter-provincial migrants moved to the two largest cities: Ho Chi Minh City (30%) and Ha Noi (11%), reflecting the growing job markets in these metropolitan areas. Overall, migration explained 42% of the population growth in urban areas in Viet Nam between 2004 and 2009.

After the 2008 global economic crisis, regional migration across the country played a smaller role in the urban population growth in Viet Nam due to the job losses in industrial and construction sectors. Instead, administrative reclassification has explained a big portion of the recent urban growth in the country. Between 2009 and 2014, administrative changes explained almost half of the population growth in urban areas, above the effect of natural growth (32%) and net migration from rural areas (21%) (Figure 1.7). For instance, the provincial city Phu Ly absorbed 21 new neighbouring municipalities in 2013, almost tripling its administrative boundary and doubling its population. Same happened with the provincial city Thanh Hoa which became one of the most populated cities in the North Coast region in 2012 after expanding its area by almost three times and thereby its population by 40%.

Figure 1.7. Contribution to urban population growth

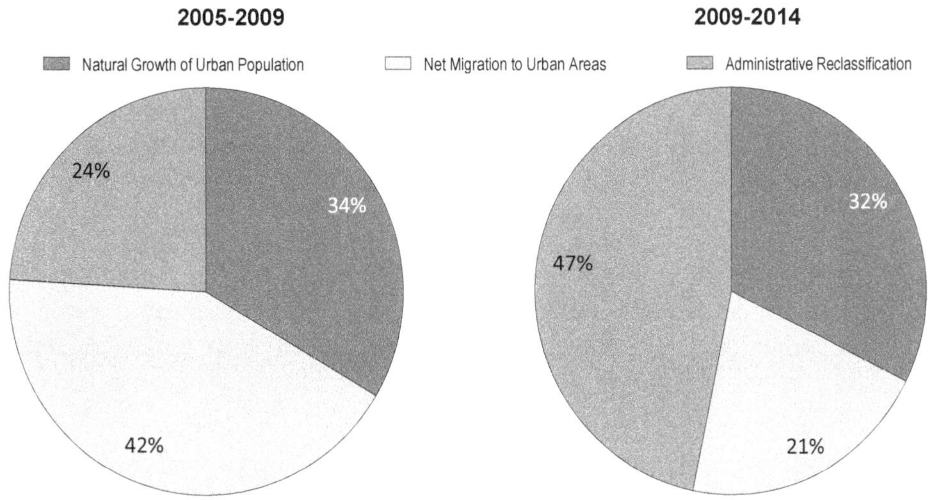

Source: OECD elaboration based on data from the General Statistics Office, Population and Housing survey (2014), "Population Census 2009 and 1999".

Viet Nam's urbanisation has been accompanied by economic growth

A country's urbanisation trajectory carries important implications for its economic growth. An important theory for rapidly urbanising countries like Viet Nam is that urbanisation *per se* is an opportunity, not a guarantee, for economic development to occur (Henderson, 2010). Some countries have become highly urbanised without growing economically (the case of many Latin American countries such as Brazil), although no country has achieved high levels of per capita income without becoming predominantly urban, as illustrated by the large empty space in the upper left of Figure 1.8. In contrast, Korea reduced the per capita income gap with the US by two-thirds, while its urbanisation rate doubled between 1970 and 2016. In the case of Viet Nam, the slow urbanisation before 1990 came together with an unchanged growth of GDP per capita relative to US, while other countries with similar initial levels of urbanisation like China and Thailand experienced a faster economic growth parallel to urbanisation. Since 1990, however, Viet Nam has quickly filled the GDP per capita gap relative to US while its urbanisation rate has increased almost six times faster than before 1990s (Figure 1.8).

Figure 1.8. Economic convergence and urbanisation (1970-2015)

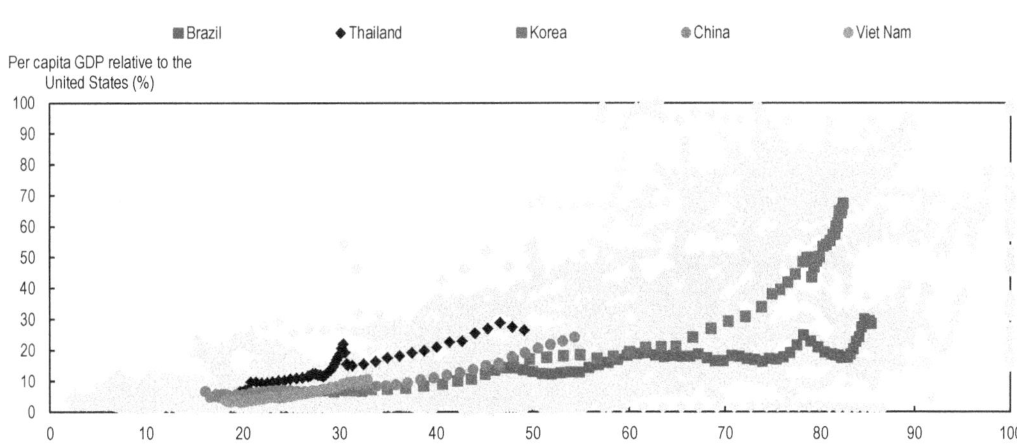

Notes: Data cover 91 countries for the period 1970-2015, GDP per capita gap vis-à-vis the US is based upon PPP GDP per capita in constant 2011 international dollars.

Source: OECD calculations based on World Bank (2016), *World Development Indicators* (database), http://data.worldbank.org/data-catalog/world-development-indicators.

Viet Nam's urbanisation process has also come together with poverty reduction and increase of quality of life. The share of people living in extreme poverty has fallen from about 50% in 1990 to 3% in 2014, which is lower than the average of East Asia and Pacific countries (4%) and also below the level of countries such as Indonesia (8%).[8] In urban areas the proportion of poor households (3%) is almost three times lower than in the rural areas.[9] Moreover, infant mortality rate has experienced a three-fold reduction since 1990 (15 deaths per 1 000 live births), with a more rapid decrease in urban areas (fourfold) than in rural (threefold). By 2015, almost all households had access to electricity and water, which is a major achievement given that coverage was less than half in 1990.

Viet Nam stands out for its high educational outputs of high school students. In 2015, the country ranked among the top ten countries on sciences according PISA results, not only above OECD average but also above countries like Korea and Germany (OECD, 2016b). There is evidence of a particular strong *urban advantage* in the Vietnamese education system where students living in cities of more than 100 000 inhabitants have performed better than in rural areas – with a score gap (26 score points on science) higher than in the average of OECD countries (OECD, 2013b). This performance gap can be attributed to different factors, such as better equipment or more qualified staff in schools of urban areas (OECD, 2016b).

Viet Nam's growth appears to be benefiting from agglomeration economies

Typically, the urbanisation process releases labour that shifts from agriculture to more productive employment in the manufacturing and service sectors. Since these sectors benefit from agglomeration economies, production should be increasingly located in high-density areas (Henderson, 2010). Consistent with economic theory, there is a fairly positive relationship between the urban population size and income in Viet Nam where provinces with a larger urban population enjoy on average a higher level of income per capita (Figure 1.9). Furthermore, economic growth has been led by centrally-administrated cities. Between 2010 and 2015, the average GDP growth of these cities (11%) has been higher than the rest of the country (7%).

Figure 1.9. Urban population size and income per capita in Vietnam's TL3 regions, 2014

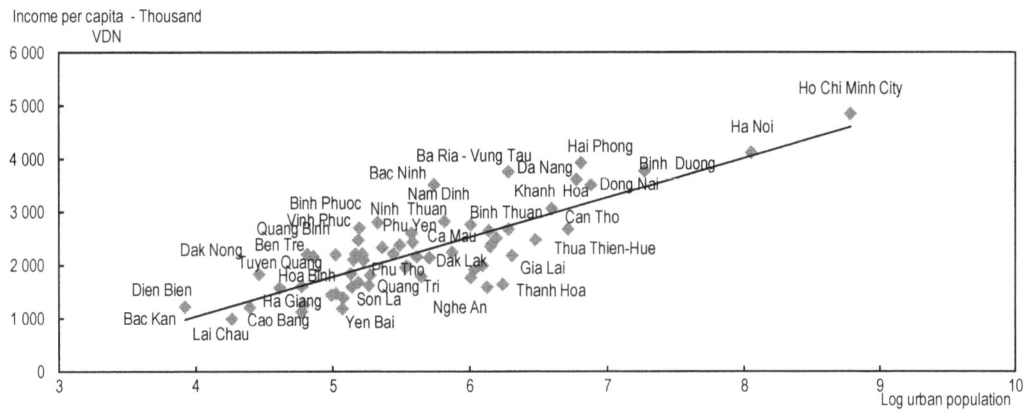

Source: Urban Development Agency (2015), Survey 2015 on national cities provided by the Ministry of Construction of Viet Nam.

Viet Nam concentrates most of its economic activities in two urban poles: Ho Chi Minh City and Ha Noi. By 2014, the income per capita in these two cities was four times higher than the country average and almost tripled the average income of the other three centrally administrated cities. By 2015, the two cities produced more than one third of the national GDP, hosted more than 25% of the national employment and contributed more than 50% of the national government's revenue (five times higher than the other three centrally-administered cities). Across OECD countries, city size is positively related with labour productivity (Ahrend et al., 2017). This trend is also followed by Vietnamese cities where Ho Chi Minh City's labour productivity is double of Ha Noi's and three times higher than the average of centrally-administered cities.

The concentration of people and firms in high density "economic growth centres" is a key element if Viet Nam wishes to harness the benefits of agglomeration economies. However, city size and population density alone are not sufficient. OECD research suggests that only well managed, well-connected cities do support economic growth, by allowing countries to enjoy agglomeration economies while mitigating the costs of agglomeration (Box 1.3).

Box 1.3. Managing agglomeration economies

Metropolitan areas and dynamic medium-sized cities have enormous potential for job creation and innovation, as they are hubs and gateways for global networks such as trade or transport. In many OECD countries, labour productivity (measured in terms of GDP per worker) and wages can be observed to increase with city size.

Stronger productivity levels are a reflection of a bonus intrinsic to being in a city, known as the agglomeration benefit. On average, a worker's wage increases with the size of the city where he/she works, even after controlling for worker attributes such as education level. OECD estimates suggest that the agglomeration benefit in the form of a wage premium rises by 2-5% for a doubling of population size (Ahrend et al., 2014), which is in line with comparable studies for individual countries (Combes et al., 2012). However, agglomeration benefits do not accrue homogeneously across cities, and they show sizeable variations within countries.

Box 1.3. Managing agglomeration economies (*cont.*)

Higher productivity is due in part to the quality of the workforce and the industrial mix. Larger cities on average have a more educated population, with the shares of both very high-skilled and low-skilled workers increasing with city size. A 10 percentage-point increase in the share of university-educated workers in a city raises the productivity of other workers in that city by 3-4% (Ahrend et al., 2014). Larger cities typically have a higher proportion of sectors with higher productivity, such as consulting, legal or financial services, etc. They are also more likely to be hubs or service centres through which trade flows and financial and other flows are channelled. These flows typically require the provision of high value-added services.

Living in large cities does provide benefits, but it also has disadvantages (see figure above). While productivity, wages and the availability of many amenities generally increase with city size, so do what are generally referred to as agglomeration costs. Some agglomeration costs are financial: for example, housing prices/rents and, more generally, price levels are typically higher in larger cities. In addition, a number of non-pecuniary costs, such as pollution, congestion, inequality and crime, typically also increase with city size, while trust and similar measures of social capital often decline. Survey data from European cities confirm that citizens in larger cities – despite valuing the increased amenities – are generally less satisfied with the other aspects mentioned, notably air pollution.

To some extent, city size is the outcome of a trade-off between these benefits and costs. Mobility across and within cities implies that – at least in the medium to long term – wage levels, commuting costs and other urban (dis)amenities are reflected in land prices, and more generally in a city's cost of living. This is supported by findings suggesting that for increasing population size, these agglomeration benefits and costs go up at a broadly comparable pace (see Combes et al. (2012), for evidence on France, and Gibbons et al. (2011), for the United Kingdom). A similar picture emerges when looking directly at cities' productivity and price levels. Evidence from Germany shows that, on average, increases in a city's productivity, and hence wages, are matched by similar increases in local price levels.

Agglomeration costs and benefits

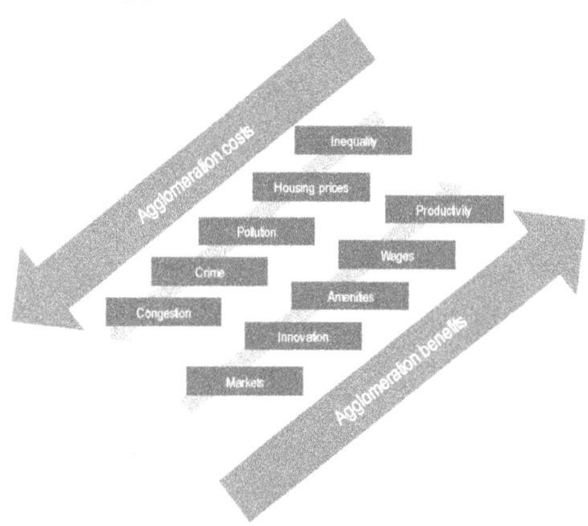

Source: OECD (2015b), *The Metropolitan Century: Understanding Urbanisation and its Consequences*, OECD Publishing, Paris, http://dx.doi.org/10.1787/9789264228733-en; OECD (2014), *OECD Regional Outlook 2014: Regions and Cities: Where Policies and People Meet,* OECD Publishing, Paris, http://dx.doi.org/10.1787/9789264201415-en; Ahrend, R., et al. (2017), "What Makes Cities More Productive?: Agglomeration economies and the role of urban governance: Evidence from 5 OECD Countries", *OECD Productivity Working Papers*, No. 6, OECD Publishing, Paris, http://dx.doi.org/10.1787/2ce4b893-en; Combes, P.P., G. Duranton and L. Gobillon (2012), "The costs of agglomeration: Land prices in French cities", *CEPR Discussion Papers*, No. 9240, Centre for Economic Policy Research, London; Gibbons, S., H.G. Overman and G. Resende (2011), "Real earnings disparities in Britain", *Spatial Economics Research Centre Discussion Papers*, No. 0065, London School of Economics and Political Science, London.

Key challenges for Vietnamese cities

Urbanisation poses several challenges for cities around the world, and Vietnamese cities are not the exception. For example, rapid urbanisation requires massive investments in local and inter-city infrastructures and modern social structures in a short time. This section will present key urban challenges for Vietnamese cities at the TL3 level with a focus on labour, housing quality and environment.

Low skilled labour and informal jobs accompany disparity in wages

Despite the rapid economic growth and positive educational performance of high school students, the education attainment of the economically-active population in Viet Nam continues to be an acute challenge. By 2015, 80% of the labour force in Viet Nam did not have any type of technical or professional education (college, university or higher) and only 10% had completed upper-secondary education. The latter is far below the average for OECD countries (83%) and even below countries in the same region like Philippines (75%) and Indonesia (52%). Within urban areas, almost two thirds of the labour force did not have any type of qualification and just 20% had completed upper-secondary education (GSO, 2016).

The large unskilled labour force in Viet Nam is feeding an economy with a high degree of insecure and temporary jobs. The informal economy is the second source of employment in the country (24% of employment), after the agricultural sector (48%), and much higher than local private sector (16%) and public sector (10%) (Cling et al., 2014). In 2015, the self-employed workers without paid employees– considered as vulnerable workers without stable jobs and no social security (GSO, 2016) – accounted for 38% of the whole employed population in Vietnamese urban areas. There is a great disparity of the amount of these workers across urban areas. For instance, Ho Chi Minh City has 29% of their population as self-employed workers without paid employees, while in Ha Noi the proportion raises to almost 45%.

Figure 1.10. Wage per capita and size of urban population in Viet Nam's TL3 regions, 2014

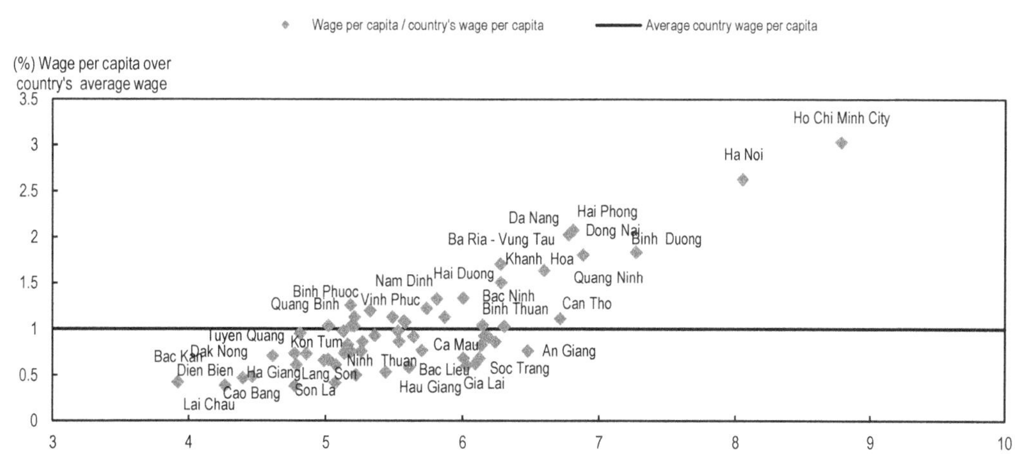

Note: Districts over the line have a higher wage per capita than the country's average.

Source: Urban Development Agency (2015), "Survey 2015 on national cities" provided by the Ministry of Construction of Viet Nam.

In addition, income inequality among urban areas poses another challenge. In 2014, Ha Noi and Ho Chi Minh City had a wage per capita almost three times higher than the country's average, while the wage per capita in region such as Lai Chau is just 40% of the national average wage (Figure 1.10 above). When it comes to international comparisons, the regional income disparity in Vietnam is relatively high. The per capita income in the top income TL2 region (Red River Delta which includes Ha Noi) is three times higher than the bottom income region (Central Highlands region), which is above the average regional disparity in OECD countries (income gap of 1.6 times) (Figure 1.11).

Figure 1.11. Income per capita gap between top income region and bottom income region for OECD and selected non-OECD countries, 2014

TL2 level regions

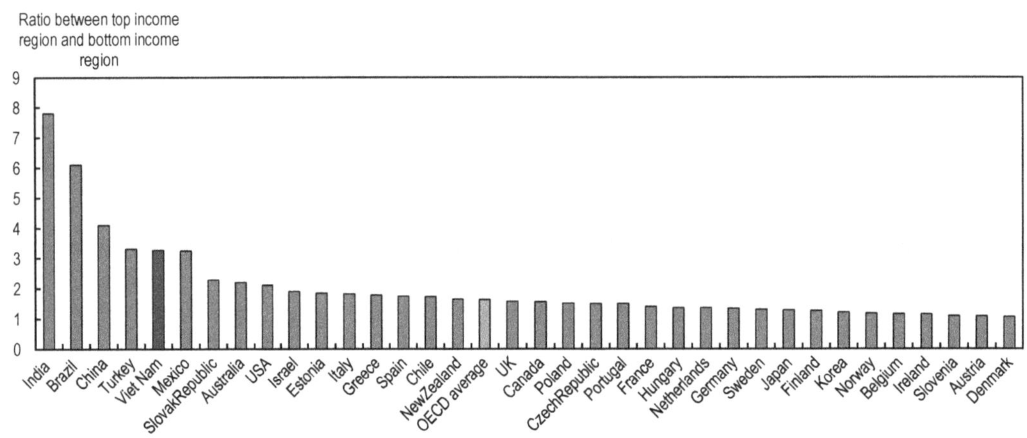

Note: Data for India refers to 2013. Gap for India, Brazil and China is calculated deducted the income form GDP per capita level.

Source: OECD (2016a), *OECD Regions at a Glance 2016*, OECD Publishing, Paris. http://dx.doi.org/10.1787/reg_glance-2016-en; Data of Viet Nam from Urban Development Agency (2015), survey 2015 on national cities provided by the Ministry of Construction of Viet Nam.

Housing and living standards in urban areas

Despite the large improvement in electricity and water supply coverage in Viet Nam, challenges on housing conditions still remain. In 2014, almost 27% of households in urban areas still received their water from sources different to pipe water such as rain water (2%) or water from protected hand-dug wells (23%). Disparities in safe water coverage are also evident across cities in the country. Class I cities such as Da Lat have almost full coverage rates, while provincial cities Class III cities such as Kon Tum or Tay Ninh have less than 65% of household connected to tap water (Ministry of Construction of Viet Nam, 2017). Even among centrally-administered cities, while Ha Noi and Ho Chi Minh City have an almost full coverage (99%) of safe water, in Can Tho the coverage is still below 90%. Furthermore, a low proportion of households with access to internet may undermine competitiveness in cities. Only 21% of households in the country have access to internet, far below the average of OECD countries (78%) (Figure 1.12). Urban areas have a proportion of 42% households connected to the internet, while in rural areas this rate drops to 10%. Taking information of urban areas at the province level (TL3), there is also an important disparity, with just six provinces with more than 45% urban households connected to internet, while almost nine provinces have connection rates smaller than 25%.

Figure 1.12. Share of Households connected to the internet in OECD and South East Asian countries

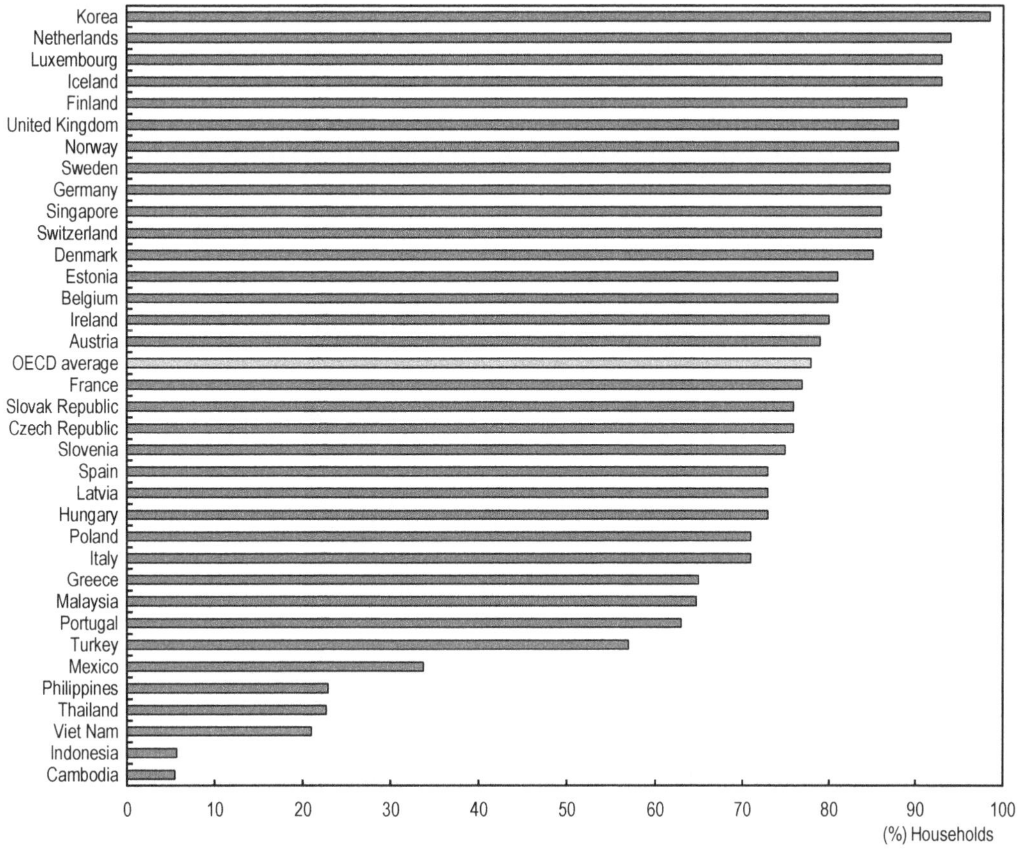

Source: OECD (2017e), "Regional well-being", *OECD Regional Statistics* (database). http://dx.doi.org/10.1787/data-00707-en; For South East Asian countries: UN-ESCAP (2016), A Pre-Feasibility Study on the Asia-Pacific Information Superhighway in the ASEAN Sub-region.

Increased motorisation along with a low use of urban public transport

An increasing motorisation rate, coupled with the difficulties of providing efficient public transport alternatives, constitutes a critical policy challenge for urban areas in Viet Nam. The country has the highest per capita motorcycle ownership in the world with motorbikes accounting for 96% of the total number of vehicles. In the case of Ha Noi and Ho Chi Minh City, the proportion of motorcycles of total vehicles registered amounts to 90% and 92%, respectively. Motorcycles have become popular not only because of their relatively low price but also because of the lack of public transport alternatives and the ease of using them (in Viet Nam, motorbikes with 50 cc engines or less do not require a license).[10] Ho Chi Minh City has almost one motorbike per person (979 motorbikes per thousand people). The rate is even higher than in cities such as Jakarta, Indonesia (910 motorbikes per 1000 inhabitants) and Manila, the Philippines (561 motorbikes per 1 000 people) (OECD/ITF, 2017). In terms of the transport mode, motorbike is by far the most common transport mode, transporting more than half of total number of passengers in less than 100 km length, which is more than two times the number of passengers transported by buses (Figure 1.13). This share is even higher in some big cities such as Ho Chi Minh City where bus trips account for less than 10% of the trips within the city (Department of Transport of Ho Chi Minh City, 2011). This widespread use of motorbikes could be used as an advantage for the country's sustainable urban mobility, if government policies encourage the use of electric or eco-friendly motorbikes along with public transport instead of the use cars.

Figure 1.13. Share of passengers mobilised in less than 100 kms distance, 2008

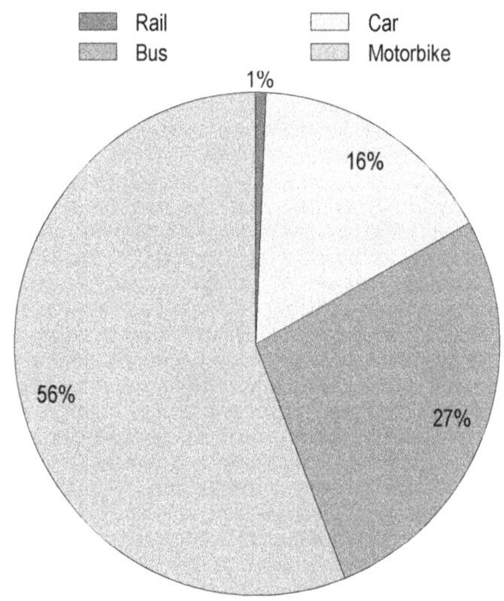

Source: VIETRANS and JICA (2008), "The comprehensive study on the sustainable development of transport system in Viet Nam", Ministry of Transport of Viet Nam.

The low quality of roads imposes an extra challenge for mobility in Vietnamese cities. In 2008, almost 80% of local roads' network was either gravel or earth roads (VIETRANS and JICA, 2008). Low road quality comes together with a high level of traffic accidents. According to the 2014 census, traffic accident is the second cause of death in the country (accounting for 5%). With 25 road traffic deaths per 100 000 people in 2014, the country registers one of the highest rates of road traffic deaths in Southeast Asia (average 18 deaths per 100 000), above countries such as Indonesia (15) and the Philippines (10), and far above OECD countries such as Australia (5), Spain (4) or Mexico (12) (WHO, 2017).

The big threat: the increasing demand of cars

The mobility situation in Viet Nam might worsen in light of the rapid increase of private cars. Boosted by a growing middle-class, Viet Nam registers the fastest growth in car sales in the region, with an average annual growth of 39% since 2012 (Figure 1.14). In fact, the number of cars per 1 000 people has been growing faster than motorbikes (Figure 1.15).

It is often claimed that the limited space for streets in Vietnamese city centres would be one of the main causes of congestion. However, while the number of secondary streets is indeed low in certain areas, a general expansion of the network without improve public transport alternatives is likely to mainly increase the traffic with little or no permanent effects on congestion. A study made for US cities extending the "the fundamental law of highways" into metropolitan areas (Duranton and Turner, 2011), demonstrated that widening and building more roads increase the car traffic. The elasticity found between roads and vehicle miles driven is one, meaning that one percent increase of roads will lead to a similar increase in driving. This is related to different factors such as changes in individual behaviour, economic activity and migration. Viet Nam also has room to improve the enforcement of traffic rules in cities. People are used to occupying sidewalks with motorbikes and parking vehicles along the roads.

Figure 1.14. Non-commercial car sales in Southeast Asia

Average growth between 2012-15

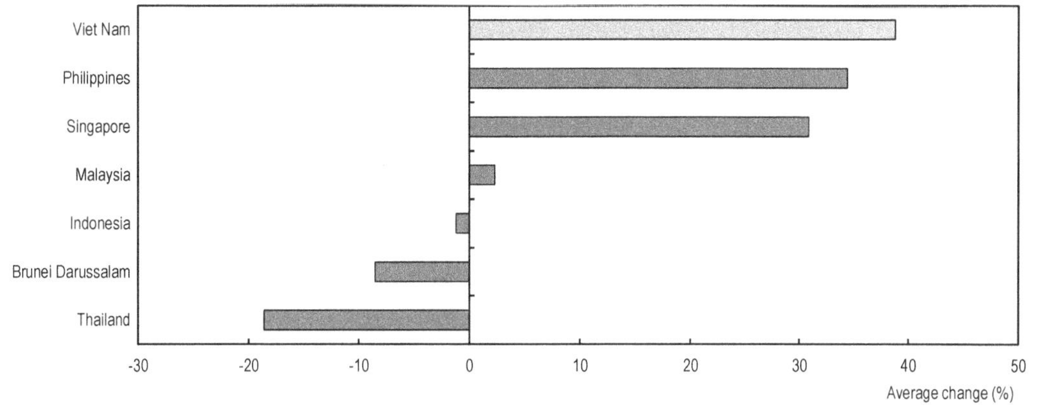

Source: ASEAN Automotive Federation Statistics (2016), www.asean-autofed.com/statistics.html.

Figure 1.15. Growth of vehicles by type in Viet Nam

Average annual growth 2007-2016

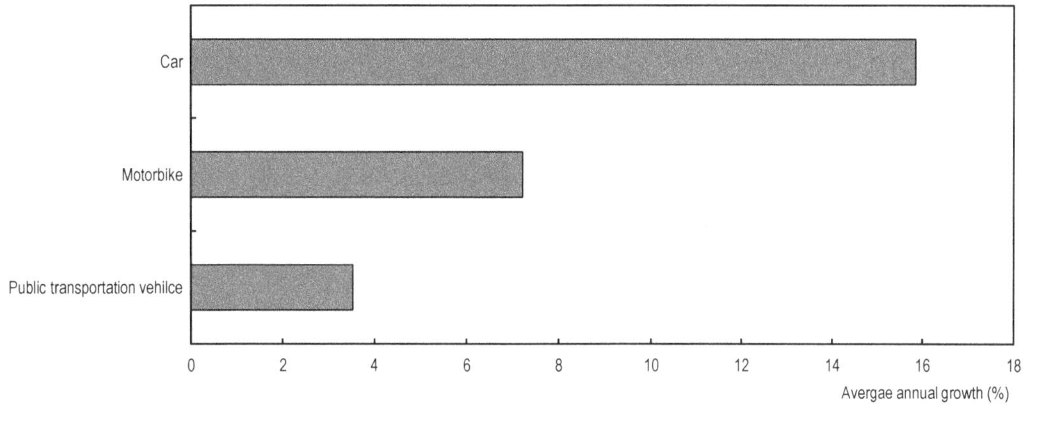

Source: Viet Nam Register; Answers to the OECD background questionnaire provided by the Ministry of Construction of Viet Nam, June 2017.

Environmental challenges

Air pollution is a rising concern in Viet Nam, putting at risk the health of its population. Globally, 25% of lung cancer deaths and about 17% of respiratory infection deaths in 2012 can be attributed to exposure to fine particulate matter (WHO, 2014). Viet Nam's average annual concentration of particular matter smaller than 2.5 microns (PM2.5) was reported to be 28 μg/m^3, one of the highest in Southeast Asia above Thailand (26 μg/m^3) and the Philippines (23 μg/m^3). It is also higher than the OECD average (15 μg/m^3) and far above the World Health Organization guideline (10 μg/m^3).

Air pollution tends to be more severe in urban areas. Limited access to public transport networks and high use of private vehicles intensify traffic and thus air pollution. Levels of air pollution in larger Vietnamese cities are higher than those in cities in other countries with a comparable level of development. The average concentration of annual particular matter smaller than 10 microns (PM10) in Ho Chi Minh City (96 µg/m³) is higher than in cities such as Shanghai, Manila and Bangkok and far above the level recommended by the World Health Organisation (20 ug/m³) (Figure 1.16).

Figure 1.16. Air pollution level in selected cities

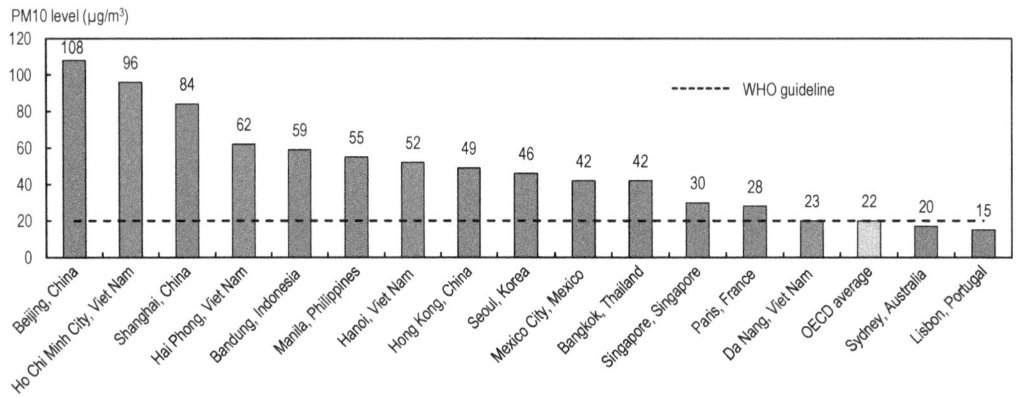

Notes: Data of Chinese and Filipino cities is from 2013. Data of Hai Phong is from 2010 and Da Nang is average between 2010 and 2014. Data for the rest of cities is from 2014. Indicator for OECD average is urban population weighted average of annual concentrations of PM10 in residential areas of cities with more than 100 000 residents.

Source: Fr Ho Chi Minh City, data is from Ho Chi Minh City Department of Natural Resources and Environment; For Hanoi and Danang, data is from Ministry of Natural Resources and the Environment of Viet Nam; For Hai Phong, data is from Hai Phong Department of Transport; For OECD average of urban areas, data is from OECD (2015), *Better Life Index 2014,* http://dx.doi.org/10.1787/socwel-data-en; For the rest, data is from World Health Organization (2016), Data Base on atmospheric pollution.

Cities in Viet Nam have also a high rate of solid waste generation when it comes to international comparisons (Figure 1.17). The available data shows that Ha Noi produces almost 800 kg per capita of solid waste per year which is relatively high compared with the average of OECD countries (516) and other cities of the region such as Bangkok (640) and Hong Kong (490). The increasing waste raises the pressure on an already weak waste treatment system in the country. In urban areas, only 60% of the waste produced is being treated by sanitary landfill or recycled. Urban areas in the country register a total of 98 open landfill sites in operation, with only 16 are considered hygienic (MONRE, 2011). There is a great disparity in waste treatment across cities, less than 15% of Class IV and V cities meet the national quality standards, while most of Class I cities (87%) and the two special cities achieve them. The situation is worst when it comes to waste water treatment where less than 5% of cities of Class V and IV meet the national criteria (Figure 1.18).

Figure 1.17. Municipal solid waste generation in selected OECD and non OECD cities

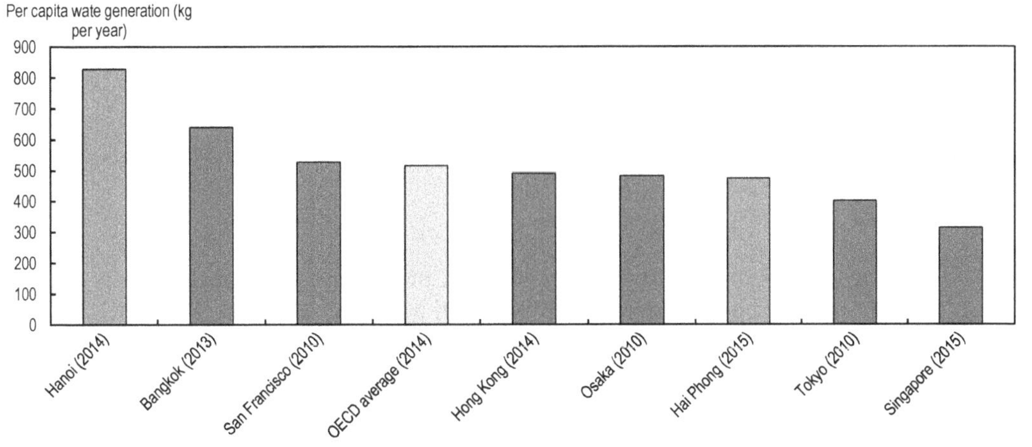

Source: OECD (2016c), *Green Growth in Hai Phong, Viet Nam,* OECD Publishing, Paris, http://dx.doi.org/10.1787/9789264260207-en.

Figure 1.18. Quality of solid waste and wastewater treatment by city rank, 2014

(%) Share of cities meeting national quality requirements

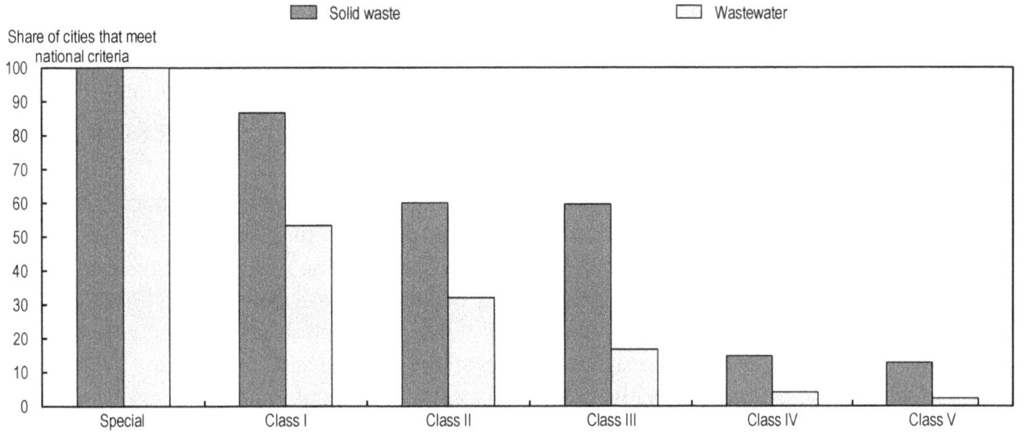

Source: General Statistics Office (GSO) (2016), Report on labour force survey 2015, Ha Noi, www.gso.gov.vn/default_en.aspx?tabid=515&idmid=5&ItemID=16027.

Notes

1. The recognition of private property in 1992, the foreign trade liberalisation in 1995, the right of business freedom in 1999 as well as the accession to WTO in 2006 were some of the policies adopted since 1990.

2. The decree 62/2011/NĐ-CP states criteria to become a township or ward. Beyond population density and share of non-agricultural labour force it includes minimum characteristics of urban infrastructure and having master or development plans approved. To become a township, the area needs also an approval to be classified as class V urban centre.

3. Infrastructure development thresholds (for inner areas) are comprised in Annex 1 of the resolution 1210/2016/UBTVQH13. It contains 38 indicators divided in four main groups: Social infrastructure (e.g. share of permanent and semi-permanent house, number of city-level education facilities, healthcare facility coverage, etc.), other infrastructure (e.g. share of public transport trip, share of households that have access to safe water, number of Internet subscription per 100 citizens, etc.), environment conditions (e.g. share of collected solid waste, density of the urban drainage system, average green area per person, etc) and Urban architecture and landscape (e.g. number of urban renovation projects, etc.)

4. This report shows the results based on the LandScan Global Population Database, which estimates ambient population (average presence of people in the area over a certain time span) and not residential population. LandScan's population grid differs from a residential population grid and its accuracy varies between different parts of the world. The Global Human Settlement (GHS) population grid is a new data source developed by the Joint Research Centre of the European Commission. It combines data on built-up areas with fine scale residential population data from national censuses. A preliminary result based on the GHS population grid indicates that the level of urbanisation in Viet Nam would be far higher than the 41% calculated using LandScan (for example, the population share living in urban centres in Viet Nam would be 54%, double the 27% calculated with LandScan). The GHS population grid will be used to develop a global, people-based definition of cities, under the forthcoming global city definition project conducted by OECD together with European Commission, Food and Agriculture Organisation (FAO) and World Bank (for further information, see http://ghsl.jrc.ec.europa.eu/degurba.php).

5. Due to data availability, it was only possible to build FUAs population for the years 2004 and 2013.

6. The system was introduced firstly in 1954 through the official document 495 and then formally extended in 1960s to the entire country (See Hardy, 2003).

9. The 2007 Law on Residence lessened the requirements for temporary residents to apply to permanent registration in centrally-governed cities and eliminated geographic restrictions for birth registration.

10. Extreme poverty is measured as the percentage of the population living on less than USD 1.90 a day at 2011 international prices (World Bank database, 2017).

11. Data of poverty in urban and rural areas is calculated according to the Viet Nam government's definition of poverty line for households. By 2015, the threshold for rural areas was 615 thousand dongs monthly per household, while for urban areas it was 760 dongs (GSO, 2017).

12. A typical motorcycle costs USD 1 000- 2 000 which represents between 30% and 60% of GDP per capita in Hanoi and 20%-40% in HCMC (Urban transport in crisis, 2011).

References

Ahrend, R. et al. (2017), "What Makes Cities More Productive? Agglomeration economies and the role of urban governance: Evidence from 5 OECD Countries", *OECD Productivity Working Papers*, No. 6, OECD Publishing, Paris, http://dx.doi.org/10.1787/2ce4b893-en.

Ahrend, R. et al. (2014), "What Makes Cities More Productive? Evidence on the Role of Urban Governance from Five OECD Countries", *OECD Regional Development Working Papers*, 2014/05, OECD Publishing, Paris, http://dx.doi.org/10.1787/5jz432cf2d8p-en.

Ahrend, R. and A. Schumann (2014), "Does Regional Economic Growth Depend on Proximity to Urban Centres?" *OECD Regional Development Working Papers*, 2014/07, OECD Publishing, Paris, http://dx.doi.org/10.1787/5jz0t7fxh7wc-en.

Angel, S. (2012), *Planet of Cities,* Lincoln Institute of Land Policy, Cambridge, MA.

ASEAN Automotive Federation (AAF) (2016), Statistics, www.asean-autofed.com/statistics.html (accessed July 2017).

Cities Alliance (2013), "Cities Alliance in Action: Transforming Urban Policy Making in Viet Nam", www.citiesalliance.org/sites/citiesalliance.org/files/vietnam%20vuup%20nuup%20-the%20final.pdf (accessed July 2017).

Cling, J.P., M. Razafindrakoto and F. Roubaud (2011), "The informal economy in Vietnam", Study for the International Labour Organization, Ministry of Labour, Invalids and Social Affairs of Vietnam (MOLISA), Ha Noi, https://app.box.com/s/gfzhqao4jgj4ckgood0mf3lcsnvp6kxs.

Combes, P.P., G. Duranton and L. Gobillon (2012), "The costs of agglomeration: Land prices in French cities", *CEPR Discussion Papers*, No. 9240, Centre for Economic Policy Research, London.

Department of Transport of Ho Chi Minh City (2011), transportation data (in Vietnamese).

Dobbs, R., J. Remes, J. Manyika, C. Roxburgh, S. Smit and F. Schaer (2012), "Urban World: Cities and the Rise of the Consuming Class", McKinsey Global Institute.

Duranton, G. and M. Turner (2011). "The Fundamental Law of Road Congestion: Evidence from US Cities," *American Economic Review*, American Economic Association, vol. 101(6), pages 2616-52, October

http://www.unescap.org/sites/default/files/ASEAN%20report%20final.pdf (Accessed July 2017).

General Statistics Office (GSO) (2017a), *Administrative unit database*, Ha Noi, www.gso.gov.vn/default_en.aspx?tabid=773.

GSO (2017b), *Solid waste and waste water database*, Ha Noi, www.gso.gov.vn/default_en.aspx?tabid=773.

GSO (2016), *Report on labour force survey 2015*, Ha Noi, www.gso.gov.vn/default_en.aspx?tabid=515&idmid=5&itemid=16027.

GSO (2015), Database of administrative units, www.gso.gov.vn/default_en.aspx?tabid=773 (accessed 27 July 2017).

Gibbons, S., H.G. Overman and G. Resende (2011), "Real earnings disparities in Britain", *Spatial Economics Research Centre Discussion Papers*, No. 0065, London School of Economics and Political Science, London.

Government of Viet Nam (2015),"National Report of the Socialist Republic of Viet Nam to Habitat III".

Hardy, A. (2003), "State Visions, Migrant Decisions: Population Movements since the End of the Vietnam War", in *Postwar Vietnam: Dynamics of a Transforming Society*, H. V. Luong and M.D. Lanham (eds), Rowman and Littlefield Publishers.

Henderson, J. V. (2010), "Cities and development", *Journal of Regional Science*, Vol. 50, No. 1, pp. 515-540.

Minsitry of Construction of Viet Nam (2017), Answers to the OECD questionnaire, May 2017, unpublished.

Ministry of Construction of Viet Nam (2015), "Mekong delta region urban upgrading project – Urban poverty status and trend in Vietnam", Ha Noi.

Ministry of Natural Resource and Environment (MONRE) (2011), "National State of Environment Report 2011-Solid waste". http://cem.gov.vn/VN/BAOCAO_Content/tabid/356/cat/177/nfriend/3741672/language/vi-VN/Default.aspx (accessed June 2017)

Obaco, M., V. Royuela and X. Vitores (2017) "Computing Functional Urban Areas Using a Hierarchical Travel Time Approach: An Applied Case in Ecuador", Regional Quantitative Analysis Research Group, *Working Paper 2017/03*, www.ub.edu/aqr/documents-de-treball_en.php.

OECD (2017a), *Economic Outlook for Southeast Asia, China and India 2017: Addressing Energy Challenges*, OECD Publishing, Paris, http://dx.doi.org/10.1787/saeo-2017-en.

OECD (2017b), "Metropolitan areas", OECD Regional Statistics (database), http://dx.doi.org/10.1787/data-00531-en

OECD (2017c), *OECD Urban Policy Reviews: Kazakhstan*, OECD Publishing, Paris.

http://dx.doi.org/10.1787/9789264268852-en

OECD (2017d), "OECD Territorial Grids", Better Policies for Better Lives, OECD Centre for Entrepreneurship, SMEs, Regions and Cities, Paris, www.oecd.org/regional/regional-policy/territorial-grids-2017.pdf.

OECD (2017e), "Regional well-being", OECD Regional Statistics (database). http://dx.doi.org/10.1787/data-00707-en

OECD/ITF (2017), ITF Transport Outlook 2017, OECD Publishing, Paris. http://dx.doi.org/10.1787/9789282108000-en

OECD (2016a), *OECD Regions at a Glance 2016*, OECD Publishing, Paris, http://dx.doi.org/10.1787/reg_glance-2016-en.

OECD (2016b), *PISA 2015 Results (Volume II): Policies and Practices for Successful Schools*, OECD Publishing, Paris, http://dx.doi.org/10.1787/9789264267510-en.

OECD (2016c), *Green Growth in Hai Phong, Viet Nam*, OECD Publishing, Paris, http://dx.doi.org/10.1787/9789264260207-en.

OECD (2015a), *OECD Urban Policy Reviews: China 2015*, OECD Publishing, Paris, http://dx.doi.org/10.1787/9789264230040-en

OECD (2015b), *The Metropolitan Century: Understanding Urbanisation and its Consequences*, OECD Publishing, Paris, http://dx.doi.org/10.1787/9789264228733-en.

OECD (2014), *OECD Regional Outlook 2014: Regions and Cities: Where People and Policies Meet*, OECD Publishing, Paris, http://dx.doi.org/10.1787/9789264201415-en.

OECD (2013a), "Metropolitan areas", *OECD Regional Statistics* (database), http://dx.doi.org/10.1787/data-00531-en (accessed January 2018).

OECD (2013b), *PISA 2012 Results: Excellence through Equity (Volume II): Giving Every Student the Chance to Succeed*, OECD Publishing, Paris, http://dx.doi.org/10.1787/9789264201132-en.

OECD (2012), *Redefining Urban: A New Way to Measure Metropolitan Areas*, OECD Publishing, Paris, http://dx.doi.org/10.1787/9789264174108-en.

Sala-i-Martín, X. and K. Schwab (2014), "Global Competitiveness Report 2014-2015", World Economic Forum, Global Competitiveness and Benchmarking Network, Geneva, http://www3.weforum.org/docs/WEF_GlobalCompetitivenessReport_2014-15.pdf.

Sanchez-Serra, D. (2016), "Functional Urban Areas in Colombia", *OECD Regional Development Working Papers*, No. 2016/08, OECD Publishing, Paris, http://dx.doi.org/10.1787/5jln4pn1zqq5-en.

Storper, M. (2013), "Keys to the City: How Economics, Institutions, Social Interaction, and Politics Shape Development", Vol. 90/3, Princeton University Press, Oxford, pp. 341-344.

United Nations Conference on Trade and Development (UNCTAD) (2017), "World Investment Report 2017", http://unctad.org/en/PublicationsLibrary/wir2017_en.pdf (accessed June 2017).

United Nations Department of Economic and Social Affairs UNDESA (2014), "World Urbanisation Prospects: The 2014 Revision", United Nations Department of Economic and Social Affairs, https://esa.un.org/unpd/wup/ (accessed June 2017).

United Nations Economic and Social Commission for Asia and the Pacific, ESCAP (2016), *A Pre-Feasibility Study on the Asia-Pacific Information Superhighway in the ASEAN Sub-region*.

VIETRANS and Japan International Co-operation Agency (2008), "The comprehensive study on the sustainable development of transport system in Viet Nam", *Interim Report*, Ministry of Transport of Viet Nam.

Thanh, N. X. and D. Dapice (2009), "Vietnam's Infrastructure Constraints", Ash Center for Democratic Governance and Innovation, Series on Vietnam's WTO Accession and International Competitiveness Research, *Policy Dialogue Paper* , No. 3, https://www.innovations.harvard.edu/sites/default/files/653317.pdf.

World Bank and Ministry of Planning and Investment of Vietnam (2016), *Vietnam 2035: Toward Prosperity, Creativity, Equity, and Democracy*, World Bank, Washington, DC, doi:10.1596/978-1-4648-0824-1.

World Bank (2016), *World Development Indicators (database)*, http://data.worldbank.org/data-catalog/world-development-indicators (accessed July 2017).

World Bank (2011), "Vietnam urbanization review: technical assistance report", Washington, DC, http://documents.worldbank.org/curated/en/225041468177548577/Vietnam-urbanization-review-technical-assistance-report.

World Health Organization (WHO) (2017), "Global Health Observatory Data, Road traffic death rate by WHO region and income level", www.who.int/gho/road_safety/mortality/traffic_deaths_rates/en/ (accessed 27 July 2017).

WHO (2016), "Global Urban Ambient Air Pollution Database", http://www.who.int/phe/health_topics/outdoorair/databases/cities/en/ (accessed 27 July 2017).

WHO (2014), "Global Health Observatory Data, Road traffic death rate by WHO region and income level", www.who.int/gho/road_safety/mortality/traffic_deaths_rates/en/ (accessed 27 July 2017).

Annex 1.A1

Defining Viet Nam's functional urban areas

This Review proposes a new methodology to address the issues that result from the gap between an administrative definition of urban areas and actual settlements patterns of people by using and adapting the OECD- European Commission method of functional urban areas (FUAs) to the case of Viet Nam.

The OECD, in collaboration with the European Commission (EC), has developed a methodology to defining metropolitan areas as functional economic places in a consistent way across countries. Using population density and travel-to-work flows (commuting data) as key information, FUAs emerge as characterised by densely inhabited "urban cores" and less-populated municipalities whose labour market is highly integrated with the urban cores "commuting zones" (OECD, 2012). The methodology consists of the three main steps presented below, where commuting data is required to define interconnected urban cores (step two) and the commuting zone (step three):

1. Identification of contiguous densely inhabited urban cores.
2. Consolidation of interconnected urban cores that are part of the same functional urban area.
3. Definition of the commuting zone of the FUA, linked by commuting flows to the urban cores.

Approximation of FUAs' methodology in the case of Viet Nam

Due to the lack of commuting data for Viet Nam's municipalities, the OECD- EC methodology had to be adapted to identify the interconnected urban cores and the commuting zone of FUAs. Therefore, while the first step (the definition of the city core) was conducted following the original OECD-EC methodology, the step two and three were developed following the adapted method described below[1].

The first step: identification of the urban cores

This first step follows the original OECD-EU methodology: the distribution of the population at a fine level of spatial disaggregation – 1 km^2 – is used to identify the urban cores which are constituted by aggregations of contiguous municipalities that have more than 50% of their population living in high-density clusters. These clusters are made of contiguous 1 km^2 grid cells with a population density of at least 1 500 inhabitants per km^2 and a total population of at least 50 000 people.

Adaptation of the OECD-EC methodology

The interconnected urban cores and the commuting zones are defined by using isochronous polygons of travel time from the centroid of each urban core, given a maximum travel time for urban core and an average speed. In order to provide some foundation to the choice of the travel time threshold, the method proposed by Obaco et al. (2017) was examined and considered. The idea of the authors is to look at the travel time patterns in a country where actual commuting data is also available and to see how such driving time changes (increases) with the size of urban cores. The paper applied this exercise for Colombia, one of the countries in the OECD FUAs' database with the most similar level of development to Viet Nam.

The authors find a relationship between actual commuting patterns and travel time which is estimated using temporal accessibility from the core as a substitute for commuting flow data. The adaptation assumes that the area of the commuting zone (A_z) is a function of the area of the core, (A_c): $\ln(A_z) = \ln(\alpha) + \beta \ln(A_c)$.[2] Given that the radio of the commuting zone is also a function of the maximum travel time (T_z) required to cross the functional urban area: $r_z = T_z * speed$, it is possible to determine the commuting zone of a specific urban core by using this maximum travel time to find the surrounding municipalities no included in the core. The equation that links the maximum travel time and the area of urban core is:$T_z = \alpha'' A_c^{\beta''}$.[3] The authors calibrated parameters α'' and β'' using the OECD-EC method of FUA's information for Colombian along with the maximum travel time to cross the FUAs (using google maps and Open street maps). After conduct a linear regression between the area of urban cores and the maximum travel times for each core, the linear equation becomes: $T_z = 4.5\, A_c^{1/3}$. These parameters are the ones used to define maximum travel time for Vietnamese FUAs (for further information about the equation underlying see Obaco et al., 2017).

In the case of Viet Nam, the methodology of Obaco et al (2017) was modified to adjust it to the country's commuting patterns. The high use of motorbike in intra-urban trips and the country's infrastructure gap requires an adjustment to the speed in Vietnamese urban areas. Based on Google Maps medium speed for Vietnamese urban areas and information collected in the field interviews, it was assumed an average speed of 25kms/hr to transit within the Viet Nam's FUAs. Furthermore, after different scenarios of sensitivity analysis,[4] the urban cores identified in the first step were divided, depending on their area size, into three different groups. The maximum travel time for each urban core was calculated using the above-mentioned parameters from Obaco et al. (2017) and the average area size in each group (Table 1.A1.1).

Table 1.A1.1. Thresholds of maximum travel time per urban core area

Maximum travel time (minutes)	Number of Urban Cores	Total population	Area size for each group (Km2)
70	3	13 421 524	>500
35	51	7 662 414	30-500
25	25	2 793 942	<30

Given the maximum travel time to cross Vietnamese urban cores and the road network of Open Street Maps for Viet Nam, an isochronous polygon of travel time was built for each urban core. This polygon defines the distance between the centroid of each core and the co-ordinates furthest away inside the FUA.

Adaptation of second and third step

Connecting non-contiguous urban cores that are part of the same functional areas. Two urban cores are considered belonging to the same (polycentric) FUA when more than 50% of the population of one urban core is within the travel time polygon of other urban core. Hierarchy among urban cores is based on the size of their areas. Therefore, when two urban cores are within the travel time polygon of another, the urban core with smaller area size will be assigned to the one with bigger area size.

Definition of commuting zones. The commuting zone of an urban core is deduced taking into account the municipalities with more than 50% of population living within the travel time polygon each urban core. A polycentric FUA includes the commuting zone area for each urban core.

The results of this methodology for Viet Nam are consistent with FUAs' characteristics for OECD countries. The relationship between the area of urban cores and commuting zones in the 63 Viet Nam's FUAs is located on the lowest part of the OECD FUAs' distribution (Figure 1.A1.1). It implies relatively smaller commuting zones in Viet Nam comparing to OECD countries, which results in line with the lower driving speed and the infrastructure gap in the country.

Figure 1.A1.1. Area of urban cores and area of commuting zones for OECD and Vietnam FUAs

Log of area in km²

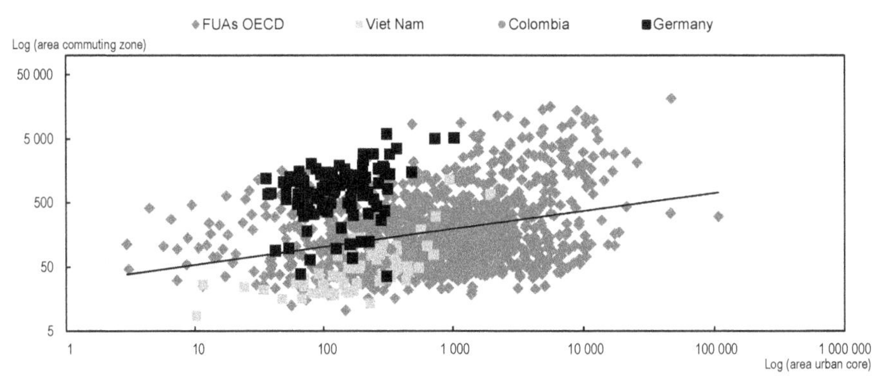

Source: OECD elaboration base on OECD (2015), OECD Metropolitan areas (database), General Statistic Office Viet Nam.

Notes

1. This adaptation to the OECD-EC methodology has also been applied by the OECD in the case of Casablanca, Morroco (forthcoming report) and it builds on the method developed in Obaco, M., Royuela, V. and Xavier, V. (2017) "Computing Functional Urban Areas Using a Hierarchical Travel Time Approach: An Applied Case in Ecuador", AQR Working Paper 2017/03, available at www.ub.edu/aqr/documents-de-treball_en.php.

2. Where, α is a coefficient of expansion and β a coefficient of adjustment

3. This formula is obtained after solving the empirical mode that makes possible to estimate the maximum travel time as a function of the area of the core $\log(T_z) = \left(\frac{1}{2}\ln\left(\frac{\alpha}{2\pi}\right) - \ln(\text{speed})\right) + \frac{\beta}{2}\ln(A_c)$, knowing that $r_z = \sqrt{\frac{A_z}{2\pi}} = \sqrt{\frac{\alpha\, A_c^{\beta}}{2\pi}}$

4. Three models with different travel time thresholds were evaluated and compared among them and with the average of OECD FUAs. The model selected (70, 35 and 25 minutes) is the one that best fits the relative conditions of the country in comparison with OECD average (high density in comparison with the national level and high share of urban core area over the total FUAs).

Chapter 2

Viet Nam's National Urban Policy Framework

This chapter focuses on the urban policy frameworks at the national level which determine possibilities and incentives for sustainable urban development at the local and regional levels. It begins by outlining the complex structures of current national urban policy frameworks. A distinctive element of Viet Nam's approach to urban policy is a heavy emphasis on city classification, and this too will be considered. The chapter will then give attention to key urban policy areas: urban transport, housing, land management and the quality of the urban environment.

In Viet Nam, urban policy and planning have been deeply affected by the far-reaching economic liberalisation that characterised the *Doi Moi* reforms of the late 1980s. As highlighted in Chapter 1, Viet Nam has made impressive economic and social achievements and powerful imperative towards immediate economic development carries obvious weight as a public policy goal. Yet in the longer term, approaches which better address goals of green and inclusive growth should offer the surest paths to lasting and sustainable development for all urban areas. Addressing this challenge necessitates the timely application of a clear and workable urban policy framework. However, the adoption of ambitious national level urban policies since 2000s has not necessarily been successful at least in two ways. First, the succession of plans and programmes has introduced complexities that had the net effect of allowing ad hoc approaches to urban development to prevail. Here lies one of the most fundamental challenges: that of simplifying and rationalising the complexities of policies and legislation that have been superimposed on one another over an extended period. As a result, in many cases policies are inconsistent and even contradictory, meaning that everyday decision-making has to contend with the conflation of disparate goals and values. Second, with the overall prospect of socio-economic prosperity depending disproportionately on the two largest urban areas – Ha Noi and Ho Chi Minh City – the prioritisation of public and private investment in these locations has meant that investment in small and medium-sized cities has always been in danger of taking second place. This may have reduced Viet Nam's potential to fully capitalise on the rapid urbanisation.

This chapter begins by outlining the complex structures of current national urban policy frameworks. A distinctive element of Viet Nam's approach to urban policy is a heavy emphasis on city classification, and this too will be considered. The chapter will then give attention to key urban policy areas such as transport, housing, land use management and the quality of the urban environment.

The national-level policy framework in Viet Nam

Urban policy by its nature is complex in the sense that it involves multiple levels of government and diverse constituent policy areas, which characteristically raises the potential for the creation of an administrative logic and a discrete silo approach. A key to 'getting cities right' is a holistic and integrated approach to cross-cutting urban challenges, which could be well applied to the Vietnamese urban context (Box 2.1). This section applies the approach to the current national-level policy frameworks in Viet Nam, which are characterised by a complex network of policies and plans.

Box 2.1. Getting cities right: the OECD approach to urban policy

Cities are the economic engines of national economies and, thanks to global urbanisation trends, the places in which most people across the world live. By getting cities right (see the table below), governments can serve a greater share of the population and economy. Accordingly, cities have become increasingly important policy targets for national governments.

Box 2.1. Getting cities right: the OECD approach to urban policy (*cont.*)

Moving from	Towards
An administrative logic, where cities are seen as administrative entities, solving problems within boundaries, even if the impact extends beyond	A functional logic, where cities are seen as functional economic areas, and solutions need to be adapted to the area of impact
Problem-driven, with a focus on issues such as air pollution, congestion, poor economic performance, failing neighbourhoods	Strategic, with a focus on opportunities (e.g. how cities of all sizes can grow and contribute to national policy objectives)
A narrowly defined urban agenda (e.g. national urban policies limited to one or two urban issues, such as infrastructure provision or revitalising distressed neighbourhoods)	A holistic approach (with national government awareness of the full range of policies that can profoundly shape urban development)
A silo approach, with sectoral, fragmented responses to specific challenges (e.g. transport, land use, water, waste, economic development)	Integrated approaches to cross-cutting urban challenges, based on co-ordinating economic, social and environmental policies (e.g. improving the quality of life and citizens' well-being, and green growth strategies)

Source: OECD (2014), *OECD Regional Outlook 2014: Regions and Cities: Where Policies and People Meet*, OECD Publishing, Paris, http://dx.doi.org/10.1787/9789264201415-en.

Viet Nam needs a coherent vision for co-ordinated urbanisation

The planning and management of urban areas in Viet Nam depends on a complex network of policies and plans which are divided between different sectors (Coulthart et al., 2006), all controlled by different ministries: socio-economic development planning by the Ministry of Planning and Investment (MPI), spatial and infrastructure planning by the Ministry of Construction (MOC) and sectoral planning such as transport and land by the Ministry of Transport (MOT) and the Ministry of Natural Resources and Environment (MONRE), respectively. These plans are then implemented by three levels of government: national, provincial and local (district and ward level). However the initial planning decisions are taken by the central government, which then inform the lower levels of planning.

The foundational element of the Vietnamese spatial and infrastructure planning is the 2009 Adjustment of Orientation Master Plan to Develop Viet Nam's Urban System until 2025 with a Vision to 2050 (AOMP). The AOMP – as stated in its name – provides the goals for urban development until 2025 and the vision for a further quarter-century. It is the highest level spatial plan and is the basis upon which other, lower-level spatial plans are developed. As is discussed more below, this top down approach to spatial planning is reminiscent of a planning model from an era when Vietnamese construction was predominantly undertaken by the state (Coulthart et al., 2006). The AOMP is complemented by two national urban development programmes:

- The 2009 National Urban Upgrading Programme (NUUP) was developed to directly support the implementation of the AOMP, and more particularly, to address the need for more targeted interventions in underprivileged urban areas. The NUUP is also aimed at more directly addressing the implementation of the 2002 Comprehensive Strategy for Growth and Poverty Reduction in urban areas by facilitating upgrading to low-income areas in order to increase access to standardised water supply, drainage, and collection and disposal of solid waste, transport, roads and public lighting (Government of Viet Nam, 2009a).
- The 2012 National Urban Development Programme (NUDP) was developed in the context of a perceived need for better-defined implementation mechanisms for the 2009 AOMP and to more strongly align the NUDP and the AOMP with the Socio-economic Development Strategy (Government of Viet Nam, 2012 and Hau,

2016). The NUDP sets targets for both the development of the urban system and for the quality of the urban area with objectives set for both 2015 and 2020.

In addition to the three documents mentioned above, the Socio-economic Development Strategy 2011-2020 (SEDS) and the Viet Nam Sustainable Development Strategy 2011-2020 also provide overall directions for development, all of which together with other sectoral policy documents constitute the national level urban policy framework in Viet Nam (Table 2.1).

Table 2.1. Viet Nam's current major national urban policy documents

Name	Decision	Ministry in charge	Context
Adjustment of Orientation Master Plan for Urban Development until 2025 with a vision to 2050 (AOMP)	Decision of the Prime Minister, No. 445, 2009	Ministry of Construction (MOC)	The Adjustment Orientation replaced the initial Master Plan for Viet Nam until 2020 (Decision 10/1998). Foundational document of the national framework for the spatial planning system and provides a foundation for the implementation of Urban Development Plans and the system of Urban Classification. Intends to develop a progressive urban system, outlining successive phases. Based on the requirements of socio-economic development plans, attempts to minimise scattered development and shift towards an urban network-based development model.
National Urban Development Programme 2012-2020 (NUDP)	Decision of the Prime Minister No. 1659, 2012	MOC	MOC is assigned to be the standing agency of the Programme Steering Committee, and to lead and co-ordinate with other ministries, agencies and guide localities in formulating, appraising and approving urban development programmes. Elaborated in 2012 to remedy limitations of the implementation of AOMP. Serves as a basic policy framework for provincial and local governments to develop action programmes in line with the core national goals of urban development until 2020. Aims to address the perceived disregard of the AOMP by cities and towns resulting in the development of their own plans and objectives, leading to difficulties in control, inefficient use of resources and detrimental competition between territories.
National Urban Upgrading Programme (NUUP)	Decision of the Prime Minister, No. 758/QĐ-TTg, 2009	MOC	MOC is in charge, although in collaboration with other ministries and with the support of investment sponsors such as the World Bank and the Asian Development Bank. In 2000, Viet Nam sought international assistance to upgrade informal and low income urban areas and in 2004 the World Bank agreed to fund a first project The project aimed to improve the living conditions and environmental sanitation of poor areas in 4 major cities: Ho Chi Minh, Can Tho, Hai Phong and Nam Dinh. Following the success of this initial programme, the government upscaled it in 2009 with the National Urban Upgrading Porgramme (NUUP) to 2020. A comprehensive investment programme for basic infrastructure services in low income areas with a focus on poverty reduction that identifies infrastructure needs to direct upgrading and infrastructure investments for different urban areas in accordance with socio-economic planning.
Socio-Economic Development Strategy, 2011-2020	Decision of the Prime Minister No. 432/QĐ-TTg, 2005	Ministry of Planning and Investment (MPI)	Identifies basic development goals to achieve sustainable growth, with emphasis on social progress and equality and environmental protection. It builds off of the previous Strategy by continuing to promote industrialisation and modernisation, and reiterates its commitment to its socialist orientation by insisting on sustainable development and equitable social progress.
The Viet Nam Sustainable Development Strategy 2011-2020	Decision of the Prime Minister No. 432/QĐ-TTg, 2012		Provides a supporting policy framework for development of provincial and localised programmes to achieve the core national goal of sustainable development until 2020.

Source: Author.

The current AOMP-led policy model does not provide many tools and incentives to co-ordinate across other urban related policies and their supporting programmes to ensure coherence. While the social and economic prerogatives of the SEDS and the spatial focus of the AOMP should work in tandem, in reality, spatial master plans frequently lack considerations for social and economic questions, and investment plans based on SEDS typically do not consider their spatial implications. This lack of co-ordination between sectoral policies manifests itself even simply in the duration of the respective plans at the regional, provincial and local levels of government. For example, some sectoral master plans and transport plans have a longer duration than the SEDS, and therefore frequently are not reflecting the up-to-date socio-economic policy objectives of the country.

The complex urban policy frameworks that have become entrenched over time also affect the development of Vietnamese urban areas. The layered goals of values of entirely different eras – going back in some cases to the era preceding Viet Nam's entry into the World Trade Organisation in 2007, and even before that to the most active era of the Doi Moi reforms – have been conflated in everyday decision-making. This is reflected by sometimes disparate targets in the various policies or decrees, and inter-relationships and priorities among them that are not clearly defined. For example, within NUDP, targets are set for the percentage of the population in Class IV and Class V cities which would have access to clean water by 2020 (90% and 70%, respectively). NUUP, on the other hand, sets a target of 100% of urban inhabitants having access to clean water by 2020. Moreover, while the ambitions are commendable, Viet Nam has failed to meet some of these goals and targets. For example, the NUDP sets a target of having 90% of the urban population in Class III cities supplied with clean water and a standardised water supply in 2015. However, selected Class III cities still have less than 65% of households connected to municipal water sources (Ministry of Construction of Viet Nam, 2017). Accordingly, one of the most pressing challenges will be to simplify the complexities of policies that have been superimposed on one another, and to provide more concrete policy direction for urban policies in Viet Nam.

A more explicit urban policy can clearly spell out the urban policy direction in Viet Nam

A promising policy option for Viet Nam is to restructure the current complex framework to adopt an explicit National Urban Policy (NUP). The experience of some OECD and non-OECD countries shows that a well-designed NUP can promote linkages between sectoral policies and thus provide a basis for co-ordination within and amongst ministries responsible. It can also strengthen urban, peri-urban, and rural links through more integrated national level territorial development and support a stronger connection between national, regional and local governments, while defining closely the roles and responsibilities of each (UN Habitat, 2016b).

An explicit NUP is clearly referred to (or titled) as "National Urban Policy" or a variant such as "National Urbanisation Policy", "National Urban Strategy" or "National Urban Development Strategy". In contrast, a partial, or implicit, NUP has many of the elements of an NUP but is not yet brought together as a formal NUP and could consist of a framework of national level urban policies, often sectoral policies, which together form an implicit guidance at the national level for urban development (UN Habitat and OECD, 2017, forthcoming). This distinction is ultimately useful to review the degree of clarity with which a NUP is spelled out. A more clearly formulated NUP could be expected to induce a larger degree of coherence of different urban policies undertaken at the national level (OECD, 2017a). Explicit NUPs have been formulated in both OECD countries such as Australia, Czech Republic, Chile, France, the Netherlands and Poland, and non-OECD countries such as Colombia, Egypt, Morocco, Rwanda, and South Africa (OECD, 2017a; UN Habitat and OECD, 2018, forthcoming).

It would seem at first sight that the country's National Urban Development Programme 2012-2020 (NUDP) could be regarded as constituting an explicit NUP. However, in reality, NUDP is only one part of an interconnected network of policies. The NUDP does not provide the policy vision of how Vietnamese government and society want cities to develop in the long-term. Viet Nam needs to formulate a simple, explicit policy document which provides an overall guidance to the nation's urban development with policy instruments and a co-ordination mechanism across sectors.

A NUP can also work as a key tool to implement global urban agendas

A NUP has been increasingly identified as an important tool for governments to implement and monitor the progress of recent global urban agendas (the New Urban Agenda, the 2030 Agenda for Sustainable Development, the Paris Agreement for Climate Change, and the Sendai Framework), and adapt them to national contexts (OECD, 2017d; United Nations, 2016a). In particular, the New Urban Agenda (NUA), adapted at the United Nations Conference on Housing and Sustainable Development (Habitat III), identified National Urban Policies (NUPs) as an essential tool for its implementation (Box 2.2). In this context, restructuring the current national urban policy frameworks and formulating an explicit NUP could be a timely effort for Viet Nam to support the implementation of global urban agendas.

Box 2.2. Implementing global frameworks through National Urban Policies

In preparation for the Habitat III process, NUP was selected as one of the ten thematic Policy Units, affirming its instrumental nature for the implementation of the New Urban Agenda (NUA). The OECD and United Nations Human Settlement Programme (UN Habitat) co-led the Policy Unit and developed the Policy Paper on NUP, which was a key input to the drafting process of NUA. Subsequently, NUA has put explicit emphasis on NUPs as one of its five implementation pillars, and called for measures to enhance the ability of governments to develop and implement such over-arching policies (United Nations, 2016a). In addition, NUPs have been proposed as a monitoring tool for the SDGs through Indicator 11.a.1, where they are acknowledged as a "way to connect national policy to local action" (United Nations, 2016b). The above developments therefore provide a unique window of opportunity to upscale the uptake of NUPs as a powerful policy process to help governments shape and implement better urban policies for better lives, in a shared responsibility across local, regional and national levels.

In 2017, UN Habitat has elaborated the Action Framework for the Implementation of the New Urban Agenda (AFINUA), providing a non-exhaustive list of the foundational elements required for urbanisation including (1) national urban policies (2) urban legislation, rules and regulations, (3) urban planning and design (4) urban economy and municipal finance and (5) local implementation (UN Habitat, 2017). In order for a NUP to support the implementation of the ethos of the New Urban Agenda, AFINUA recommends that a NUP, at a minimum:

1. Formulates medium and long term demographic projections and trends, with geographic disaggregation, taking into consideration the interplay consideration the interplay of economic, social and environmental forces;
2. Establishes national rules to determine land suitability for urbanisation and for environmental and cultural heritage protection and disaster risk reduction while taking into account its equitable distribution and accessibility;

Box 2.2. Implementing global frameworks through National Urban Policies (*cont.*)

3. Defines the roles and jurisdictional responsibilities of all levels of government and local authorities regarding urbanisation and urban planning and management;
4. Aligns national urban policies with national and sectoral development plans and policies at all territorial levels to harness the transformative power of urbanisation with urban plans (e.g. energy, water, transportation and other infrastructural corridors);
5. Adopts a framework to reduce urban and territorial disparities by promoting an inclusive and productive system of cities and human settlements, and strengthening urban-rural linkages; and
6. Promotes jurisdictional co-ordination and coherence through horizontal co-ordination of policies and plans across jurisdictions for the efficient, equitable and affordable delivery of basic services and infrastructure, according to an agreed set of standards (UN Habitat, 2017).

Source: United Nations (2016a), "The New Urban Agenda: Key Commitments", Sustainable Development Goals, 17 Goals to Transform our World, New York; United Nations (2016b), *Policy Paper 3: National Urban Policy*, A/CONF.226/PC.3/16, New York; UN Habitat (2017), *Action Framework for the Implementation of the New Urban Agenda*, Nairobi.

The Principles of Urban Policy of the Czech Republic is an example of an explicit NUP. Originally launched in 2010 and revised in August 2017, it is a framework document that provides guidance and aims to help co-ordinate urban development activities at all levels of government. For example, the Principle One clearly states the need for creating a link between urban and rural policy and other relevant policies at different level of government (Box 2.3). South Africa's Integrated Urban Development Framework (IUDF) is another example. It aims at building more inclusive cities by putting an end to decades of social exclusion and urban poverty, and establishing rural-urban linkages for sustainable development (Box 2.4). Two key lessons for Viet Nam are that the IUDF acknowledges the different types of cities and towns and their different roles and requirements in the urban system; and that the policy levers must be understood in conjunction with the cross-cutting issues of rural-urban interdependence, urban resilience and urban safety.

Box 2.3. Principles of Urban Policy in the Czech Republic

The *Principles of Urban Policy* was first launched in 2010 and revised in 2017. The principles constitute a guiding document pronouncing the views of society and state administration bodies on the standing and importance of cities for economic and regional development in the Czech Republic. The five principles are as follows:

- ***Principle 1: Strategic and integrated approach to the development of cities.*** Cities development requires a long-term vision and adequate planning tools. Urban and regional development cannot be disunited. Adoption of the concept of 'smart cities' for the promotion of planning at the local level. Links between urban and rural policy and other relevant policies at different level of government need to be created.
- ***Principle 2: Polycentric development of the settlement system.*** Growth and development of urban areas should not be in detriment of the development of medium-sized and smaller cities.

Box 2.3. Principles of Urban Policy in the Czech Republic (*cont.*)

- ***Principle 3: Cities as poles of development in the territory.*** To promote the development of rural areas, knowledge economy, innovation in the production process. Brownfield redevelopment, investment in public transport, and improving the access to housing and public services are some of the key priorities.
- ***Principle 4: Protection of the urban living environment.*** Strategic direction include adopting measures to prevent negative impacts of climate change, efficient use of resources and energy, preservation of green areas, balance the relationship between rural and urban areas, and environmental education and awareness of the public.
- ***Principle 5: Ensure the implementation of the New Urban Agenda.*** A framework for the implementation of the New Urban Agenda is to be prepared.

Source: Ministry of Regional Development of the Czech Republic (2017), www.mmr.cz/cs/Regionalni-politika-a-cestovni-ruch/Podpora-regionu/Koncepce-Strategie/Zasady-urbanni-politiky.

Box 2.4. Integrated Urban Development Framework in South Africa

To face South Africa's urban development challenges, the Ministry of Cooperative Governance and Traditional Affairs adopted the "Integrated Urban Development Framework – a new deal for South African cities and towns" (IUDF). Its key outcome is spatial transformation. It is expected that the Framework will unlock the synergy that comes from the co-ordinated investments in people and places and build inclusive, resilient and liveable cities.

The Framework provides a new approach to urban investment by the public and private sectors and households. The vision is to build cities that are liveable, safe, efficient, and that are socially integrated and economically inclusive. The IUDF is expected to contribute to strengthening rural-urban linkages, and promote urban resilience and urban safety.

The IUDF has four overall strategic goals: spatial integration, inclusion and access, growth, and governance. These goals inform the priority objectives of nice policy levers: i) integrated urban planning and management; ii) integrated transport and mobility; iii) integrated sustainable human settlements; iv) integrated urban infrastructure; v) efficient land governance and management; vi) inclusive economic development; vii) empowered active communities; viii) effective urban governance; and ix) sustainable finances.

Source: South Africa's Ministry of Cooperative Governance and Traditional Affairs (2016), "Integrated Urban Development Framework".

Stronger legislative frameworks can help concretise the urban policy direction set by a NUP

The urban legislative framework in Viet Nam will play a key role in implementing the urban policy directions set by an explicit NUP. The current urban legislative framework in Viet Nam, despite its considerable extent (*e.g.*, laws, plans, strategies and programmes) (Table 2.2), has a very similar caveat as the current urban policy frameworks. A lack of hierarchical alignment among the networks of laws, government decrees and circulars, as well as the resulting complexity for compliance and enforcement, has gone beyond being an inconvenience to become a contributing factor to the ad hoc urban development that so frequently occurs at the local level. This is one of the most potent and pressing threats to sustainable and inclusive urbanisation in Viet Nam. For example, while *the Law on Urban Planning* is mandated to dictate the planning of urban areas, laws in other sectors such as land, socio-economic development, and real estate encroach on the mandate of the planning law, and each adds its own layer of stipulations that govern urban development. For example, the Land Master Plan based on *the Land Law* may allow for conversion of land from agricultural to urban use, while the Construction Masterplan based on *the Law of Urban Planning* may list the same parcel of land as rural area. The lack of clarity in terms of the hierarchy, along with the contradictions that exist within and among the laws, is complicated by the reality that the implementing (and enforcing) ministries of these laws are also different.

Table 2.2. The current urban legislative framework in Viet Nam

Area	Law	Contexts
Urban planning and urban development management (2 laws, 9 decrees, 13 decisions)	Law on Urban Planning (2009)	• provides detailed stipulation of urban planning formulation, appraisal of urban planning approval, revision of urban planning, implementation organisation and management of urban development according to planning
	Law on Construction (2014)	• focuses specifically on urban construction planning
Technical infrastructure management (9 decrees and 5 decisions)	n.a.	• There are no laws particularly for technical infrastructure management in cities, but are nine decrees and five decisions which support the implementation of infrastructure elements of other laws.
Housing and real estate market (two laws, 6 decrees and 10 decisions)	Law on Housing (2014)	• Approved 2014 and took effect November 2015, topics that are given particular attention are provision for recognition of self-built housing, the inclusion of the private sector in the production of housing stock, and provision of affordable housing for low income groups.
	Law on Real Estate (2014)	• Approved 2014 and took effect November 2015
Urban land management (one law, 5 decrees and 2 decisions)	Law on Land (2013)	• stipulates regulation on urban land use and land management including urban residential land

Source: Adapted from Hau, D. (2016), Technical Assistant Project, Vietnam National Urban Development Strategy, Report of Tasks A, B and C, Urban Development Agency, Viet Nam.

Moreover, one of the main challenges of the current legal framework is that it does not specify government's policy position to guide the future growth and management of urban areas. This is not surprising for, as elaborated above, a policy vision which is *both* cohesive and long term, has not been defined. Therefore, the legal framework serves as a guide on process and procedures however is not able to act as a reference point in terms of policy direction for ministries and cities. Subnational governments consider that there is a lack of clarity regarding urban definitions, criteria for urban identification, and a policy framework on financial mobilisation for urban development.

A key opportunity for Viet Nam is to strengthen the legislative framework by concretising government's urban policy directions which will be set by an explicit NUP, in addition to serving as a guide on process and procedures. The expected new legislation on urban development management, which is currently under discussion led by the Ministry of Construction, will be a good window of opportunity for the government to make necessary amendments or additions to the whole legislative framework and provide clearer demarcation of responsibilities among the existing laws, government decrees and other policy documents across relevant ministries. Developing a clear urban policy direction in the form of an explicit NUP, prior to the process of the development of the

Urban Management Law is imperative, to ensure that the Law functions as a mechanism to implement the to-be-developed NUP.

It is also important to make sure that the current urban-related legal frameworks and general rplans are well-integrated into the framework of the newly approved *Planning Law*, which will take effect from January 2019. It is an ambitious attempt affecting more than 25 laws across ministries, aiming to reduce overlaps in planning work and reduce the number of plans in the national planning system. This is another good window of opportunity for the urban sector to ensure legal consistency with other relevant policy sectors.

An evidence-based approach will be key to effective development and implementation of NUP and to the success of the implementation of the current policy framework

In addition to the development of an explicit NUP, existing Vietnamese policies and plans (including a NUP) must be more closely aligned to a realistic assessment of projected growth, and national spatial plans should become more strategic, prescriptive and allow more flexibility and adaptability at the local level. Currently, the development and implementation of national level policies and programmes in Viet Nam is severely hindered by insufficient capacity for the national government to analyse demographic, socio-economic and environmental trends at the urban scale during the policy development process and to translate them into planning processes at the subnational level. This has resulted in an under-forecasting of urban growth. Accordingly, the reality of urban development has, in some cases, drastically outpaced the rate of development forecast within the plans, leaving it up to the localities to make up the difference and find ways of providing for unforeseen demand. For this reason, localities will often redefine the development objectives that are found in the AOMP in the local Detailed Plans, so that they are suitable for the reality of urban growth in their area. This often results in difficulty in achieving national-level goals such as public service provision, and more generally feeds the ad hoc planning which has been detrimental to sustainable urban growth in Viet Nam.

Moreover, although the AOMP provides the targets and vision towards 2025 and 2050 respectively, it provides no guidance regarding the resources needed in order to achieve these targets and no indication of where these resources may be coming from. In practice, the AOMP provides an "idealized top-down representation" (Coulthart et al., 2006) of spatial planning in Viet Nam, and lacks any concrete resource allocation. Thus, it has no mechanisms to guarantee implementation or enforcement. The absence of a realistic assessment of funding needs for implementation of the current policy framework has led in turn to a growing funding gap for necessary infrastructural development and the increasingly ad hoc nature of the implementation of the policies at the local level. This opportunistic reliance on developers has significant implications for the quality of the urban environment in Viet Nam, with profitability often overriding a consideration of the needs and quality of life of urban dwellers.

An evidence-based approach will be key to remedy these problems. Basing the NUP and other policies and programmes on reliable urban growth projections and trends at the urban scale and assessment of associated infrastructure needs (including assessment of funding needs) would allow policymakers to set more realistic goals and targets tailored to local contexts. Germany has developed strong monitoring systems on spatial data at central and local levels (Box 2.5). In addition, the experience of Poland's NUP demonstrates the importance of planning the development of cities through their functional areas, instead of their administrative borders (Box 2.6). As presented in Chapter 1, the identification of 63 FUAs and 12 corresponding metropolitan areas in Viet Nam and an urbanisation rate of 41%, as opposed to the 32% indicated by national statistics, underlines the need for accurate measurements of current and projected urbanisation, and makes this example especially relevant for Viet Nam.

Box 2.5. Spatial monitoring in Germany

Germany has a long tradition of monitoring spatial structures and development processes. National spatial development reports exist since 1963, with the 16th volume just released in autumn 2017. Similar reports exist for some federal States. The metropolitan regions of Frankfurt/Rhine-Main and Nuremberg have intermittently published atlases on their regions. At the local level, cities such as Dusseldorf, Cologne, Bonn, Berlin and Osnabrück also publish social monitoring reports, by using statistical data as a basis for displaying spatial disparities.

The basis is good statistical data with high spatial resolution, ranging from urban wards to counties. Germany has 402 counties and cities, and this is the main reference system for analytical work on the whole country. For example, the city of Cologne (with about 1 million inhabitants) is divided into 86 urban quarters, which enables analysis for small spatial units. There is a broad thematic variety of indicators (e.g., economy, demographic and social issues, land use, rents, fiscal aspects, and infrastructure). Most of the data come from statistical offices, but also from alternative sources such as renewable energy production, activities at airports and harbours. All the empirical work is based on capacities of counties and cities to collect, analyse and interpret the information in a reasonable way.

Source: Bezirksregierung Düsseldorf / Bezirksregierung Köln (2016), "Metropolregion Rheinland Datenatlas 2016" Düsseldorf; Bundesinstitut für Bau-, Stadt- und Raumforschung (2012), "Raumordnungsbericht 2011", Bonn; Hauptstadtregion Berlin-Brandenburg (2013), "Raumordnungsbericht (ROB) 2013", Berlin; Stadt Osnabrück (2012), "Soziale Ungleichheit in Osnabrück, Ein kleinräumiger Ansatz mit besonderer Berücksichtigung von Kindern und Jugendlichen Osnabrück", www.osnabrueck.de/fileadmin/user_upload/Bericht_SozialeUngleichheit.pdf.

Box 2.6. National Urban Policy in Poland

Poland's National Urban Policy (NUP) is a document that sets forth the planned actions of the governmental administration in the area of urban policy, considering the objectives and directions in mid-term national development strategy and the national strategy for regional development. It aims at territory-oriented action of the state for sustainable development of cities and their functional area as well as for using their potential in the development process of the entire country.

The ultimate goal of the NUP is for Polish cities to take a big step towards making cities competitive, powerful, spatially coherent, sustainable, compact and efficiently managed. Its strategic objective is to strengthen the capacity of the cities in urbanised areas for sustainable development and creating jobs, as well as improving the quality of life of residents. Its five specific objectives are:

- Establishing the conditions for effective, efficient, and partner-like management of development in urban areas, in particular in metropolitan areas;
- Supporting the sustainable development of urban centres, including preventing the negative phenomena of uncontrolled suburbanisation;
- Restoring the development capacity through revitalisation of socially, economically and physically degraded urban areas;

Box 2.6. National Urban Policy in Poland (*cont.*)

- Improving competitiveness and the capacity of main urban centres to promote development, growth and employment;
- Supporting the development of sub-regional and local urban centres, primarily in the thematic areas of the urban policy (including some rural areas) through strengthening their function and through preventing their economic collapse.

Source: Ministry of Economic Development, Government of Poland (2016), "National Urban Policy 2023", Warsaw.

The city classification system in Viet Nam: ensuring coherence with the AOMP and other urban strategies

Viet Nam ranks "urban areas" through a national assembly resolution (No. 1210/2016/UBTVQH13). Centrally-administered cities, provincial cities, towns and townships are all considered within the classification and therefore defined as "urban areas" (for readability purpose, this report uses "cities" hereafter). They are classified hierarchically into six classes – Special and Class One (I) to Five (V) – based on a threshold of infrastructure development, population size and socio-economic characteristics (Chapter 1).[1] In 2016, Viet Nam had 799 cities, with two cities with Special Class (Ha Noi and Ho Chi Minh City) and 17 cities with Class I. Between 1999 and 2009, the number of cities increased by 29% (from 604 to 779). Most of the increase was accounted for by Class V cities. The increase was slowed down between 2009 and 2016; only 20 cities were added during the seven years, although Class I cities increased drastically from 5 to 17 (Table 2.3).

Table 2.3. Number of cities in Viet Nam by city class

City class	1999	2009	2016	Change between 1999 and 2016
Special	0	2	2	+2
Class I	2	5	17	+15
Class II	8	12	25	+17
Class III	12	40	42	+29
Class IV	64	95	83	+18
Class V	518	625	630	+110
Total	604	779	799	+189

Source: Ministry of Construction of Viet Nam (2017), Answers to the OECD questionnaire, May 2017, unpublished.

The city classification system has been, since its initiation in an early form in 1990, a key tool for urban management in Viet Nam. The system, as first envisaged, was enacted by the Ministry of Construction. It subsequently underwent major updates in 2001 and 2009. The amendment made in 2009 clarified four essential purposes. The first was to organise, arrange, and develop the national system of urban centres. As well as its practical implications for approaching urban development in many areas of the country, this principle was and remains noteworthy for its explicit avowal that the urban areas of

Viet Nam should be treated in a policy sense as a system, with all the interdependence and intended coherence that this implies. The second purpose was to formulate and approve planning for construction activity in urban areas. The third purpose was that it was intended that the classification system should provide appropriate criteria for raising the quality of urban centres in all respects, and notably with regard to sustainability. The fourth purpose was to provide for the ongoing formulation of policies and mechanisms for urban management and development.

Accordingly, all urban areas receive one of six classifications as previously mentioned in Chapter 1 (Table 1.1). The threshold population level for Class V, the lowest level, is 4 000. Thus, the urban system is taken to include centres that are themselves quite small places; however, the classification serves to distinguish these townships (*thi tran*) from the rural areas that typically surround them. In ascending order, the cities denoted as Class IV to Class I are urban areas that range from relatively small centres of intra-provincial regions to central to regions that transcend provincial boundaries. Especially significant is that Hanoi and Ho Chi Minh City, since the 2009 update, have their own distinctive classification as special cities, superimposed upon the numerical classification. This status accurately reflects not only the immense size of these conurbations, but also the recognition that they require a unique level of administrative autonomy. Indeed, the entire system is characterised by an ascending degree of autonomy and, accordingly, of financial transfers from the national government. National oversight is maintained even in the largest cities, and is guided by the principle of preserving the coherence of the national approach to urban development. Cities are seen as drivers of economic growth in the district or province to which they are central and – in the case of the special cities – in a national sense. For the central government, the city classification system has become a central element of the ability of the national government to shape urban development and undertake continuing urban management, notably through regulating the allocation of resources and administrative authority.

From the perspective of individual cities and their administrators, the greater autonomy and increased financial flexibility that comes with the higher classifications creates an incentive to move upwards within the scale. This may be seen as a positive factor, in encouraging urban administrators to be ambitious on behalf of their cities and the provinces they serve, but it also carries certain significant disadvantages. For example, within the classification system, cities must achieve a score of 70 out of 100 in order to move up in the ranks. Each of the six elements in the criteria is weighted differently. The highest weight of points target urban infrastructure, GDP, and population (55, 15, and 10 points respectively). Urban density, on the other hand, constitutes only 5 points in the overall scheme. Emphasis, therefore, is disproportionately put on infrastructure development and population growth. As a result, local infrastructure development is prioritised above adherence to the AOMP and other urban strategies which place stronger focus on sustainability.

Furthermore, since population is a key measure of the significance of a city within the system, administrators may favour expansion of city boundaries to include neighbouring areas. In fact, some cities in Viet Nam have expanded their boundaries to rezone villages outside of the city to "boost" population growth (Chapter 1). While this process may be predicated on the idea that increases in autonomy and financial transfers will benefit the absorbed areas as well as the original city, in reality there are no guarantees that the social and physical infrastructure will be adequate for what may now be a greatly expanded and more complex area. This is especially the case, as changes in the city classification are not synchronised with any new assessment of changing needs with respect to administrative capacity. Another concern is that, given that population density is given little regard, this results in cities paying less attention to developing dense and well-connected urban environment, by instead favouring ad-hoc development which can quickly add to their population figures. This will make the provision of public services, such as wastewater treatment, solid waste collection and mass public transport extremely costly and inefficient.

Besides, the classification system, while embracing in principle the need for healthy and sustainable urban growth, provides no penalties for urban growth that ignores these criteria and instead takes little or no regard for living quality, adequacy of infrastructure, the creation and preservation of green areas that may also contribute to food security, preservation of cultural heritage, or any other form of environmental safeguard. In this way, the classification system may also have an impact in limiting longer-term economic investments that may suit the particular characteristics of a given city. Certain cities have cultural or heritage attributes – or scenic endowments – that with appropriate investment could become the basis for an ongoing tourist industry. However, the existing framework is highly ambiguous with respect to such unique characteristics. For example, National Assembly Resolution No.1211, which outlines the criteria for the establishment of provincial cities, towns, urban districts, wards and townships, gives special status to areas with unique characteristics,[2] by allowing the population threshold and density detailed in the Resolution to be lessened by up to 50% of the outlined criteria (Government of Viet Nam, 2011), but a lack of hierarchical delineation between the two documents means that the Resolution on City Classification does not recognise any special characteristics, or provide for their preservation, and relies only on the above mentioned criteria for upwards movement through the classification scale. Finally, the classification system makes no provision for monitoring and evaluation that could provide assessment both of the outcomes of reclassification and, in appropriate cases, of the impact of recognising special characteristics.

Based on these assessments, a number of possible improvements could be considered to ensure that the classification system can emerge as a flexible and dynamic tool for urban management. First, developing a monitoring and evaluation mechanism holds the key. More active monitoring and objective evaluation of performance of cities would be invaluable in providing for greater assurance in judging the desirability of reclassification in a timely manner. Second, ensuring that the incentive mechanism is coherent with the AOMP and other urban strategies, for example by incentivizing the quality of the urban environment, including public spaces and preservation of cultural heritage, would greatly help cities to make more effective investment decisions on urban infrastructure. Finally, the city classification system could also value interconnections between cities within a metropolitan area, fostering a stronger metropolitan approach to development.

Urban transport policies: tackling the shift from motorbikes to cars, while accelerating public transport investment

In any urban context, efficient transport linkages within cities facilitate movement of goods and people in ways that can integrate neighbourhoods and minimise environmental damage through fossil-fuel pollutants. The quality of cities' transport infrastructure not only determines the level at which growth can be communicated to the national economy as a whole but also is a crucial factor in both attracting foreign investors in cities and in elevating the quality of life of urban residents. In particular, accessible urban transport is an essential component of facilitating urban mobility for low-income households, allowing them to access better job and education opportunities. These observations are relevant to Viet Nam in particular ways that arise from the nature of Vietnamese urbanisation. Despite the focus on infrastructure development in Viet Nam, infrastructure, along with institutions and innovation, continues to be recognised as one of the most central drags on Vietnamese international competiveness, with road infrastructure being the most problematic (World Economic Forum, 2017).

This section will analyse Viet Nam's urban transport policies as one of the key policy areas which can affect the overall performance of cities. While inter-connection of urban clusters and their linkage to international transport networks is invariably crucial to national economic development, this review will focus more specifically on transport within urban areas, as opposed to inter-urban transport, given the urgent transport challenges observed especially within large urban areas in Viet Nam.

Current major transport-related investment in urban areas has a heavy focus on road and street construction

The current national policy framework for transport is centred on *the 2013 Adjusted Strategy for Development of Vietnam's Transport through 2020, with a vision toward 2030* (Decision No. 355/QD-TTg), which replaced the original transport development strategy in 2007. Taking a balanced approach to transport development, this policy framework gives attention to transport needs in rural as well as urban areas, while also acknowledging the interdependence of rural and urban transport systems. The 2013 adjustment has given priority to the development of mass transit systems, initially in Ha Noi and Ho Chi Minh City, in order to decongest these cities and to improve safety. Mass transit that is efficient enough to offset daily motorbike and car usage is the only practicable solution for Viet Nam, as the 2013 adjustment strategy already recognises.

The current major transport-related investment in urban areas in Viet Nam has a heavy focus on road and street construction. For example, more than 50% of the World Bank's ten-year Hanoi Urban Transport Development Project was allocated towards road development (World Bank, 2007). Such an approach may be justified in the short term. In 2008, the total road area in inner cities and towns represented only 16% of total buildable area (as opposed to the government's standard of 20 to 25%). Based on a survey of 41 Vietnamese urban areas, the average road density in large urban areas (2.2km/km^2) is much lower than the target set by the government in Circular 34 (26km/km^2) (CTTPP, 2016). However, the investment on road and street construction has not always been efficient. In practical terms, local governments have been increasingly led into a constant process of addressing bottleneck situations through widening and extending roads, as well as through constructing new connectors, without long-term growth projections and impact assessments. In inner cities, there are limits to the improvements that can be made in the context of streets that are frequently narrow, and the constrained efforts to do so often involve expropriations, evictions, and demolitions that are socially and financially costly. Moreover, even insofar as the goal of allowing more cars in parts of a city is realised through these efforts, the problems of congestion may only be shifted to other parts of the city rather than being resolved in any viable sense. Finally, reliance on the expansion of the road network also raises concerns regarding the ability of the Government of Viet Nam to provide necessary road maintenance in the future. Although 94% of the national road network in Viet Nam is paved, only 43% of the thoroughfares are considered to be in "good" condition. Furthermore, when moving from the national to the provincial level, the quality is significantly worse, with almost a quarter (24%) of provincial roads being unpaved (ADB, 2010). Worryingly, it is estimated that the necessary maintenance of the road network is currently being funded at 50% or less of what is required to have the current network kept at a reasonable standard (ADB, 2010). It is imperative that the future road maintenance costs should be factored into the decision whether more new roads should be built or not.

Viet Nam urgently needs to tackle the rapid shift from motorbikes to cars

As discussed above, much more attention is needed to manage the rapidly increasing number of cars in Viet Nam (Chapter 1). Indeed, one of the most urgent urban policy agendas for Viet Nam is to tackle the rapid shift from motorcycles to cars and ensure smooth transition to public transport. The exceptionally high rate of motorcycle use has meant that usage of larger vehicles has so far been restrained. Even so, significant traffic congestion is evident. With each car on average occupying some $14m^2$ of space by comparison with the $1.8m^2$ of a motorcycle (Bertaud, 2011), the shift from motorcycles to cars will ultimately overwhelm street transport routes unless counter-measures are taken. Road improvement may continue to have its place in locations where it can be demonstrated to be socially and environmentally justifiable – and where proper maintenance can be provided – but only in a broader context of other measures. For these reasons, policy recommendations must embrace broader solutions to problems that are long-term by their nature while also attempting to offer short and medium term measures that can assist with increasing the quality of life in Vietnamese cities by making efforts to make transportation safer and greener.

In the short and medium term, Vietnamese policy-makers could consider the following measures. First, with road accidents being the second highest cause of death in Viet Nam (Chapter 1), urban road safety is a pressing issue that must be urgently addressed. The 2012 National Road Safety Strategy by 2020 and a vision to 2030 (Prime Minister's Decision No: 1586/QĐ-TTg) addresses the road safety problem in Viet Nam and demonstrates the government's recognition of traffic safety challenges. An immediate measure would be better regulated motorcycle traffic by offering dedicated lanes, more stringent enforcement of regulations on helmet manufacturing and use, and bans on sidewalk parking with strict penalties. Considering that these deaths disproportionately are affecting young people, targeted measures for young drivers could be considered, such as stricter requirements for learner drivers through a graduated driver licensing (GDL) programme.

Second, to address air and noise pollution, the use of electrically-powered bicycles and scooters (e-bikes and e-scooters) could be promoted. As highlighted in Chapter 1, 25% of lung cancer deaths and about 17% of respiratory infection deaths in 2012 can be attributed to exposure to fine particulate matter air pollution (WHO, 2014). E-bikes and e-scooters have clear advantages in urban settings where they facilitate fast and energy-efficient transport while avoiding air and noise pollution. This approach is not only fiscally responsible in that it pre-empts costs associated with expanding use of cars, but also environmentally responsible, contributing to de-carbonising transport. Policy makers could consider a purchase subsidy programme to encourage the usage of e-bikes and e-scooters, instead of subsidising car ownership. Subsidy programmes have been used in both OECD and non-OECD countries with considerable amounts of success. Typically, the most successful subsidy schemes are efforts that work at all levels of government. For example, Austria, which now has the highest sales rates of e-bikes in Europe, had an effective three tier subsidy system (Box 2.7). Experience from these countries shows that a thorough review of the transport-related legislative framework is needed to ensure certain important things are clear, such as: distinction between different modes of electronic bikes/scooters, whether or not a license is needed, whether or not a helmet is needed, and whether dedicated lanes are required. Although the 2013 national technical standard for e-bikes distinguishes between different types of e-bikes, care should be taken to ensure consistency in all legislation and policy.

Box 2.7. Promoting e-bikes in Austria

Austria is the only country to the present time to operate incentives at all three levels of government. Within this pattern, there are complexities in the sense that such initiatives were pioneered at the local and regional levels in 2010 and 2011, and yet many such programmes have now lapsed and have been effectively superseded by incentives offered by the national government. However, the more localised schemes played a vital role in what has been rightly considered a breakthrough for the use of e-bikes, so that Austria now has one of the highest rates of sales and usage per capita in Europe. The incentive programme offered locally by the city of Vienna was especially important. Provided to individuals, it supplied a grant equal to 30% of the purchase price of an e-bike, to a maximum of €300. In 2010, this subsidy was applied to the purchase of no fewer than 2540 units, out of total nation-wide sales of 20 000. At the same time, regional subsidies elsewhere varied in amounts – more or less than in Vienna, depending on the region, and in some cases available to organisations as well as to individuals – and collectively also made a notable contribution to making the e-bike a common form of transport.

As approaches have tended to coalesce in more recent years around the national subsidy programme, nevertheless some regional and local incentives persist. The region of Styria, for example, has chosen to focus on cargo e-bikes – models with reinforced frames that support cargo-carrying platforms and baskets – and since 2016 has offered subsidies of EUR 400 for companies and EUR 500 for individuals. A corporate initiative in the Tyrol region, meanwhile, has seen the regional electricity provider Tiroler Wasserkraft provide a rebate on electricity bills valued at up to EUR 150 to a customer who purchases an e-bike.

At national level, the incentive programme applies to the purchase of e-bikes and cargo e-bikes, as well as in some cases to cargo trailers. Payable not to individuals but rather to organisations of many kinds and to local authorities, the scheme provides subsidies of EUR 300 for e-bikes and EUR 500 for cargo e-bikes. Taken together, the incentive programmes – at a relatively modest fiscal outlay, and with clear benefits both fiscal and environmental – have substantially increased the proportion of e-bike usage throughout Austria.

Source: European Cyclists' Federation (2016), "Electromobility for All: Financial Incentives for E-Cycling", Brussels, https://ecf.com/sites/ecf.com/files/final%20for%20web%20170216%20ecf%20report_e%20for%20all-%20financial%20incentives%20for%20e-cycling.pdf.

Third, policy-makers could consider allocating a greater proportion of the real cost of car usage to vehicle owners through fiscal measures. It is estimated that traffic congestion in Ho Chi Minh City is costing the city about VND14 billion a year which is roughly 6.25% of the city's GDP (ESMAP, 2014). Fiscal measures such as vehicle licencing fees, parking charges and congestion charges are effective to shifting the cost of car usage more fully to vehicle owners. In particular, congestion charges have seen significant results in some OECD and non-OECD cities. In cities like London, Singapore and Stockholm, congestion charge systems have resulted in an average of 13-30% congestion reductions, 15-20% greenhouse gas reductions and reductions of fine particulate pollution (Pike, 2010). Congestion charges can also be used as a policy tool to raise revenue for further infrastructure investment in alternative transport modes, such as bicycle lanes, reflecting the local urban contexts. The case of Stockholm highlights a number of important considerations which should be taken into account by Vietnamese policy makers if designing a congestion charging system (Box 2.8). It is important to note that such fiscal measures could help not only reduce congestion but also improve environmental performance of cities. For example, introducing higher congestion charges to cars and traditional motorbikes than e-bikes and e-scooters could accelerate the shift to these environment-friendly vehicles.

Box 2.8. Congestion charges in Stockholm, Sweden

The implementation of the congestion charge in Stockholm, Sweden, highlights a number of important lessons:

- Although the system has the potential to raise revenue, there will also be significant setup and running costs. The running costs could indeed equal 10 to 30% of revenues (Perkins, 2011). In parallel, significant investment in public transport systems is required to accommodate increased ridership that can be an expected outcome of a successful congestion charge system and to ensure that low-income groups retain their mobility (ITF, 2010; Pike, 2010). If it is local governments to make investments, thought must be given to the ability of localities to make this large initial investment.
- A trial period was useful in order to build public consensus and to determine which type of system would work best in each city context. Stockholm saw a substantial transformation of public approval levels, following a six-month trial period. During the trial, in 2006, traffic volumes within the controlled area fell by approximately 20%, while public transit ridership increased by some 6 to 9% (Pike, 2010). The initial public view of the system had been negative, with a disapproval rate of 55%, but following the trial period this had changed to 53% taking a positive view. This shift took place in a context where the area involved was extensive – some 34 square kilometres – and where a modest charge could nevertheless add up significantly: vehicles entering at one of 17 charging pints would pay up to 20 Swedish Krona SEK, roughly USD 3, with a daily maximum of 60 SEK and daily passes available.
- Technical details are vital to its success. In the case of Stockholm, varied payment methods and daily passes made the system more user-friendly. A variety of payment options can be used, including automatic account debiting, online payment, or in-person payment at shops and banks. In terms of technology, implementation based at first on detection of vehicles through a combination of automatic license plate recognition and transponders, but subsequently this has been adjusted so that the system relies mainly on cameras that have the capacity to identify license plate numbers automatically. This has made the system more effective.
- Time must be taken to build consensus and policy-makers must take the initiative to clearly communicate the policy goals and expected impacts to the public. The favourable public view of the congestion charge has been justified by the results that have been observed over time. While there was a considerable upfront investment – equivalent to some USD 200 million in setting up the system, and some USD 300 million in buses, other transit options, and park-and-ride facilities – operating costs have proved to represent some 25% of annual revenues, rendering the investment cost-effective. Moreover, other benefits have been estimated on an annualised basis at some USD 85 million deriving from shorter travel times, USD 18 million from enhanced road safety, and USD 13 million from health and environmental benefits. Moreover, no effect was observed on the level of retail sales.

Box 2.8. Congestion charges in Stockholm, Sweden *(cont.)*

Overall, Stockholm's experience has shown that, while implementation of a congestion charge is not a step to be taken lightly or without proper preparation – and with consideration to whether it could be pursued with complementary measures such as parking regulation and the optimisation of license plate fees – nevertheless it can bring clear and significant benefits in a context of public support.

Source: ITF (2010), Implementing Congestion Charges, OECD Publishing, Paris, http://dx.doi.org/10.1787/9789282102855-en; Perkins, S. (2011), "Green Growth and Transport", International Transport Forum Discussion Papers, No. 2011/02, OECD Publishing, Paris, http://dx.doi.org/10.1787/5kg9mq57s8wb-en; Pike, E. (2010), "Congestion Charging: Challenges and Opportunities", International Council on Clean Transport, White Paper, Washington DC, https://www.theicct.org/sites/default/files/publications/congestion_apr10.pdf.

Accelerate investment in public transport systems in Viet Nam

In the long term, Viet Nam's policy priority should be to accelerate investment in urban transport systems. Policy makers are aware of this and the transport master plans of Ho Chi Minh City and Ha Noi both have ambitious targets for expanded public transport systems (both aim for public transport to account for 45-50% of the urban transit share by 2020) (ADB, 2010). However, these ambitious targets are not coherent with national targets. For example, the minimum public transport use targets for cities under the city classification system lack ambition, with only 10% and 6% for Special Class cities and Class I cities, respectively (Table 2.4). Given the magnitude of transport-related problems in cities, the government should consider revising these targets. Viet Nam's economy has grown rapidly in the past twenty years and, as highlighted in Chapter One, is expected to maintain its path of expedited growth (OECD, 2017a). In line with this growth, levels of overseas development assistance (ODA) have declined, both in absolute terms and relative to GDP (ESMAP, 2014; ADB and AFD, 2012). In addition to adjusting the targets for public transport, Vietnamese policy makers have two key considerations: how to design effective public transport systems and what options they have available to pay for them.

Table 2.4. Minimum public transport use target set under the city classification system

	Special Class	Class I	Class II	Class III	Class IV	Class V
Percentage of public transport carriage (%)	10	6	4	2	0	0

Source: Government of Viet Nam (2016a), Resolution No. 1210/2016/UBTVQH13, City Classification.

Designing effective public transport systems in Viet Nam

Integrated and well-located public transport offers key opportunities for Viet Nam to address social segmentation and to offset the danger that urban growth will increase urban inequalities. However, there are significant obstacles to urban transport system integration in any comprehensive form. They range from rushed implementation that has produced conflict and confusion, to inadequate technology for secure collection of fares and recognition of tickets, to disparities in equipment and infrastructure maintenance between municipalities (Hidalgo and Carrigan, 2010). Two types of challenges can be particularly noted:

- The spatial challenge: designing an effective public transport system will require accurate understanding and future projections of urban development directions and subsequent travel patterns. For example, fast-growing cities in Viet Nam, as elsewhere, lack public transport to accommodate travel from suburb to suburb as opposed to a purely radial system designed to move people only between a given suburb and the core of the city. In addition, silo approaches, in which the transport sector lacks co-ordination with other sectors such as construction, land use and housing development, often create a spatial mismatch between the demand and supply of public transport, resulting in inefficient public transport networks and perpetuating inequality. Housing will be built in areas where land is cheaper, meaning most frequently that low-income residents will be located in outlying and peripheral areas where public transport is either non-existent or is so expensive that ridership is limited and investment is accordingly difficult to mobilise.
- The co-ordination challenge: metropolitan agglomerations often face a challenge of cities co-ordinating the transport policies and practices of neighbouring suburban municipalities, notably in the context of transport planning, which frequently needs to operate within the functional boundaries of urban areas, as opposed to the administrative ones (Aguilar-Jaber and Glocker, 2015). Indeed, nearby municipalities may come into conflict with one another if they perceive that a neighbour is lacking in commitment to transport integration or is unwilling to invest in a way that is equitable to all partners.

The Hanoi Bus Rapid Transit (BRT) system illustrates well these challenges and how the Vietnamese government has been trying to address them. Launched in December 2016, the 14.5 km route has 23 stops. The BRT system largely parallels a metro line under construction, with the important distinction that the metro line will run through more densely populated areas and thus may take ridership away from the BRT. In addition to common criticisms that the BRT is taking up significant space on the already congested roadways, an important question has been raised: whether the route is attracting the ridership that it initially aimed for. Intermodal connectivity with the BRT system is limited, and a lack of station accessibility may pose additional restraints (Fjellstrom, 2017). While it is certainly too early to make definitive judgements on the likely impacts of the BRT initiative, it is noteworthy that more powerful regulatory and fiscal instruments may be required to attract urban development along the BRT route with the principles of Transit-Oriented Development (TOD) and to invest in intermodal connectivity, in order to make the overall BRT investment effective (Box 2.9). In Cape Town, well-designed public transport has contributed crucially to inclusivity of urban areas (Box 2.10). The TOD has gained recognition as an approach that offers a promising solution to the inherent challenges involved in transport integration in Cape Town. It is an avowedly long-term strategy of more effective co-ordination of transport with land use that implies conscious and decisive determinations of where and how development should take place. However, considering the crucial potential benefits for inclusiveness, fostering TOD could be considered as a key long-term objective for Viet Nam. More specifically, the government could consider the following policy options:

- Provide effective market incentives to attract more private development and promote mixed-use development in priority areas supported by public transport systems. In addition, the government could gradually introduce public transport linkages as a condition for public support for housing development (for low and middle income households) to make sure that their locations are supported by public transport systems.

- Consider to form a metropolitan transit authority which could co-ordinate investment and provide integrated operational service across different transport modes. As is elaborated in Chapter 4, facilitating urban collaboration at the metropolitan level could have multiple benefits for different sectors in Viet Nam, including urban transport infrastructure development.

Box 2.9. BRT systems and transit-oriented development

Bus Rapid Transit (BRT) systems have rapidly gained widespread attention as an alternative to urban rail that promises greater cost-effectiveness and a degree of flexibility that is gained from combining use of existing road infrastructure – often with dedicated BRT lanes – with the creation of new roads and stations where required. Worldwide, more than 160 cities have adopted such systems, with Latin America and China especially active. Studying general trends in the light of particular studies of Bogotá (Colombia) and Ahmedabad (India), however, it has been noted that in the absence of specific efforts to leverage more general forms of urban development through a BRT system, the result may fail to realise the limited goal of decreasing traffic congestion if concentrated on the building of low-cost corridors where land is cheapest. Case studies have revealed "that in the absence of proactive planning and attempts to entice private development near stations, few land-use changes occur" (Cervero and Dai, 2014). Transit-Oriented Development (TOD) approach, by contrast, emphasises the co-ordination of transit enhancements with development planning, so that the one reinforces the other and healthy urban growth is enhanced as a result. There is no reason why BRT should not be an effective route towards TOD, but this is unlikely to take place if traffic mobility is the only or the over-riding motivation.

Source: Cervero, R. and D. Dai (2014), "BRT TOD: Leveraging transit oriented development with bus rapid transit investments," in *Transport Policy*, No. 36, pp. 127-138.

Box 2.10. Building an inclusive city: Cape Town's TOD strategic framework

Cape Town's Transit-Oriented Development (TOD) Strategic Framework was adopted by City Council in March 2016. In the context of the city's broader Integrated Development Plan, the TOD Strategic Framework has become central to Cape Town's long-term development strategy. The framework recognises the profound challenges that currently exist, and in particular the legacy of apartheid-era spatial planning, with its privileging of certain areas at the expense of others – notably placing lower-income residents on the outskirts of the urban area. Also, public transport is unduly expensive, and in an era of rapid urbanisation this has favoured the unplanned growth of areas without regard to creating and maintaining a viable public transport system.

To address these problems, while also maintaining healthy urban growth and maximising economic opportunities, the TOD framework operates from a simple principle: that residential developments and transport infrastructure must be planned together, not separately. Notably in five carefully-defined areas, residential growth will be promoted at the same time as existing public transport routes are made more efficient, and new rail links are created where needed. Major stations and bus terminals will also be developed as areas for shopping and for socialisation.

Box 2.10. Building an inclusive city: Cape Town's TOD strategic framework (*cont.*)

Thus, by optimising the location of future residential areas, and co-ordinating them with transport planning, the prescription of how developments should be designed and implemented will encourage more compact urbanisation. While having advantages for all income groups, Cape Town's approach will be especially beneficial for lower-income households, which currently may expend some 45% of monthly income on transport and will have lengthy journeys of up to 70 km each day, frequently on congested and poorly-maintained roads, in order to reach their workplace.

In all of this, the city will be a "catalyst investor," while stimulating and regulating the identified development projects. The TOD Strategic Framework sets out to transform Cape Town's spatial reality through its integrated approach. Executive Mayor Patricia De Lille commented that, "this is a continuation of our work to build an opportunity and inclusive city where the future of our residents is not defined by where they live but by the increasing opportunities that they will have access to."

Source: Transport for Cape Town (2016), "Transit Oriented Development", www.tct.gov.za/en/transit-oriented-development (accessed 15 August 2017).

Funding public transport in Viet Nam through PPPs and land value capturing mechanisms

Infrastructure investment in Viet Nam accounts for 2-3 percent of the country's GDP.[3] The recent decline in ODA in Viet Nam (see Chapter 4) has resulted in a large gap in available financing for planned and future transport infrastructure projects in the country, in particular for urban public transport. For example, the estimated total investment costs necessary to achieve the transport masterplan targets (including road and public transport targets) by 2020 for Ha Noi and Ho Chi Minh City are about USD 12.7 billion and USD 21 billion respectively (ADB, 2010). Viet Nam is not alone in facing a funding gap when it comes to infrastructure development: according to the Addis Ababa Action Agenda, the infrastructure funding gap in developing countries can be estimated to between USD 1 and 1.5 trillion (United Nations, 2015).

Overall, policy makers must make the most of the existing funding by re-allocating a higher proportion of public income to financing public transport systems (see Chapter 4 for details). However, considering the clear resource gap, Viet Nam urgently needs to devise complementary funding strategies. One of these mechanisms, as highlighted above, could be to price against negative externalities of car usage, through congestion and parking charges, and redirect this revenue into public transport infrastructure development.

Public-private partnerships (PPPs) would be another instrument which can be used to fund urban transport systems, and they have been shown to be particularly suited for BRT systems, rail links, and shared-use vehicle and bicycle systems (Ang and Marchal, 2013). PPPs can facilitate greater private sector participation and allow the government to spread the risk associated with infrastructure development. However, the necessary policy framework must be put in place in Viet Nam in order to ensure a balance between the social and environmental concerns, such as affordability, and the financial viability of projects. To date, Viet Nam has had a mixed history with PPPs. Having relatively limited examples of PPPs in the country, government is seen as lacking a credible PPP history and ongoing projects have been criticised for long processes and a lack of transparency when it comes to project approvals (ADB and AFD, 2012). In 2015, the Ministry of Planning and Investment (MPI) launched *Decree 15 on Public Private Partnerships*. This Decree aims to address these challenges through setting out a specialised project cycle for PPPs, including necessitating a feasibility study which, in theory, should ensure the balance between social, environmental, and financial interests within the proposed projects. In parallel to the decree, MPI also launched a training course for provincial authorities, entitled the *PPP Foundations Course*, to enhance capacity at the provincial level on the key points of identifying, preparing and tendering PPP projects. Since its launch, the course has trained over 600 public sector representatives (Boots, 2016). The success of future PPP projects in Viet Nam will rely on the successful implementation of the goals in *Decree 15* and the continued enhancement of capacity of national and local government officials.

Public transport systems can also be financed through value capture mechanisms, as they almost inevitably lead to increasing land values. Land value capture can facilitate the government's ability, through a variety of mechanisms, to capture, at least in some part, the increasing value of the land and feed this revenue into the funding of the system. Value capturing mechanisms are not new tools and have been successfully used in OECD and non-OECD countries. Tokyo, Japan, has used a model that combines privatisation of transport service and joint development. Brazil and Colombia have had significant successes with the use of betterment levies, or *contribución de valorización* (Walters, 2012). London has successfully used a package of value capture mechanisms to raise 25% of the necessary funding for the London Crossrail project (Box 2.11). Among non-OECD countries, India launched in February 2017 the *Value Capture Finance Policy Framework*. This document charts the way forward for the use of value capture financing within the country (MoUD, 2017). Value capture mechanisms are diverse, and examples include tax increment financing (TIF) districts, development charges, development rights and joint development (Ang and Marchal, 2013). It is important to recognise that a package of different policy mechanisms is often more effective.

Viet Nam demonstrates many of the characteristics of an emerging middle-income economy which would be amenable to successful value capture – strong economic growth, rising incomes, increasing motorisation, and congestion – all which can instigate the increase of land value around public transport projects (Suzuki et al., 2015). However, in order to avoid potential negative consequences of value capturing, such as displacement of informal or vulnerable populations, or corrupt practices that can be associated with value capture, the necessary policy, legal, and financial frameworks must be put in place to support the successful use of value capture tools. Therefore, it is recommended that first, a regulatory review is undertaken to ensure that the necessary mechanisms, such as clear and transparent regulatory framework, are in place to ensure a fair and transparent value capture process, as well as to reinforce core values that increase quality of life in urban areas (UN Habitat, 2016a). Secondly, all levels of government must be adequately trained to be able to select and implement a package of value capture mechanisms. UN Habitat's Global Land Tool Network provides a training programme particularly focusing on land based finance for local governments (UN Habitat, 2016a).

Box 2.11. Land value capture: funding the Crossrail project in London

As an overall provider of public transport, Transport for London (TfL) was created in 2006 and reports directly to the Mayor of London. TfL has wide-ranging responsibilities that include rail-based infrastructure, but also a range of regulatory responsibilities involving streets – these include implementing the city's congestion charge, as well as providing for bicycle routes and pedestrian infrastructure. London has been active in launching innovative transport initiatives that have required substantial investment. Accordingly, the city has looked to value capture strategies to render these measures cost-effective. One advantage has been the continuing rise in commercial property values, which has greatly enhanced the value of TfL's own real estate holdings. In addition, the rising trend has enabled the city to use a supplement to an existing property tax on commercial buildings as a powerful value capture mechanism.

The Business Rates Supplement (BRS) has been especially important in financing a significant proportion of the construction for the new 21-kilometer Crossrail project. This large infrastructure development will provide an entirely new east-west rail linkage across the city. The project also draws revenues, as well as from the BRS, from a tax on new commercial development that will gain value from proximity to the Crossrail line. While this tax has proved to have some sensitivity to the ups and downs of construction activity, it also represents an effective value capture device. More generally, TfL is making ongoing efforts to persuade the government of the United Kingdom that all business rates paid in London should be devolved to local and regional governments for direct provision of services – which potentially could offset a decrease in the infusion of funds from outside London – although the outcome of this advocacy has yet to be determined.

Source: Salon, D. (2014), "Value Capture Opportunities for Urban Public Transport Finance", White Papers Prepared for the Transit Leadership Summit, London, Institute of Transportation Studies, University of California Davis, pp. 101-12, http://transitleadership.org/docs/TLS-WP-Value-Capture-Opportunities.pdf.

Housing policies: addressing the growing informal housing market

Housing stock in Viet Nam

The urban population of Viet Nam was 31 million in 2015, and is projected to rise to 44 million by 2020, representing a 3% annual growth (Chapter 1). With the average household size also projected to diminish, an annual average of 370 000 additional housing units will be required, and a total of 4.8 million units will need to be serviced, upgraded or rebuilt in urban areas by 2020 (Government of Viet Nam, 2016b). As of 2009, Viet Nam had 476 million m^2 of housing stock in urban areas which increased to 689 million m^2 in 2014 (World Bank, 2015a). The housing stock in Viet Nam is also relatively new, with 59% of the total stock being built after 2000 (World Bank, 2015a). Types of housing in Viet Nam are divided between permanent, semi-permanent, less permanent and simple housing.[4] As of 2014, only about 40% of urban dwellings were permanent housing (Table 2.5).

Table 2.5. Types of housing in urban areas Viet Nam (%), 2009 and 2014

Type of housing	2009	2014
Permanent housing	41.4	42.4
Semi-permanent housing	52.7	54.1
Less permanent housing	3.3	2.4
Simple housing	2.6	1.1

Source: Adapted from CTTPP (2016).

Viet Nam's housing stock is primarily owner-occupied, although demand for rental housing is increasing especially in urban areas. The 2009 Census recorded that 15% of all Vietnamese housing is rented and 85% is owner-occupied (UN Habitat, 2014b), although the share of rental housing is higher both in cities (26% in Ho Chi Minh City, for example) and amongst certain population groups (64% of immigrants in Ho Chi Minh City and Hanoi, for example) (CTTPP, 2016). A large portion of demand in rental sector is also from industrial zone workers. Approximately 40% of industrial workers are between the age of 15 and 29, of which approximately 78% (1.75 million people) rent their homes (World Bank, 2015a). The rental sector is mainly informal, with 90% of the rental supply nationwide remaining informal (Waibel et al., 2007). The affordable, or social, housing sector in Viet Nam is particularly stressed, with only 6.9% of the demand being met as of 2014 (CTTPP, 2016).

The current housing policy frameworks in Viet Nam have boosted private housing development but left behind the informal sector

Development of the housing legislative frameworks in Viet Nam

Before the *Doi Moi* economic reforms, Viet Nam did not have an articulated housing policy nor a real estate market. Considered as a social good rather than a commodity, housing was built and rented out by the government to state cadres and workers in urban areas, meeting only one third of housing needs for this population (Gough and Tran, 2009). With the 1986 reforms and the transition to a socialist-oriented market economy, the subsidy and state supplied system of housing gave way to a real estate market, with policies and legislation on land and housing regulating equitable access. *The 1993 Land Law* established land use rights for private persons and the possibility to sell and exchange it, and in 1994, the state-owned housing stock was privatised. *The 2006 Housing Law* established a framework for the provision of social housing to targeted populations through financial incentives and relaxation of construction standards. These new conditions ensured an influx of investment in housing and created favourable conditions for construction activities and renovation of existing housing, ensuring a housing boom in many urban centres. In 2015, *the Housing Law* was given a substantial revision in order to address a number of the below-highlighted challenges in the Vietnamese housing sector. Topics that are given particular attention are provision of affordable housing for low income groups, provision for recognition of self-built housing, and the inclusion of the private sector in the production of housing stock.

In addition to the 2015 revised Housing Law, the current legal environment regulating the housing market also comprises the Land Law (2013); the Construction Law (2003), the Investment Law (2005), the Enterprise Law (2005), the Real Estate Business Law (2006) and the Urban Planning Law (2009). Taken together, these measures are designed to ensure the right to use land and own property, and to regulate the transfer and sale of these rights, while also providing mechanisms to ensure that the housing and real estate markets are fair and accessible. They also illustrate the degree to which, as policy areas, housing and land – while separable for analytical purposes – are closely linked. The main agency overseeing the housing sector is the National Steering Committee for Housing and Real Estate Market Policy, established by the prime minister and headed by a deputy prime minister, guiding the implementation of housing and real estate business laws, and developing and supervising housing policies (UN Habitat, 2014b). In terms of the relationship to broader policy formulation, the Socio-Economic Development Plan recognises housing as a strategic sector, and a dedicated strategy was established in 2011:

the National Housing Development Strategy to 2020, with a vision to 2030 (NHDS). The NHDS states that housing development is a joint task of the state, society and the people, and aims to increase housing development and to support specific groups of people with difficulty in accessing adequate housing, such as low income people, industrial workers, or students. Some programmes targeted urban centres specifically (Wilson, 2016). In particular, the NHDS aims to:

- Provide adequate residential floor area: average floor area to be 26 m2/person in urban areas and 22 m2/person in the whole country;
- Increase stock of social housing: to build at least 10 million m2 of social housing for low-income earners in urban areas;
- Enhance quality of housing: rate of "firmly built" houses will reach 65% in urban areas and to increase the rate of households having adequate sanitation to 95% in urban areas; and
- Increase rental stock: in urban centres of Class III or higher, rental houses will account for at least 20% of total housing stock.

The challenge: shortage of housing supply and growing informal housing market

Despite these national targets, providing access to affordable and decent quality housing is one of the foremost challenges for Viet Nam's urban areas. As discussed above, official statistics show a substantial shortage of housing supply, rental housing in particular. Indeed, the modern housing sector that emerged from the real estate and housing market reforms represents a minority of actual urban housing production in Viet Nam. The formal housing sector and market in Viet Nam today is still out of reach of large segments of the population. Indeed, the current housing and rent prices in urban areas mean that most housing, even modest, is unaffordable for low to middle income households, even if they are eligible for a loan.

Consequently, an informal market has been developed in the housing sector in Viet Nam, which in practice provides the largest proportion of housing.[5] Catering to the urban poor and unregistered rural migrants, the informal sector indeed embodies an estimated 75% of housing production, and 75 to 80% of housing finance (Wilson, 2016), leaving only about 20% of actual urban housing to the modern and formal production mechanisms (UN Habitat, 2014b). The informal housing market creates low-quality housing stocks in cities, some of which are even in unsafe conditions. It may also hinder the development of the skilled and competitive construction sector. Moreover, informal housing development tends to occur in areas with concentrated poverty or with high risks of floods and other natural disasters. These areas are also often spatially segregated from other urban neighbourhoods, which, in turn, is associated with other social problems.

A number of factors may have perpetuated the existence of a large informal housing market:

- Inability of local governments to meet social housing quotas. The NHDS has targets for social housing provision, and the *2013 Decree on developing and managing social houses* (No. 188/2013/ND-CP) also mandates localities to allocate 20% of land from commercial development to social housing. Nonetheless, already limited budgets are strained by other demands and therefore do not extend to provide for this allocation or the meeting of these targets. The role which the private sector should play in such commercial development is not well defined, either.

- Underestimation of real housing needs, both in number and in type. This can be partially explained by the household registration system (*Ho Khau*) which was put in place in 1964 (Work Bank and Vietnam Academy of Social Sciences, 2016) (Box 2.12). A technical problem is that migrants who are registered as short-term (seasonal or temporary) or returning migrants in the system are left out of urban statistics. This distorts the actual demographic estimations in urban centres. The most recent census counted 8.6% of the population (about 6.7 million people) as migrants. However, as this number does not include short-term or returning migrants, the total number of "migrants" could be much higher (GSO, 2011). In addition, the complex requirements for migrants to obtain a permanent residence status may also prevent them from entering the formal housing market, as discussed in details later.
- Existence of non-registered migrants. Migrants who are not registered in the household registration system are also left out of urban statistics. It is estimated that they represent approximately a third of urban population growth (UNFPA, 2007). Non-registered residents are restricted from home and land ownership, pushing them towards informal and substandard types of rental housing.
- A lack of access to housing finance. Housing financing institutions are reluctant to engage with certain groups of populations, such as low income households and the elderly. Such clients are frequently seen as too risky, given their lack of collateral, and also with issues of income verification when the client comes from the informal economic sector. In Viet Nam, it is estimated that 68% of the labour force generates their income from the informal economy, which does not allow them to access traditional financing sources (World Bank, 2015a).

Box 2.12. Viet Nam's household registration system

Established in 1964 in the context of a planned economy, the Household Registration System (*Ho Khau*) mandated the registration of every citizen at the place of the permanent residence of their household. This system was intended as an instrument of security, economic planning and migration control, as movement had to be permitted by local authorities. Moreover, permanent residence was attached to the provision of rationing, land, housing, education, health services and employment, thus strongly restricting internal migration.

With the *Doi Moi* reforms of 1986 and the *Residence Law* of 2006, the system has been relaxed to enable migration and urbanisation. Migrants no longer required a departure permit from their local authority or the provision of a proof of employment or university enrolment to move to another city, and a temporary registration status was introduced. In 2013, the local authorities were granted the responsibility of setting their own policies for registration. As a result, some local authorities, especially in large cities, went back on the previous relaxation and for instance increased the period of temporary residence necessary to obtain a permanent status to two years, and three years in Hanoi.

It is estimated that migrants lacking permanent residence status in Viet Nam represent 5.6 million people, and account for 18% of the population in Hanoi, and 36% in Ho Chi Minh City (Work Bank and Vietnam Academy of Social Sciences, 2016). Despite recent reforms, and although the Constitution of Vietnam guarantees its citizens the freedom to move with equal social, economic and political rights ensured, the household registration system may have affected the access to social and economic opportunities and benefits for migrants without permanent residence status (UNDP, 2010).

Box 2.12. Viet Nam's household registration system (*cont.*)

For instance, children of migrants with temporary residence status tend to have lower instances of enrollment in secondary school, especially girls; access to health insurance is also limited, even for children under 6 years old that are supposed to be guaranteed free health care. Migrants without permanent residence status also tend to be excluded from the "poor list", granting eligibility for social assistance programmes (Duong et al., 2011). Such undesirable consequences can be considered to slow down necessary structural transformations and economic growth that could result from a sustainable urban development process.

Source: World Bank and Vietnam Academy of Social Sciences (2016), "Vietnam's Household Registration System", Hong Duc Publishing House, Ha Noi, https://openknowledge.worldbank.org/handle/10986/24594 ; UNDP (2010), "Urban Poverty Assessment in Hanoi and Ho Chi Minh City", UNDP, Hanoi, http://www.un.org.vn/en/publications/government-agency-publications/doc_details/264-urban-poverty-assessment-in-ha-noi-and-ho-chi-minh-city.html; Duong et al. (2011), "Social protection for rural-urban migrants in Vietnam: current situation, challenges and opportunities", CSP Research Report 08. Institute for Social Development Studies: Ha Noi.

In addition to these factors, a fundamental problem is a lack of recognition of the informal housing sector in the current national housing policy framework. This policy blind spot has created a distortion in the offer of housing options, which do not reflect the variety of needs, preferences and abilities to finance of different households. Indeed, housing policies have mainly focused on modern, suburban developments, while a majority of urban dwellers remain in degraded inner city housing or in peripheral areas lacking urban infrastructure. Moreover, policies for social and affordable housing have also historically forgotten large parts of the poor urban population (Gough and Tran, 2009), as it is mostly reserved for specific population groups such as officially employed and permanent residents, excluding unregistered migrants and workers from the informal economic sector.

Increasing affordable housing supply

In order to address these problems, it is urgent to consider policy options for increasing supply of affordable housing, both owned and rental, and both in the formal and informal housing market.

In 2006, the government took up the responsibility of ensuring access to housing for socially disadvantaged groups. However, the governmental social housing projects under *the 2006 Housing Law* targeted a set of very specific social groups, namely "state employees, officials, government staff, government officers, and workers in economic zones, industrial, productive and high tech areas" (2006 Housing Law, article 53). Projects that have impacted urban areas for instance included housing support for such categories as "meritorious people", social housing for students, housing for workers in industrial zones, and housing for officials. In fact, the scheme meant supporting some privileged groups and leaving out large segments of the urban poor such as the unemployed, low paid workers, privately or informally employed people, thereby illustrating a segmented and unco-ordinated approach to social housing. Recent projects, however, have benefited larger portions of the urban poor. This recent governmental shift committing to addressing the actual needs and demands of the urban poor is a first step towards a more comprehensive approach to social and affordable housing (World Bank, 2015a):

- The social housing programme for low income people in urban areas, which provided financial incentives and benefits to private developers for the construction of social housing, resulting in the completion of 19 686 units, with 55 830 still in implementation; and
- The housing finance project, which ran from 2003 to 2012 with the support of the Asian Development Bank to develop housing finance for the urban poor.

As previously noted, in 2015 *the Housing Law* was given a substantial revision, including provision of affordable housing for low income groups and inclusion of the private sector in the production of housing stock. In order to operationalise the law and to increase affordability for the lowest income, Vietnamese policy-makers may consider the following recommendations.

First, the priority target population for social housing in the NHDS should be redefined, based on the existing housing stock and resource availability and align with those target populations of the National Urban Upgrading Programme. Household poverty should take into account multi-dimensional poverty criteria, not just income thresholds (Box 2.13). An urgent action could be taken to recognise short-term (seasonal or temporary) or returning migrants, as defined in the household registration system, and take their housing needs into account within the housing strategy. Currently they are not counted in official estimates of housing needs within the NHDS (International Institute for Environment and Development, 2013). Recognising these migrants as urban population is crucial to better understand the real housing and other infrastructure needs, and to design housing and other urban policies accordingly. Continued efforts are also needed to encourage proper registration of migrants, to minimise policy challenges which may arise from non-registered migrants.

Box 2.13. Measuring poverty: the concept of multi-dimensional poverty in Viet Nam

The concept of "Multi-dimensional Poverty" moves away from a strictly economic view of poverty by giving attention also to a series of other – though related – forms of deprivation that may be suffered by households and individuals. They include limited access to education, inadequate health care, restricted opportunities for employment, poor-quality housing, and lack of physical safety. In the case of urban areas where monetary poverty can be, in some contexts, relatively limited but where the other deficits present serious and urgent problems, traditional poverty measures may be inaccurate and misleading, in that they may fail to take adequate account of urban residents who are not monetarily poor but face severe obstacles in the other areas.

Migrants in Ha Noi and Ho Chi Min City were particularly deprived in areas of housing services and housing quality and area, in comparison to residents. Indeed, while in Viet Nam urban areas the rate of poverty based on income is relatively low, measures of poverty in Viet Nam that include degraded housing and bad living conditions, show the rate to be placed at a much higher level.

Source: United Nations Development Programme (UNDP) (2010), "Urban Poverty Assessment in Hanoi and Ho Chi Minh City", UNDP, Hanoi, UPS09_report_final.pdf.

Second, different regulatory and fiscal measures to encourage the private sector to supply affordable housing could be considered. Options include:

- Introduce development charges to be used for local governments to supply affordable housing. Localities will continue to struggle with meeting the necessary quotas of land stipulated in the *Decree 188* to meet social housing targets, as the private sector can only provide localities with land, without resource to actually provide social housing. Such value capturing mechanism would generate extra revenue for localities and help to enable actual affordable housing and relieve pressure on social public housing demands.
- Introduce mixed-income development requirement for private housing projects. Experience in certain OECD countries indicates that "another way of approaching the housing affordability gap is by adopting an inclusionary approach" (OECD, 2017b). Central to this approach is the provision of incentives to private developers to incorporate affordable housing into projects that are primarily aimed at market-driven housing development, as illustrated in the example from Ireland (Box 2.14).
- Increase land supply for affordable housing provision in urban areas. Many OECD countries and cities have introduced taxation and/or charges for vacant or underutilised land in primary urban areas, as observed in Ireland (Box 2.14). This could disincentivise investors from land banking and open up more available land for affordable housing for the urban poor. This and other fiscal measures – for example, providing incentives for development of infill sites – could also augment the overall supply of affordable housing.

Box 2.14. Mixed-income housing developments in Ireland

The Irish Planning Act was revised in 2003 and 2006 in order to address affordable housing needs and to alleviate problems of social segregation. Previously, builders could exchange money or land instead of setting aside up to 20% of new developments for social or affordable use, a provision under Part V of the Planning Act and therefore, some developers have been able to build the social portions of new developments elsewhere. However, now social units must be predominantly on site, making it mandatory for developers to set aside up to 10% of new developments for social use.

In addition, a vacant site levy of up to 5% of the value of derelict sites was introduced, aimed at avoiding vacant sites in urban areas and facilitating inner-city development. A "use-it-or-lose-it" clause regarding land zoned for development to reduce speculation or land hoarding. This is likely to oblige developers to begin on site or to have a portion of the development built within five years of receiving planning permission.

Source: National Economic and Social Council (NESC) (2014), "Review of Irish Social and Affordable Housing Provision", *NESC Secretariat Papers*, Paper No. 10, http://files.nesc.ie/nesc_secretariat_papers/No_10_Review_of_Irish_Social_and_Affordable_Housing_Provision.pdf.

Another important policy option is to develop an implementation mechanism for affordable housing, such as housing corporations/associations. The development and operation of housing corporations/associations has been a successful model in many OECD countries, such as Australia, Germany, the Netherlands, and the United Kingdom. In these countries, the associations vary in their mandates – whether it be to provide housing for disadvantaged populations or to manage rental market properties, however, they are similar in that any profits are re-invested in new housing projects or used to maintain existing stock. Although they are independent of the government, they receive preferential benefits, such as public subsidies and tax benefits. In many countries, housing corporations/associations have been very productive in delivering housing stock – in the United Kingdom, for example, housing associations started 9 063 homes in the first Quarter of 2017 and completed 9 291 homes during the same period (NHF, 2017). In the Netherlands, the Dutch Social Housing Associations own 75% of the housing stock (Box 2.15).

Box 2.15. Dutch Social Housing Associations or "toegelaten instellingen"

There are about three million rented homes in the Netherlands. About 75% of them are owned by social housing associations, which are organisations that build, let or sell accommodation and provide homes for households with lower incomes, older people and people with a disability. They are not-for-profit organisations which reinvest their profits/reserves in social housing, to maintain the housing stock. Main activities of social housing associations are:

- housing households with lower incomes, older people, people with a disability and those needing assisted housing;
- building and letting social property such as neighbourhood libraries, women shelters, and primary schools;
- appointing caretakers and neighbourhood managers; and
- maintaining houses and the immediate surroundings, such as alleyways and parking spaces.

Source: Government of the Netherlands (n.d), Housing associations, www.government.nl/topics/housing/housing-associations.

The Vietnamese government should try to reduce housing production costs to allow affordable housing provision. This can be achieved by supporting technological innovation (e.g. low-cost and sustainable construction materials) and process innovation (e.g. efficient construction methods), and improving skills of the workers to enable production of diverse housing types to different needs, incomes and lifestyles. The central government has a crucial role in creating greater efficiency and more transparent market conditions of the construction sector. In addition, it is very important to remove administrative burden to land acquisition, registration and construction with a review and reformulation of existing rules, regulations and procedures. Improving transparency of the housing market would also be crucial through improved public communication on market trends and transactions, which would reduce information asymmetry and speculative behaviour (UN Habitat, 2014a).

Improving the low-quality informal housing stocks

At the same time as increasing supply of affordable housing in the formal sector, the government also needs to directly address the existing low-quality informal housing stocks. It is important to recognise that investment only in the formal housing sector, even in social housing models, will not solve the entrenched challenges that citizens face in order to enter the formal/social housing market. This will continue to precipitate the growth of an informal housing market, and be detrimental to efforts to address concerns of multidimensional poverty in urban areas.

As demonstrated in certain informal settlements, there have been signs in recent years of a changing governmental approach to informality: from demolition, eviction and resettlement for informal areas to the recognition of self-built housing, upgrading, and sites and services schemes. In 2000, the government relied on international assistance to deal with informal settlements, which led to detailed studies of the housing and infrastructure needs of the urban poor and an action plan for the city of Can Tho (Government of Viet Nam, 2008; Cities Alliance, 2013). Based on this study, the Viet Nam Urban Upgrading Project was initiated in 2004. This project consisted in upgrading infrastructure, providing housing improvement loans and building capacity in four selected cities which led to the upgrading of 295 low-income areas, benefiting 2.5 million people. This demonstrated the benefits of a more flexible approach to informality, and of trying to enable people to stay in their homes through upgrading. Following the success of the project, the government upscaled it in 2009 into *the National Urban Upgrading Programme to 2020*. The programme covers 95 cities of Class IV and above, which has reached 90 000 households, servicing unplanned housing areas and providing financial assistance for housing improvement and tenure regularisation (World Bank, 2015b).

Building on this experience, Vietnamese officials may consider having further consideration for the informal sector in national level housing policies. The following options could be considered:

- Include explicit reference to the informal housing sector in the National Housing Development Strategy (NHDS). The NHDS could be revised to include informal settlement and upgrading of existing housing stocks both in its objectives and subsequent implementation measures. Furthermore, overall housing objectives could be re-oriented to focus not only on the quantitative targets but also on the provision of adequate and accessible housing.
- Strengthen inspection and guidance to improve the housing quality.
- Develop an effective micro-finance mechanism to upgrade the existing low-quality housing stock and living arrangements. Although wide spread slums do not exist in Viet Nam, there is reference to "vertical slums," which are multi-floor buildings which are divided into small living spaces and rented to the low income market. Given the financial constraint in the public sector, incremental upgrading and maintenance of the existing housing stock by individuals could be encouraged. One way to do so is to provide access to micro finance, since micro-finance for housing purposes remains an underused phenomenon in Viet Nam (Thanh et al., 2013). Expanding such a programme towards the housing sector offers a valid way of offsetting the tendency of state banks to concentrate on mortgage loans to the wealthier strata of society (UN Habitat, 2014b).

Finally, the current household registration system (*Ho Khau*) could also be improved. As previously stated, it has contributed to a growing informal housing sector, partly because short-term (seasonal or temporary) or returning migrants are not taken into account within the NHDS. Furthermore, it is reported that the system precipitates some socio-economic inequalities for migrants without permanent residence status (UNDP, 2010). Considering the increasing rate of rural to urban migration, simplifying the procedures for obtaining permanent registration could be an effective option to help migrants getting integrated into the society and avoid unnecessary inequity in urban areas. Two concrete steps could be considered. Firstly, one of the most pressing needs is to remove the stipulation on housing square footage. The current system requires prior to obtaining permanent registration status that applicants must reside in housing that abides by a minimum living space per person. Considering that migrants already are disproportionately living in poorer living conditions when compared to residents, this stipulation is highly problematic. According to the 2009 Viet Nam poverty survey, residents in cities have, on average, 20.3 m^2 of living space, while migrants typically reside in only 8.4m^2 (UNDP, 2010). Secondly, the requirement to prove formal employment may also be relaxed to some extent, as many migrants into cities are employed in the informal sector.

Land policies: streamlined regulations for efficient urban development

Due to rapid urbanisation, the pressure for developing land has been strong in Vietnamese cities, which necessitates efficient and transparent land usage and management. However, the complexity and ambiguity of the current system seriously hinders efficient land transformation for Vietnamese cities. The state is responsible for the allocation of land to institutions, organisations, individuals and households for long term use, and it grants and limits the rights of land use and exchange. The role of the state is hence crucial for ensuring efficient operation of the land system and addressing the increasing development needs in cities.

Current land policy frameworks present co-ordination and consistency challenges

Legislative and institutional frameworks

Until 1986, Viet Nam had a planned economy model in which private property was not formally recognised. Not until the *Doi Moi* reforms, which initiated the transition of the country to a socialist-oriented market economy, did a market for urban land emerge. *The 1993 Land Law* recognised land rights for private persons, and established the mechanisms for their trade and pricing. This concept was also enshrined in the Constitution in 1992, which specifies that "land falls under the ownership of the entire people. The state assumes the unified administration of land according to overall planning and in conformity with the law and ensures its appropriate and effective use", and that "citizens have the right to use the land allocated by the state and have the right to undertake construction of housing in accordance with planning and law" (UN Habitat, 2014b). As indicated by this constitutional stipulation, although ownership of land is attributed to the people, and individual land use rights are recognised, the role of the state in the land sector is still dominant. In *the 2003 Land Law*, land is subject to the exclusive administration of the state, acting as the people's representative.

Since its emergence, the sector of land has been the subject of a vast array of governmental legislation and regulations, as detailed below. The primary law overseeing land use and management issues is *the Land Law*, updated every ten years since the first *Land Law* of 1993, under the Ministry of Natural Resources and the Environment (MONRE). *The Land Law* establishes the rights of the government and of land users, stipulates the requirements of land use planning, and the mechanisms for land allocation, renting and withdrawal. It also regulates land use right registration, and land financing and pricing. *The 2003 Land Law* further opened the land market, and guaranteed and concretised land rights through the system of building ownership and land use certificates (BOLUCs) and land use rights certifications (LURCs), which constitute a form of "title", on the basis of which the market exchange developed. *The 2013 Land Law* further clarified the mechanisms of the land market through regulations on the rights and responsibilities of the government and individuals, on allocation, acquisition and compensation of land, and access to the market. MONRE and its attached departments and agencies are responsible for land policies and the regulation of land management bodies, and evaluate and guide land use plans.

Another important agency regarding land is the Ministry of Construction (MOC), responsible for physical and spatial planning, and the housing and real estate markets. Under its purview is *the 2003 Law on Construction*, which decentralises the granting of building permits to the districts, and details the spatial plans required at different scales. *The 2009 Law on Urban Planning* adds to and updates the stipulations of *the Law on Construction*. It regulates the classification of cities and towns, the development, evaluation and approval of regional and urban construction plans and the management and usage of urban land, while decentralising many urban planning responsibilities to the districts and provinces.

Land usage is therefore determined by the multiple requirements and regulations of plans from different sectors: the Land Use Plans under the responsibility of MONRE, the spatial plans of the MOC, and of plans under a large number of other sectoral laws such as *the Housing Law, the Law on Real Estate Business, the Investment Law, the Law of Residence, the Law of Enterprise, and the Law of Commerce*. This variety of laws, regulations, plans and institutions reveals a key limitation of the land policy framework: its inherent lack of any co-ordination or consistency. Not only is each of the institutions divided at the subnational level in departments and branches at the province and city levels, but even more importantly land and land use planning issues are regulated by multiple plans under entirely different agencies.

Complex and ambiguous land management system results in delays in project developments and opens the door to corruption

These different agencies approach land from their own policy perspectives, and follow different schedules and processes. They use different definitions, classifications and projections for decision-making, resulting in sometimes contradictory or incoherent requirements for land use (World Bank, 2011, and UN Habitat, 2014b). For instance, the land use plans of MONRE and construction plans of the MOC define urban land differently and have different classifications of land, relying on different criteria. *The Land Law* lists different land use purposes, classifying it between agricultural, non-agricultural and non-used land, while *the Law on Urban Planning* is concerned with "urban planning land" – it distinguishes civil, non-civil and other lands, with uses classified as residential, public, commercial, service and industrial. These classifications and plans serve as a basis for land use transfer, transaction and leasing, and yet their relationship is not specified. This complexity and ambiguity leads to delays in project development, as actors cannot decide which one takes precedence, or how to harmonise both classifications (Wilson, 2016). It also creates serious administrative burden for cities' officials who operationalise land use changes, BOLUCs and LURCs.

The complexity and ambiguity also leads to informal developments that seriously undercut efforts to make rational sense of the system. Following the formal procedures, development projects have to wait for and comply with a series of land use plans at different scales and from different institutions (see Box 2.16). Under intense development pressure, many projects eventually go ahead without waiting for the finalisation of all relevant plans. As the result, private developers change the spatial and economic reality on the ground and the calculations and projections on which land use plans are based end up obsolete and inadequate. For instance, certain industrial zones in Viet Nam remain unused because they no longer respond to an actual demand.

Box 2.16. Development approvals process in Viet Nam

The infrastructure and development approval procedure in the country depends on the nature and size of project (projects are classified according to the four categories of national, A, B or C), the investment capital status (private, foreign direct investment, ODA, state enterprises, and/or individual), and the category of land use right. There are three types of development approval (investment approval; issuance of land use right certificate; and development approval and building or construction certificate) and most projects require all three.

The four categories are in descending order of the scope and scale of the project. National projects require the approval of the Prime Minister within a framework established by the National Assembly. Group A projects are approved at the level of national ministries, while Group B and Group C projects are assessed by agencies at the provincial level. After investment approval has been attained, and the environmental impact favourably appraised, the proponent must submit a request for land allocation to the local Department of Natural Resources and Environment. A construction permit based on detailed design of the project is also required. Under the relevant Construction Law, construct permits are issued either by the Ministry of Construction, the provincial Department of Construction, or the District-Level People's Committee, depending on the complexity of the project.

Investment projects that require land allocation for development go through a pre-planning process with the local Department of Planning and Investment for investment approval and the local Department of Construction for guidance on the project location. After approval, the project proponent negotiates the compensation and resettlement plan. The Land Law requires that the project be consistent with the annual land use planning process of the District-Level People's Committee.

Source: Dang, G and L.S. Pheng (2015), Infrastructure Investments in Developing Economies: The Case of Vietnam, Springer, Singapore; Coulthart, A., N. Quang and H. Sharpe (2006), "Urban Development Strategy: Meeting the Challenges of Rapid Urbanization and the Transition to a Market Oriented Economy", World Bank, Vietnam Country Office, Hanoi; Indochina Legal (2012), "Legal Overview of Construction in Vietnam", Indochina Legal.

Furthermore, the complexity and opaqueness of the current system open the door to corruption, with informal gifts or payments being requested for the granting of BOLUCs, LURCs and other construction related permits (World Bank/International Finance Corporation, 2009). A further expedient to which many developers may turn is to respond to impenetrable recommendations by simply requesting a waiver or exemption, following which they will be at liberty to proceed as they wish – but again at the price of providing informal gifts and payments, and at the deeper price of further undercutting any semblance of consistency in the land management system.

Complexity of requirements also means bottlenecks for households to formalise land registrations

The sheer accumulation of regulations on land use also constitutes an administrative burden for households to regularise their land holding through being granted a BOLUC or LURC. The complex procedures and high costs and fees often discourage households, especially the poor, from regularising their land or self-built housing, keeping them in the informal housing sector. Fees are normally determined at the provincial level, and therefore can vary from province to province (Government of Viet Nam, 2009, Article 28). For instance, the granting of a building permit requires a detailed drawing of the construction project for which many people do not have the technical skills, nor the financial capacity to hire an architect. Also required is a LURC, meaning that documentary evidence of property must be provided, which is often difficult as the majority of land transactions occur informally. Granting processes for BOLUCs and LURCs are also lengthy and involve costs for the cadastral survey, mapping and registration in the form of taxes, levies and fees that most people cannot afford and avoid by deferring regularisation (Wilson, 2016). The complexity of land registration procedures can be illustrated by the multiplicity of agencies involved: the Land Use Right Registration Office, the tax office, the state treasury and the notary's office.

In this context, the impact of the policies on housing and land use are closely interlinked, and lack of co-ordination in each area greatly exacerbates the challenges that citizens face when attempting to regularise their land and housing arrangements. Often, major challenges in the land sector are also due to a lack of information dissemination, leading to a lack of public knowledge on how to undertake complex procedures. This, in turn, can invite corruption, where any public ignorance can be an entry point for uncouth practices.

Selling land is becoming an income generator for local governments – at the expense of urban sprawl

The involvement and control of the state in the land market based on *the Land Law* is reflected in the two-tiered land price system in place in Viet Nam, which was established to encourage direct investment in land. All activities and transactions between the state and land users, such as compensation, acquisition, allocation, renting or taxing, are based on a set Land Price Framework (LPF), at rates lower than the market price. Since 2003, the LPF has been determined by provincial governments annually, at about 70% of market price (Thu and Perera, 2011). The state can acquire land from displaced land use right holders at this price. However, the imposed price does not adjust to the rise actual market price and the state can then allocate such rights to developers that can then resell to individuals at market price, thus disproportionally benefiting developers and investors over land users. This is precipitated by lack of any substantial land value capture mechanisms in urban development, meaning that the revenue local governments are receiving is significantly less than what it could and should be.

Another important fact to note concerning land transaction in Viet Nam is that governments and their agencies at local and regional levels are permitted to keep land revenues. This is in strong contrast with other government revenues which are collected by the central government and redistributed. This encourages local governments to sell as much land as possible to increase their revenue, particularly when their revenue from other sources does not reach their annual expectation, leading to urban sprawl and an inadequate allocation of land uses, notably infrastructure inefficiencies (World Bank, 2011). In the absence of a consistently enforced land policy framework, the selling off of periphery land proceeds independently of either rational development principles or an accurate reckoning of consequences immediate or long-term.

Enhance urban land management in Viet Nam

Streamline building permits and development approvals processes

Given the rapid urbanisation in Viet Nam, the land use planning system under *the Land Law* needs to be better adapted to the dynamic circumstances of urban development led by the market economy. This would imply adopting plans that are more dynamic and offer guidance, rather than being definitive and having too detailed prescriptions. This would allow for plans and developments to better answer to socio-economic needs and to adjust more quickly to the needs of rapid urbanisation. The Vietnamese government could consider the following options:

- Strengthen inspections and enforcement. Along with the simplification of the permit/approval, the government needs to ensure that the permitted/approved developments are completed as planned. Reducing administrative burden by simplifying certain permits/approvals could also help to reserve human resources for this type of work.
- Consider reducing the fees for smaller-scale developments, while introducing high penalties for non-compliance. This could help reducing financial burdens for households and help with formalising land registration.
- Use the private sector for certain types of building permits and inspection. In many OECD countries, such as Japan, building permits and inspection are being operated by the private sector under public supervision. This also addresses the shortage of resources in the public sector and ensures speedy processes (Box 2.17).
- Introduce and enforce a standard processing time for different types of permits/approval. This allows private developers to anticipate when they can receive the results of their applications. It also enables cities to ensure necessary resources to be able to deal with the applications in time.
- Introduce "one-stop" service for development/building permits. Although scattered examples of one stop models exist in Viet Nam (for example, the one-stop service centre at the Vietnam-Singapore Industrial Park in Quang Ngai province), officials should consider scaling up these initiatives, and transitioning the physical one stop centres online to ensure transparency and efficiency. For example, in Prague, Czech Republic, facing the complicated building approvals process, an amendment to the Building Act has been proposed to integrate a zoning procedure and a building procedure into a joint permit (OECD, 2017c) (Box 2.18). Rwanda met a similar challenge by centralising development approval processes through both physical and online "one stop centres". These clearly articulate the exact requirements for development, including the timeframe and the cost, thus making large strides in increasing transparency around development processes (Box 2.19).

Box 2.17. Reforming building confirmation and inspection system in Japan

In Japan, it is necessary for a building owner to obtain a building confirmation that the building plan conforms to the building standards, prior to the start of construction work. In addition, when the construction work is completed, it is necessary to undergo a final inspection and get a certificate of inspection before starting to use the building. While the system aimed to ensure the building standards, administrative capacity of local governments posed a severe challenge. In 1996, there were about 1 800 building officials in Japan, who had to be responsible for approximately 1.1 million construction starts. In 1998, it was estimated that only 40% of new buildings received a final inspection.

In 1999, the revised Building Standard Law introduced a new system where authorised private institutions could also carry out building confirmation and inspection. The Ministry of Land, Infrastructure, Transport and Tourism or prefectures are responsible for designating and overseeing such institutions. Those who carry out building confirmation and inspection in the private institutions are required to have the qualification equivalent to building officials.

The new system drastically increased the number of total inspectors. In 2014, approximately 4 500 people, including public building officials and private inspectors, were engaged. Private institutions accounted for 86% of building confirmations (in 2014) and 80% of final inspections (in 2013). The final inspection rate increased from the 40% in 1998 to about 90% in 2013. The new system also allowed public building officials to focus on conducting other important tasks such as auditing building officials and remedying non-conforming buildings.

Source: Ministry of Land, Infrastructure, Transport and Tourism of Japan.

While the administrative costs related to building approvals in Prague, Czech Republic, are relatively low compared to other European cities, the length of time that it takes to receive a permit is much longer and the process is more complex. For example, the World Bank's "Doing Business" report finds that it takes on average 247 days to obtain a planning permit to construct a warehouse in the Czech Republic. The Czech Republic ranked 183rd out of 213 countries surveyed by this measure. For more complicated projects, the Czech building permit process can take between three to seven years.

With the two-step approval process there is more space for objections, which the regional planning authorities must address. First, if any of the involved bodies do not agree with the result, it is possible to request an opinion or decision of the Ministry for Regional Development on the matter. Afterwards, there is also the possibility to appeal to the regular court. Further, the process is administratively onerous, requiring the binding opinions of 23 authorities for both steps. In some cases, opinions are also required by state authorities. In total, up to 45 different approvals may be required by state and municipal authorities. In some cases, the approvals of different levels of government or different departments can be contradictory, which presents further obstacles and delay.

In acknowledgement of the need to streamline this complicated approvals process, an amendment to the Building Act has been proposed. The amendment would permit municipal authorities to issue a joint ruling for a town and country planning (zoning) procedure, and for a building procedure. To date, these two procedures are separate. Under the proposed amendment, a binding assessment of the environmental impact of construction would form the basis of permission to build and this decision-making process would be integrated into a joint permit. These are important amendments that could reduce regulatory burden and streamline the building approvals process without reducing environmental diligence.

Source: OECD (2017c), *The Governance of Land Use in the Czech Republic: The Case of Prague*, OECD Publishing, Paris, http://dx.doi.org/10.1787/9789264281936-en.

Box 2.18. Reforming the development approvals process: the case of Rwanda

To remedy what, at the time, was a long and costly process for investors, Rwanda set up a One Stop Centre where investors could go to acquire all the titles and permits they required for their projects, with clear and transparent access to the timeline and costs. As the investment climate in Kigali improved, so too the construction industry. Combined with forward looking urban planning, focused on working with the community to improve the quality of public spaces and based on disaggregated data collected through tools such as the One Stop Youth Centres, this allowed us to guide urban development in the right direction.

The Kigali construction and urban planning One Stop Centre was created by a cabinet decision of 14th April 2010 and was assigned the following roles:

- To ensure respect for safety standards in the construction sector;
- To develop and review key area detailed physical plans;
- To ensure quick service delivery mostly in building permit issuance; and
- To monitor and advise Districts' land bureau for efficient service delivery.

The Kigali construction and urban planning One Stop Centre is also tasked with the role of implementing the Kigali Master Plan which is expected to assist the City in creating:

- A livable environment that supports sustainable growth of the city while embracing the three E's of Ecology, Equity and Economy;
- A livable community that supports a sense of belonging, co-operation and healing, and optimism;
- Guaranteed guidance and monitoring of the management and use of land;
- Ensured security of residents by setting development standards that must be abided by;
- A model of environmental protection and preservation that minimises pollution and waste disposal; and
- A foundation for economic vitality for all its citizens.

Source: Rwanda Development Board (2017), "One Step Centres", www.rdb.rw/one-stop-centre.html.

Improve the transparency of land related information

The transparency of land systems is directly related to the "openness, consistency and accountability of administrative systems" (UN Habitat, 2013a). An urgent option for the government is to ensure access to all the national and subnational plans and strategies related to land use and management. Certain information on individual BOLUCs and LURCs should also be made available to the public. "E-cadastre" and other electric information could greatly improve the accessibility to land related information and reduce the administrative costs of data management in the long run, as demonstrated by Macedonia's experience of property registration reform (Box 2.19). Currently, the MONRE is developing the national Multipurpose Land Information System (MPLIS), supported by the World Bank's *Improved Land Governance and Database* (VILG) *Project*. Such land administration systems can support the streamlining of procedures and their associated costs and timelines, standardise and digitalise cadastre maps and land use maps, and consolidate land inventory and land pricing. For the successful implementation of the LIS, Vietnamese officials are encouraged to consider its accessibility, particularly for the most vulnerable populations. In addition, the launch of the MPLIS should be accompanied by capacity development not only for public servants, but also for the community, in particular for vulnerable groups like women and those that currently reside in informal properties.

Box 2.19. Reforming property registration in Macedonia

A series of changes at the real estate cadastre in Skopje have made registering property faster and easier in Macedonia. A 2008 law streamlined procedures and set time limits. The number of property cases awaiting registration in Skopje shrank from 15 035 in 2005 to 2 082 in May 2011. The average time to process applications fell from 60 days in 2004 to 5 in 2011. All fees were cut by 50% in 2007 as part of the regulatory guillotine project and by another 10–72% in January 2010.These accomplishments won the cadastre an award of excellence from the World Bank in June 2010. The cadastre has introduced performance standards to motivate staff to work more efficiently. Staff exceeding the average can receive a salary increase of up to 25%.

The cadastre has also worked to improve its public image, by holding "open days", opening "hotlines" to answer questions and meeting with citizens in the municipalities of Skopje. A customer asked about his recent experience reported having to wait in line outside the cadastre for 4 hours in the summer heat—but considered that a huge improvement over a few years ago, when transferring property took several months. The most recent efforts to increase efficiency and effectiveness include launching an electronic cadastre and front desk in 2010. The "e-cadastre" is aimed at improving management of the workload and providing real-time dissemination and exchange of data. The "e-front desk" supported by the Netherlands, includes electronic conveyance, recording and processing of applications. Among other things, it allows notaries to check information on encumbrances and the status of applications.

Source: UN Habitat (2013a), "Tools to support Transparency in Land Administration", Nairobi.

Reflect market prices more accurately for land transactions

As discussed previously, in Viet Nam, the perpetuation of urban sprawl is exacerbated by developers seeking to purchase cheaper land on the periphery of urban areas, by governments' and agencies' land sales without rational planning principles, and by large amounts of unused land in cities due to land banking. Continuing on this path will propagate the cycle of extended commuting, high transport costs and levels of congestion, and poor quality of urban life. It is in direct contrast with the principles of TOD. Vietnamese officials may consider to:

- Encourage inner city land use through placing higher rates of tax or introducing fees/charges on unused or underutilised land. Land tax currently only accounts for 2-3% of government revenues. This is due to minimal tax rates, but also to the land valuations of the Land Price Framework, which price land below market value. An increase on land tax strengthens the incentives to develop land, as opposed to holding it. In areas of high land value, development should be particularly encouraged, thus helping development around transport hubs, and fostering denser urban areas (OECD, 2017d). Extra revenue from land taxation should be kept in the respective localities and reinvested in the inner city urban environment.
- Review the land valuation under the Land Price Framework. Land value appraisal needs to be as close as possible to prices of private land transactions. Collecting more information on private land transactions and making it available for the

public would be useful to make more accurate and timely revisions of the Land Price Framework.

- Increase local own revenues to be used to invest in local urban infrastructure. The need for local governments to sell land, particularly on the urban peripheries, can also be mitigated by more sustainable forms of local financing, as is elaborated in Chapter 4.

Policies for the quality of the urban environment

Urban public spaces are key to a city's prosperity

A high quality urban environment is essential for cities to prosper. Urban space can be a "development enabler," if planning is done in a way that provides areas not only for economic activities, but also for recreation as well as cultural and social interactions (UN Habitat, 2016c). Public spaces, both streets and public open spaces, are necessary for fostering socially cohesive and inclusive cities which, in turn, can ensure an adequate quality of life for urban citizens. Moreover, they are essential not only for people to gather and interact, but also for economic competitiveness, urban eco-systems and for cultural heritage in cities. For example, high quality of life in urban areas, together well-functioning urban infrastructure, can attract skilled people and contribute to the competitiveness of cities (OECD, 2006; 2009; 2012). Besides, the quality of the urban environments is closely linked to the success of compact city policies. Public parks, green spaces and streets in urban centres are an essential element of a compact city, and when public space is well designed and delivers high-quality services, density is perceived positively, alleviating many of the problems associated with high density (OECD, 2012).

Many organisations have long advocated cities with well-designed and quality urban environments. For example, UN Habitat has developed the Five Principles of Sustainable Urban Neighbourhoods (Box 2.20). Most recently, the importance of green, clean and safe public spaces for quality urban life has been recognised in the Sustainable Development Goals, particularly in Target 11.7 which calls for the provision of "universal access to safe, inclusive and accessible, green and public spaces, in particular for women and children, older persons and persons with disabilities". The New Urban Agenda also calls for "promoting safe, inclusive, accessible, green and quality public spaces, including streets, sidewalks and cycling lanes, squares, waterfront areas, gardens and parks" (United Nations, 2016a).

Box 2.20. Five Principles of Sustainable Urban Neighbourhood

UN Habitat, long recognising and advocating the importance of public spaces, has developed *the Five Principles of Sustainable Urban Neighbourhoods*:

1. Adequate space for streets and an efficient street network: the street network should occupy at least 30% of the land and at least 18 km of street length per km^2.
2. High density: there should be at least 15 000 people per km^2, that is 150 people/ha or 61 people/acre.
3. Mixed land-use: at least 40% of floor space should be allocated for economic use in any neighbourhood.

Box 2.20. Five Principles of Sustainable Urban Neighbourhood (*cont.*)

4. Social mix: the availability of houses in different price ranges and tenures in any given neighbourhood to accommodate different incomes; 20 to 50% of the residential floor area should be for low cost housing and each tenure type should be not more than 50% of the total.
5. Limited land-use specialisation: this is to limit single function blocks or neighbourhoods; single function blocks should cover less than 10% of any neighbourhood.

Following the five principles, UN Habitat also promote that well designed cities can work to achieve the following key characteristics:

- Vibrancy: Supporting and promoting street life by enabling a variety of activities, conducive frontage and street width, and reducing the presence and role of private transport. A high population density generates sufficient industrial and commercial service demand while mixed land use provides adequate manufacturing and service space.
- Walkability: Promoting walkability as a key measure to bring people into the public space, reduce congestion and boost local economy and interactions. A vibrant street life encourages people to walk or cycle around, while a rational street network enables necessary city administrative services to be offered within walking or cycling distance and ensures security. Walkability helps to reduce automobile reliance and thus alleviate relevant congestion, air pollution and resource depletion issues.
- Affordability: Supporting affordability of transactions and economic activities, as well as of services and housing, by promoting proximity and reducing costs and building services for a diverse group of users. The social mix principle tries to promote a rational distribution of urban public resources and provides adequate housing for different revenue groups through city planning regulations – ensuring social equity and promoting economic efficiency. An affordable and accommodating city is a core feature of a sustainable city.

Source: UN Habitat (2015), "Global Public Space Toolkit: From Global Principles to Local Policies and Practice", Nairobi https://unhabitat.org/wpcontent/uploads/2015/10/Global%20Public%20Space%20Toolkit.pdf.

Vietnamese cities are struggling for providing public spaces in pace with the urbanisation

The rapidity of Vietnamese urbanisation has posed challenges for government in terms of its ability to ensure a quality environment for urban residents. For example, Vietnamese cities are struggling for the provision of open space in dense inner-city centres. In Hanoi, between 2000 and 2010, the area devoted to parks and public gardens per capita went from 2.17m^2 to 1.58m^2 (HealthBridge, 2015). In Hoan Kiem district, Ha Noi's old quarter, the area was only 0.14m^2 per person in comparison to the national average (1.7m^2) and the target set in the 2008 Viet Nam Building Code (7 m^2) for "public-use green spaces outside of residential units" for special-grade cities such as Ha Noi (UN Habitat, 2015).

Despite the clear challenges in Viet Nam to ensure the quality of the urban environment, it is important to highlight that there have been successful initiatives aimed at improving the urban environment for urban residents in Viet Nam. For example, City of Ha Noi has created a pedestrian zone within Hanoi's Hoan Kiem, old quarter, district which takes effect between Friday and Sunday evening every weekend. Despite fears from shop owners that their revenues would decrease, since the pedestrianisation, shops within this area reported a 14% increase in revenue (DiGregorrio, 2016).

Not only dense urban centres in large cities, but most of urban areas with rapid population growth are facing difficulties in providing sufficient public spaces with decent quality. While detailed area plans set the specific uses of urban space and the quality, quantity and position of each development type and building footprint, they are often prepared without securing the necessary funding for implementation. Consequently, the urbanisation process can be heavily influenced by subjective decisions by local governments regarding development and planning permissions, a process which is open to the influence of the interests of developers (Coulthart et al., 2006). This often results in sub-quality public space, inadequate street networks, and low safety levels for those walking or cycling.

Furthermore, enforcement of policies and laws dictating environmental quality standards is a challenge. Some references to quality urban environment have been made in Viet Nam's urban policy framework. For example, the AOMP requires that urban construction and development comply with the Approved Regulations on Urban Architecture Management (ARUAM), which provides a general guideline for designing urban centres (e.g., model urban quarters, civilised urban streets and public areas for the life of urban residents). However, it is not clearly defined how to monitor and evaluate the quality of projects in the planning and/or construction stages. *The Decree 11/2013 on Urban Development Investment Management* also determines that large-scale urban development projects have to undergo a special procedure of approval at the provincial and ministerial level to ensure an orderly staged urban development synchronised with the provision of necessary technical and social infrastructure. However, it also lacks reference to the requisite regulations (and guidelines) that ensure an effective assessment of projects. Finally, as previously discussed, the overlapping responsibilities for urban management across many ministries may also jeopardise enforcement processes.

National level urban policy frameworks can help actively attract investment in public spaces

In order to move towards the achievement of quality urban space for urban residents in Viet Nam, national level urban policy frameworks can play a decisive role. The following policy options could be considered:

- Ensure that the national level planning and urban development strategies actively safeguard the quality of the urban environment, and requires each city's detailed plan to include a strategy to enhance the quality of the urban environment. This would enable each city to plan and invest in its urban environment based on its long-term vision, and allow localities to have more control over private developers to ensure that projects contribute to a high-quality urban environment.
- Consider preservation of cultural heritage in cities as a priority and integrate it into national urban policy frameworks. There must be an explicit recognition of the importance of preservation on existing cultural heritage in Viet Nam. As was elaborated above, one of the most impactful ways of doing this would be to include consideration for quality of the urban environment, including cultural heritage, within the criteria in the city classification system, thus capturing the

importance of heritage preservation in Viet Nam's most influential tool for urban management.

- Provide technical guidelines to improve street design so that the potential of streets as public spaces is maximised. When streets become recognised as public spaces in cities, they can be both planned and designed in a way that increases the quality of life of urban residents and supports more environmentally sustainable and productive cities. Designing streets as public spaces can mean planting trees and installing seating, but can also mean ensuring that streets are places that can be shared by non-motorised forms of transport. To do so, Vietnamese officials could consider providing better infrastructure for cycling through the provision of bike paths/lanes and by keeping sidewalks clear for pedestrians by enforcing laws on motorbike parking. Overall, street design should aim to enhance infrastructure, environmental sustainability, social interaction, public health, productivity and social inclusion (UN Habitat, 2013b).
- Promote compact and connected urban development through investing in public spaces. While a compact urban form can reduce urban sprawl, create efficacies in public transport and promote mixed land uses, it can also be associated with lower quality of life, due to high density. However, well-designed public spaces can lower "perceived" density and increase the quality of life of urban residents (OECD, 2012). This would be a particularly effective policy direction for Viet Nam, as its major cities typically have low-quality and dense urban centres due to a proliferation of unregulated development in the urban cores (Storch et al., 2008).
- Support replicating successful practices, such as a weekend pedestrian zone within Hoan Kiem district, in many other cities and districts.

A special development agency can help revitalising existing urban areas

Given the increasing need for investing in public spaces in existing urban areas, Viet Nam should also consider developing an implementation mechanism for inner city revitalisation which can comprehensively address inner city problems including the quality of the urban environment. Implementing urban development projects in already built-up urban areas would involve many stakeholders (e.g., landowners, tenants, businesses) and tend to get embroiled in local politics, which causes delay and indecision despite of a clear need for urgent regeneration. The experience of OECD countries shows that a special development agency could effectively address these complex issues. In the United Kingdom, Urban Development Corporations (UDCs) have been used as a mechanism to regenerate urban areas in need of revitalisation where there was a need for a new body that could take a focused, single-minded approach. While most UDCs have been created by central government, Mayoral Development Corporations (MDCs) and other forms of development corporations are recently used as delivery vehicles by local authorities (Box 2.21).

Box 2.21. Development corporations in the United Kingdom

Development Corporations have a long history in the United Kingdom. They were originally introduced by central government under the New Towns Act 1946 to drive forward the creation of high quality, mixed, new communities in areas beyond the periphery of major cities, particularly around London. These cities were undergoing major reconstruction after the end of World War II. The New Town Development Corporations (NTDCs) were given statutory planning functions and compulsory purchase powers within a defined area. They operated outside the local authority framework and boundaries being directly answerable to central government through Parliament. They had a long life, at least 30 years but most needed much longer.

In the 1980's, as part of efforts to regenerate inner city areas, Urban Development Corporations (UDCs), such as the London Docklands Development Corporation, were introduced. UDCs were designated, empowered, financed by and directly accountable to central government with extensive powers over land acquisition, finance and planning and acted independently of local authorities. Run by board members appointed directly by the government and with heavy representation from the private sector, they had substantial budgets. Unlike the NTDCs, their lifespan was much shorter (10 years or so) but with much more detailed control both regulatory and financial by central government. UDCs achieved considerable physical regeneration of their areas although their benefits in terms of houses built and jobs created did not always go to the local community.

Under the Localism Act 2011, Mayoral Development Corporations (MDCs) can be created at the request of an elected Mayor to drive regeneration in a defined area. MDCs are accountable to the Mayor rather than central government. As the statutory planning authorities within an area they have compulsory purchase powers and a brief as wide as the NTDCs ("to do anything it considers appropriate for the regeneration of the area or incidental purposes"). To date, three MDCs have been created – two in London (London Legacy Development Corporation covering the 2012 Olympic site, and another at Old Oak Common/Park Royal to regenerate an area around a High Speed Rail 2 [HS2] station), and one in the Tees Valley Combined Authority in North East England, to regenerate an area affected by a major steel plant closure.

The UK Government is now using New Towns Act powers to support the creation of garden cities, towns and villages by a widening of its reach and more devolution to local authorities. The Ebbsfleet Development Corporation, for example, was set up by Government to speed up the delivery of new homes and create a 21st Garden City in north Kent, south west of London. It is the planning authority for Ebbsfleet Garden City and is a non-departmental public body. It is run by a Board involving three local authorities and central government representatives to deliver a shared vision for the area with high quality housing and environment and opportunities to create 30 000 jobs. The Neighbourhood Planning Act 2017 also gives powers to allow local authorities to oversee the creation of garden towns and villages by enabling responsibility for any development corporation created under the New Towns Act to be transferred to local authorities.

Source: UK Department for Communities and local Government; Roberts, P. and H. Sykes (eds.) (2016), *Urban Regeneration*, 2nd Edition, Sage Publications; Tallon, A. (2013), *Urban Regeneration in the UK*, 2nd Edition, Routledge; Smith, L. and A. Pratt (2017), "Garden Cities, Towns and Villages", House of Commons Library, *Briefing Paper No. 6867*, http://researchbriefings.files.parliament.uk/documents/sn06867/sn06867.pdf.

Notes

1. According to the resolution, provincial cities must be Class I, Class II or Class III urban area; towns must be Class III or Class IV urban area; and township must be Class IV or Class V urban area.

2. As per Article 9, "unique characteristics" are defined as being as area with "a mountainous, deep-lying, remote, border or island area or an area with special values in terms of cultural, historical or natural heritages or tourism, which has been nationally or internationally recognised" (Government of Viet Nam, 2011).

3. The total investment in roads and public transport from 1999 to 2007 was USD 5.6 billion, reaching on average an equivalent level of 2.2% of annual GDP. 80% of the total investment was in roads (Japan International Cooperation Agency and Vietnam Ministry of Transport, 2009).

4. Permanent housing refers to a house having all the three important components of a house (wall, roof and floor) defined as solid (each component is defined as solid when it is made by one of the following three main construction materials: "concrete", "brick/stone" or "steel/iron/durable wood"). Semi-permanent housing refers to a house having two among the three components defined as solid. Less-permanent housing refers to a house having only one among the three components defined as solid. Simple-permanent housing refers to a house having none of the three components defined as solid (Ministry of Planning and Investment and General Statistic Office, 2014).

5. In Viet Nam, housing is regarded as informal when the builders/owners do not hold both land use building certificates (BOLUCs) and land use rights certifications (LURCs).

References

Aguilar-Jaber, A. and D. Glocker (2015), "Shifting towards Low Carbon Mobility Systems", *Discussion Paper 2015-17*, OECD International Transport Forum, Paris, https://www.itf-oecd.org/sites/default/files/docs/dp201517.pdf.

Ang, G. and V. Marchal (2013), "Mobilising Private Investment in Sustainable Transport: The Case of Land-Based Passenger Transport Infrastructure", *OECD Environment Working Papers*, No. 56, OECD Publishing, Paris, http://dx.doi.org/10.1787/5k46hjm8jpmv-en.

Asian Development Bank (ADB) (2010), "Sector Assessment (Summary): Road Transport", www.adb.org/sites/default/files/linked-documents/41433-013-vie-ssa.pdf (accessed 7 August 2017).

Asian Development Bank (ADB) and Agence Française de Développement (AFD) (2012), "Assessment of Public–Private Partnerships in Viet Nam: Constraints and Opportunities", Mandaluyong City, Philippines, https://www.adb.org/sites/default/files/publication/29922/assessment-ppp-viet-nam.pdf.

Bertaud, A. (2011), "Hanoi urban structure: Spatial Development Issues and Potential", http://alainbertaud.com/wp-content/uploads/2013/08/ab_chapter-10_transport-hanoi-_graph_aug_28_2013_final_kkb.pdf (accessed 7 August 2017).

Bezirksregierung Düsseldorf / Bezirksregierung Köln (2016), "Metropolregion Rheinland Datenatlas 2016", Düsseldorf.

Boots, S. (2016), "The PPP Decree: An Important Re-Boot for Vietnam's PPP Program", World Bank Group, https://ppp.worldbank.org/public-private-partnership/ppp-decree-%C2%A0-an-important-re-boot-for-vietnam%E2%80%99s-ppp-program (accessed 11 August 2017).

Bundesinstitut für Bau-, Stadt- und Raumforschung (2012), "Raumordnungsbericht 2011", Bonn.

Capital Aid Fund for Employment of the Poor Microfinance (Ltd.) (2017), "Introduction to CEP", www.cep.org.vn/gioi-thieu/1_may_loc_nuoc_sai_gon.html.en, (accessed 20 August 2017).

Centre for Technology Transfer of Physical Planning (CTTPP) (2016), "Part One: Vietnam Urban Situation Assessment Following 9 Selected Fields", Hanoi.

Cervero, R., and D. Dai (2014), "BRT TOD: Leveraging transit oriented development with bus rapid transit investments," in *Transport Policy*, No. 36, pp. 127-138.

Cities Alliance (2013), "Cities Alliance in Action: Transforming Urban Policy Making in Viet Nam", www.citiesalliance.org/sites/citiesalliance.org/files/vietnam%20vuup%20nuup%20-the%20final.pdf (accessed 19 November, 2017).

Coulthart, A., N. Quang and H. Sharpe (2006), "Urban Development Strategy: Meeting the Challenges of Rapid Urbanization and the Transition to a Market Oriented Economy", World Bank, Vietnam Country Office, Hanoi.

Dang, G and L.S. Pheng (2015), Infrastructure Investments in Developing Economies: The Case of Vietnam, Springer, Singapore.

Department for Communities and Local Government, Parliamentary Statement (2015), www.parliament.uk/business/publications/written-questions-answers-statements/written-statement/Commons/2015-01-16/HCWS205 (accessed 19 November 2017).

DiGregorrio, M.R. (2016), "Reimagining Public Space in Crowded Hanoi", the Asia Foundation, http://asiafoundation.org/2016/10/26/reimagining-public-space-crowded-hanoi/ (accessed 7 August 2017).

Duong, L. B., G. L. Tran and T. P. T. Nguyen (2011), "Social protection for rural-urban migrants in Vietnam: current situation, challenges and opportunities", CSP Research Report 08. Institute for Social Development Studies: Ha Noi.

Energy System Management Assistance Program (ESMAP) (2014), "Exploring a Low-Carbon Development Path for Vietnam", ESMAP, DFID (Ha Noi) and World Bank, in *Overseas Development Institute* (2015), "Mapping Current Incentives and Investment in Viet Nam's Transport Sector: Informing Private Climate Finance".

European Cyclists' Federation (ECF) (2016), "Electromobility for All: Financial Incentives for E-Cycling", Brussels, https://ecf.com/sites/ecf.com/files/final%20for%20web%20170216%20ecf%20report_e%20for%20all-%20financial%20incentives%20for%20e-cycling.pdf (accessed 19 August 2017).

Fjellstrom, K. (2017), "World Bank's First BRT in Asia is Designed to Fail", Far East Mobility, BRT and urban transport planning, www.fareastbrt.com/en/feature/hnbrtjan17 (accessed 18 August 2017).

Gough, K. V. and H. A. Tran (2009), "Changing housing policy in Vietnam: Emerging inequalities in a residential area of Hanoi" in *Cities*, Elsevier Ltd pub., Vol. 24, pp. 175-186.

Government of the Netherlands (n.d), Housing associations, https://www.government.nl/topics/housing/housing-associations (accessed 19 August 2017).

Government of Viet Nam (2016a), Resolution No. 1210/2016/UBTVQH13, City Classification.

Government of Viet Nam (2016b), "National Report of the Socialist Republic of Viet Nam to Habitat III".

Government of Viet Nam (2012), Decision No. 1659/QD-TTg, Approving the national Program on Urban Development in 2012-2020 Period.

Government of Viet Nam (2011), Decree No. 62/2011ND-CP, Establishment of provincial cities, towns, urban districts, wards and townships.

Government of Viet Nam (2009a), Decree on Grant of Certificates of Land Use Rights and House and Land Attached Asset Ownership, http://moj.gov.vn/vbpq/en/lists/vn%20bn%20php%20lut/view_detail.aspx?itemid=10697 (accessed 19 November, 2017).

Government of Viet Nam (2009b), Decision No. 758/2009/QD-TTg, "Approving the National Urban Upgrading Programing Period of 2009-2020".

Government of Viet Nam (2008), "National Urban Upgrading Programme: National Urban Upgrading Strategy and Overall Investment Planning for Urban Upgrading to 2020", Final Report, Vol. 1, Main Report.

General Statistics Office (GSO) (2011), "Migration and Urbanisation in Vietnam: Current Situation, Trends and Differentials", Statistics Publishing House, Hanoi, in Thanh, H.X., T.T. Anh and D.T.T. Phuong (2013), *Urban Poverty in Vietnam – A View from Complementary Assessments*, International Institute for Environment and Development.

Hau, D. (2016), "Vietnam National Urban Development Strategy", Report of Tasks A, B and C, Urban Development Agency, Viet Nam.

Hauptstadtregion Berlin-Brandenburg (2013), "Raumordnungsbericht (ROB) 2013", Berlin.

Hidalgo, D. and A. Carrigan (2010), "Modernizing Public Transportation: 'Lessons Learned from Major Bus Improvements in Latin America and Asia'", World Resources Institute, Washington DC, http://pdf.wri.org/modernizing_public_transportation.pdf.

Indochina Legal (2012) "Legal Overview of Construction in Vietnam", Indochina Legal.

International Institute for Environment and Development (2013), "Urban poverty in Viet Nam", *Human Settlements Working Paper Series, Poverty Reduction in Urban Areas*, No. 40, http://pubs.iied.org/pdfs/10633IIED.pdf.

ITF (2010), *Implementing Congestion Charges*, OECD Publishing, Paris, http://dx.doi.org/10.1787/9789282102855-en.

Japan International Cooperation Agency (JICA) and Vietnam Ministry of Transport (2010), "The Comprehensive Study on the Sustainable Development of Transport System in Vietnam (VITRANSS-2)", North-South Expressway Master Plan Final Report, http://open_jicareport.jica.go.jp/pdf/12000030_01.pdf.

Minsitry of Construction of Viet Nam (2017), Answers to the OECD questionnaire, May 2017, unpublished.

Ministry of Cooperative Governance and Traditional Affairs, Government of South Africa (2016), "Integrated Urban Development Framework", Pretoria.

Ministry of Economic Development, Government of Poland (2016), "National Urban Policy 2023", Warsaw.

Ministry of Planning and Investment and General Statistics Office (2014), "The 2014 Vietnam Intercensal Population and Housing Survey: Some Key Indicators", Hanoi, http://vietnam.unfpa.org/sites/default/files/pub-pdf/KeyIndicatorsBooklet.2014IPS.pdf.

Ministry of Regional Development of the Czech Republic (2017), www.mmr.cz/cs/Regionalni-politika-a-cestovni-ruch/Podpora-regionu/Koncepce-Strategie/Zasady-urbanni-politiky.

Ministry of Urban Development (MoUD), Government of India (2017), "Value Capture Finance Policy Framework", New Delhi.

National Economic and Social Council (NESC) (2014), "Review of Irish Social and Affordable Housing Provision", *NESC Secretariat Papers*, Paper No. 10, http://files.nesc.ie/nesc_secretariat_papers/No_10_Review_of_Irish_Social_and_Affordable_Housing_Provision.pdf.

National Housing Federation (NHF) (2017), www.housing.org.uk/resource-library/browse/how-many-homes-did-housing-associations-deliver-in-quarter-one-2017-18/ (accessed 23 August 2017).

OECD (2017a), *National Urban Policy in OECD Countries*, OECD Publishing, Paris, http://dx.doi.org/10.1787/9789264271906-en.

OECD (2017b), *OECD Urban Policy Reviews: Kazakhstan*, OECD Publishing, Paris, http://dx.doi.org/10.1787/9789264268852-en.

OECD (2017c), *The Governance of Land Use in the Czech Republic: The Case of Prague*, OECD Publishing, Paris, http://dx.doi.org/10.1787/9789264281936-en.

OECD (2017d), *The Governance of Land Use in OECD Countries: Policy Analysis and Recommendations*, OECD Publishing, Paris, http://dx.doi.org/10.1787/9789264268609-en.

OECD (2014), *OECD Regional Outlook 2014: Regions and Cities: Where Policies and People Meet*, OECD Publishing, Paris, http://dx.doi.org/10.1787/9789264201415-en.

OECD (2012), *Compact City Policies: A Comparative Assessment*, OECD Publishing, Paris, http://dx.doi.org/10.1787/9789264167865-en.

OECD (2009), *How Regions Grow: Trends and Analysis*, OECD Publishing, Paris, http://dx.doi.org/10.1787/9789264039469-en.

OECD (2006), *Competitive Cities in the Global Economy*, OECD Publishing, Paris, http://dx.doi.org/10.1787/9789264027091-en.

Office of the Deputy Prime Minister, United Kingdom (2004), "Assessing the Impacts of Spatial Interventions: Regeneration, Renewal and Regional Development, The 3Rs Guidance", https://www.gov.uk/government/uploads/system/uploads/attachment_data/file/191509/Regeneration__renewal_and_regional_deveopment.pdf (accessed 19 November, 2017).

Perkins, S. (2011), "Green Growth and Transport", *International Transport Forum Discussion Papers*, No. 2011/02, OECD Publishing, Paris, http://dx.doi.org/10.1787/5kg9mq57s8wb-en.

Pike, E. (2010), "Congestion Charging: Challenges and Opportunities", International Council on Clean Transport, White Paper, Washington DC, https://www.theicct.org/sites/default/files/publications/congestion_apr10.pdf.

Roberts, P., H. Sykes and R. Granger (eds.) (2016), *Urban Regeneration*, 2nd Edition, Sage Publications.

Republic of Rwanda, City of Kigali (2017), "Construction Permit System, and Master Plan", www.kigalicity.gov.rw/index.php?id=91&L=1 (accessed 20 August 2017).

Rwanda Development Board (2017), *One-Stop Centre*, www.rdb.rw/one-stop-centre.htm (accessed 20 August 2017).

Salon, D. (2014), "Value Capture Opportunities for Urban Public Transport Finance", White Papers Prepared for the Transit Leadership Summit, London, Institute of Transportation Studies, University of California Davis, pp. 101-12, http://transitleadership.org/docs/tls-wp-value-capture-opportunities.pdf.

Smith, L. and A. Pratt (2017), "Garden Cities, Towns and Villages", House of Commons Library, *Briefing Paper*, No. 6867, http://researchbriefings.files.parliament.uk/documents/SN06867/SN06867.pdf.

South Africa's Ministry of Cooperative Governance and Traditional Affairs (2016), *Integrated Urban Development Framework.*

Stadt Osnabrück (2012), "Soziale Ungleichheit in Osnabrück, Ein kleinräumiger Ansatz mit besonderer Berücksichtigung von Kindern und Jugendlichen Osnabrück", www.osnabrueck.de/fileadmin/user_upload/Bericht_SozialeUngleichheit.pdf.

Storch, H., R. Eckert and P. Pfaffenbichler (2008), "The compactness of urban areas in Vietnam, Sustainable urban development and local mobility nodes", *Reviewed paper*, Schrenk et al. (eds), www.corp.at/archive/CORP2008_48.pdf (accessed 23 August 2017).

Suzuki, H. et al. (2015), "Financing Transit-Oriented Development with Land Values: Adapting Land Value Capture in Developing Countries", Urban Development Series, Word Bank, Washington DC, http://documents.worldbank.org/curated/en/468551468165570019/pdf/936860PUB00ISB0TransportDevLV0final.pdf (accessed 4 August 2017).

Tallon, A. (2013), *Urban Regeneration in the UK*, 2nd Edition, Routledge.

Thanh, H.X., T.T. Anh and D.T.T. Phuong (2013), *Urban Poverty in Vietnam – A View from Complementary Assessments*, International Institute for Environment and Development.

Thu, T.T. and R. Perera (2011), "Consequences of the Two-Price System for Land in the Land and Housing Market in Ho Chi Minh City, Vietnam" in *Habitat International*, Vol. 35/1, pp. 30-39.

The Transport and Urban Development Authority (TDA) (2016), "Transit Oriented Development", www.tct.gov.za/en/transit-oriented-development (accessed 15 August 2017).

Transport for Cape Town (2016), "Transit Oriented Development", www.tct.gov.za/en/transit-oriented-development (accessed 15 August 2017).

United Nations (2016a), "The New Urban Agenda: Key Commitments, Sustainable Development Goals, 17 Goals to Transform our World", New York.

United Nations (2016b), *Policy Paper 3: National Urban Policy*, A/CONF.226/PC.3/16, New York.

United Nations (2015), "Addis Ababa Action Agenda of the Third International Conference on Financing for Development", Addis Ababa, www.un.org/esa/ffd/wp-content/uploads/2015/08/AAAA_Outcome.pdf.

United Nations Development Programme (UNDP) (2010), "Urban Poverty Assessment in Hanoi and Ho Chi Minh City", UNDP, Hanoi, http://www.un.org.vn/en/publications/government-agency-publications/doc_details/264-urban-poverty-assessment-in-ha-noi-and-ho-chi-minh-city.html.

United Nations Population Fund (UNFPA) (2007), "State of World Population 2007: Unleashing the Potential of Urban Growth", New York, https://sustainabledevelopment.un.org/content/documents/1109UNFPA_State%20of%20the%20World%20Report%202007.pdf.

United Nations Human Settlement Programme (UN Habitat) (2017), "Action Framework for the Implementation of the New Urban Agenda", Nairobi.

UN Habitat (2016a), "Global Land Tool Network: Leveraging Land: Land-based Finance for Local Government", Nairobi.

UN Habitat (2016b), "UN Habitat's Support for the Development of National Urban Policies", Nairobi.

UN Habitat (2016c), "Urbanization and Development: Emerging Futures", World Cities Report 2016, Nairobi, https://unhabitat.org/books/world-cities-report/#.

UN Habitat (2015), "Global Public Space Toolkit: From Global Principles to Local Policies and Practice", Nairobi, https://unhabitat.org/wp-content/uploads/2015/10/Global%20Public%20Space%20Toolkit.pdf.

UN Habitat (2014a), "The Evolution of National Urban Policies: A Global Overview", Nairobi.

UN Habitat (2014b), "Viet Nam Housing Sector Profile", Nairobi.

UN Habitat (2013a), "Tools to support Transparency in Land Administration", Nairobi.

UN Habitat (2013b), "Streets as Public Spaces and Drivers of Urban Prosperity", Nairobi.

UN Habitat and OECD (2017, forthcoming), "The Global State of National Urban Policy 2017", Nairobi.

Waibel, M. et al. (2007), "Housing for Low-income Groups in Ho Chi Minh City between Re-Integration and Fragmentation Approaches to Adequate Urban Typologies and Spatial Strategies," in *ASIEN*, Vol. 103, S. 59-78.

Walters, L. C. (2012), "Land Value Capture in Policy and Practice", paper presented at the World Bank Conference on Land and Poverty, Washington DC, www.landandpoverty.com/agenda/pdfs/paper/walters_full_paper.pdf (accessed 11 August 2017).

Wilson, L. (2016), "Overview of the current urban development framework in Vietnam and the implications for the National Urban Development Strategy (NUDS)", Ho Chi Minh City.

World Bank and Cities Alliance (2011), "Vietnam Urbanization Review: Technical Assistance Report", https://openknowledge.worldbank.org/bitstream/handle/10986/2826/669160esw0p1130review000full0report.pdf?sequence=1 (accessed 11 August 2017).

Work Bank and Vietnam Academy of Social Sciences (2016), "Vietnam's Household Registration System", Hong Duc Publishing House, Ha Noi, https://openknowledge.worldbank.org/handle/10986/24594 (accessed 31 October 2017).

World Bank/International Finance Corporation (2009), "Enterprise Surveys: Vietnam Country Profile", Washington DC.

World Bank (2015a), "Viet Nam Affordable Housing: A way forward", http://documents.worldbank.org/curated/en/240541467995097856/pdf/100706-wp-p150619-public-box393231b-2015-10-16-05-45.pdf.

World Bank (2015b), "Vietnam Urban Upgrading project: Lives Transformed, The Story of the Urban Poor in Vietnam", World Bank, Washington DC.

World Bank (2011), "Vietnam urbanization review: technical assistance report", Washington, DC, http://documents.worldbank.org/curated/en/225041468177548577/Vietnam-urbanization-review-technical-assistance-report

World Bank (2007), "Vietnam: Hanoi Urban Transport Development Project", Project Information Document, http://documents.worldbank.org/curated/en/861141468141594238/pdf/hanoi0hutdp0pid01 22806.pdf (accessed 11 August 2017).

World Economic Forum (2017), "The Global Competiveness Report 2016-17", Geneva.

World Health Organisation (WHO) (2014), "Global Health Observatory Data, Road traffic death rate by WHO region and income level", www.who.int/gho/road_safety/mortality/traffic_deaths_rates/en/ (accessed 27 July 2017).

Chapter 3

Making Vietnamese cities sustainable and productive through green growth policies

This chapter gives a special focus on Viet Nam's endeavour to foster green growth in urban areas. It begins by a short introduction highlighting Viet Nam's urgent needs for strengthening urban green growth policies. It then analyses national policy frameworks in the areas of green growth and climate change along with a selection of related sectoral policies in Viet Nam. The chapter also assesses governance structures for urban green growth policies, demonstrating how urban green growth could be implemented more effectively, through a cooperative and coordinated approach as well as improved monitoring, reporting and verification (MRV) systems.

Viet Nam's urgent needs for strengthening urban green growth policies

Viet Nam's greenhouse gas (GHG) emissions have increased six-fold since 1990 (Low Emission Development Strategies Global Partnership, 2014), mainly due to the transport, industry and energy sectors including coal-fired power generation. The country's CO_2 emissions per GDP are much higher than OECD countries and are still increasing, while the equivalent figure is decreasing in other Asian countries including China (Figure 3.1). Cities alone are responsible for 70% of Viet Nam's CO_2 emissions. Due also to the rapid increase of cars and the lack of public transport, Viet Nam's cities have some of the most polluted air in the world. The Environmental Performance Index ranks Viet Nam's air quality as 170th out of 180 countries (Yale University, 2016).

Figure 3.1. CO_2 emissions (kg per 2010 USD of GDP), 1990 to 2013

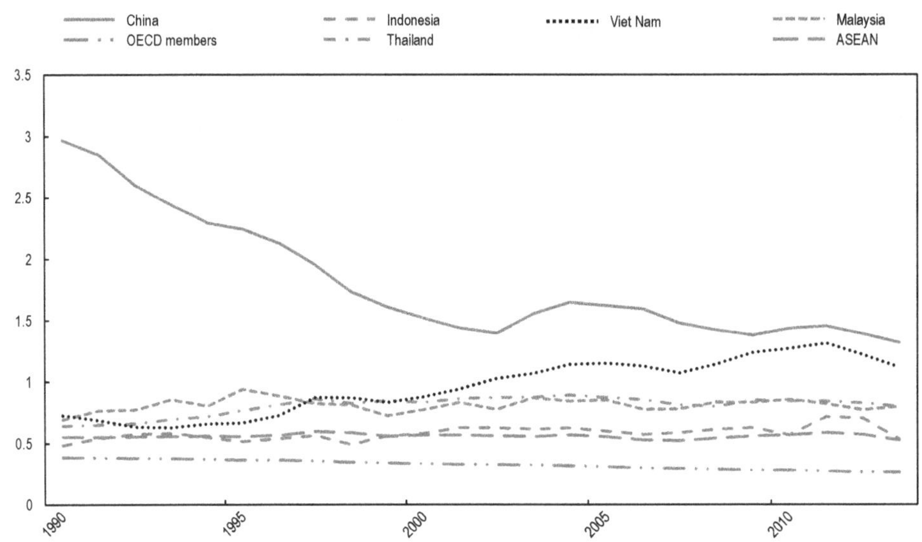

Source: World Bank (2017), CO2 emissions (kg per 2010 US$ of GDP) database, Carbon Dioxide Information Analysis Center, Environmental Sciences Division, Oak Ridge National Laboratory, Tennessee, United States, https://data.worldbank.org/indicator/EN.ATM.CO2E.KD.GD.

Viet Nam is also highly exposed to climate change. Most of Viet Nam's population and economic activity are located in the Mekong and Red River Deltas and other coastal areas. The Mekong Delta is one of the world's three most vulnerable deltas to sea level rise, estimated at 30 cm by 2050 (Smajgl et al., 2015). More generally, Viet Nam is highly vulnerable to natural disasters such as floods, droughts, saltwater intrusion (affecting water availability), landslides and typhoons. Between 2001 and 2010, the annual damage caused by natural disasters was estimated to be approximately 1.5% of the national GDP (Office of Prime Minister, 2011). Furthermore, urban development encroaches on forests and agricultural land, putting stress on soil and water resources, and agricultural runoff threatens depleted coastal mangroves (ADB, 2013).

Viet Nam urgently needs to address climate-related challenges and other environmental issues, while continuing its economic growth and social progress. Green growth has been recognised as a key policy, as it can address economic growth, social inclusion and environmental sustainability at the same time. Especially, fostering green growth in cities is critical because cities play disproportionately large roles in the economic and environmental performance of countries (OECD, 2013) (Box 3.1).

Box 3.1. Concept of urban green growth

The OECD defines green growth as "fostering economic growth and development while ensuring that the natural assets continue to provide the resources and environmental services on which our well-being relies. To do this it must catalyse investment and innovation which will underpin sustained growth and give rise to new economic opportunities" (OECD, 2011). The Global Green Growth Institute (GGGI) defines green growth as "a development approach that seeks to deliver economic growth that is both environmentally sustainable and socially inclusive" (GGGI, 2017). GGGI further details five characteristics of green growth as "(1) increases the quantity and quality of natural resources and environmental services. Given these are factors of production, their availability is critical to higher and longer-term economic growth; (2) increases the productivity of resources, i.e. it allows generating higher growth with fewer resources; (3) drives new technologies or innovative application of existing technologies. Innovation is a key driver of economic growth; (4) focuses on removing the market failures present among economic, environmental, and social goals, contributing to more efficient allocation of resources in the economy; and (5) pursues an inclusive and participatory approach, putting in place mechanisms for benefit sharing, in particular to benefit those who are dependent on natural resources and most vulnerable to climate change" (GGGI, 2017).

Policy makers' interest in green growth has led to a call for more information on the policies which can actually bring about green growth in cities. In this regard, the OECD defines urban green growth as "fostering economic growth and development through urban activities that reduce negative environmental externalities and the impact of growth on natural resources and environmental services" (OECD, 2013). What is "green" about this growth is how it is stimulated: through urban activities (including policies and programmes) that reduce either: 1) negative environmental externalities, such as air pollution and CO_2 emissions; or 2) the consumption of natural resources and environmental services, including water, energy and undeveloped land. These effects are in part the result of more readily identifiable interactions at the urban level among economic efficiency and environmental objectives. By focusing on growth, this definition recognises that polices to reduce environmental impact can only be sustained over the long term if they generate wealth (OECD, 2013).

Cities' potential for green growth can be explained by the disproportionally large roles for cities in national economic and environmental performance, and also because they are opportune levels of action. Cities are indeed responsible for a significant share of national infrastructure investments – 58.8% in the OECD countries. Policy complementarities are also more easily identifiable at the local level, as activities related to environmental protection and economic development are more integrated at the local level than at the national level. Coherent policy packages can help mitigate the trade-offs among environmental, growth and equity priorities: a properly designed policy package would address the costs of reducing environmental impact in a co-ordinated way and have less impact on the most vulnerable people. The fact that they are closer to citizens' needs, have better knowledge of local conditions, and can test and refine innovative ideas locally also creates conditions for successful policies (OECD, 2010).

Source: OECD (2013), *Green Growth in Cities*, OECD Publishing, Paris, http://dx.doi.org/10.1787/9789264195325-en; OECD (2011), *Towards Green Growth*, OECD Publishing, Paris, http://dx.doi.org/10.1787/9789264111318-en; OECD (2010), *Cities and Climate Change*, OECD Publishing, Paris, http://dx.doi.org/10.1787/9789264091375-en.

National policy frameworks for urban green growth

This section reviews national policy frameworks related to urban green growth (Figure 3.2) and assesses their respective abilities to deliver urban green growth. Such a review is timely, as the government is currently undertaking a review of the implementation of the 2012 Viet Nam Green Growth Strategy (VGGS), five years after the launch of the VGGS. In addition, the section analyses three key sectors that drive green growth in urban areas: energy, solid waste and wastewater treatment (the transport sector is not included here, as it is discussed in Chapter 2).

Figure 3.2. Key national policies related to urban green growth in Viet Nam

Source: Authors.

National level green growth policies

Socio-economic development strategies have laid a solid foundation to implement urban green growth

Viet Nam has put green economic development at the core of its socio-economic agenda. At the highest policy level, both the *Socio-Economic Development Strategy (SEDS) 2011-2020* and the *Socio-Economic Development Plan (SEDP) 2016-2020* recognise the importance of green and sustainable development and have laid a solid foundation for the implementation of urban green growth:

- The SEDS has specified one of its development approaches as *"to ensure rapid, efficient and sustainable development, economic growth is to go along with social progress and equity, and environmental protection"* (SEDS 2011–2020, Section II.2).
- The SEDP further elaborates this approach through its objectives: *"to accelerate the implementation of strategic breakthroughs, economic restructuring associated with growth model innovation and improving productivity, efficiency and competitiveness ... and to actively respond to climate change, effectively manage resources and protect the environment"* (SEDP 2016-2020, Section II.1).
- SEDP's targets for urban areas include: increasing the urbanisation rate to 38-40% and reducing urban unemployment rate to less than 4% by 2020 (SEDP 2016-2020, Section II.2.2.1 and II.2.2.2).
- The SEDP encourages to modernise urban infrastructures in large cities and to improve the quality and management of urban planning for sustainable development (SEDP 2016-2020, Section III.2).

The National Green Growth Strategy and the Action Plan could be further strengthened by clearly defining urban green growth

Viet Nam also set two milestones for the development of green growth in the country: the National Green Growth Strategy (VGGS) in 2012 and the National Green Growth Action Plan (VGGAP) in 2014. The VGGS promotes the restructuring of the economy and improving economic institutions towards more efficient use of natural resources, thus strengthening the competitiveness of the economy. More specifically, the VGGS sets out three overall objectives: i) restructure the economy and improve economic institutions by greening existing sectors and encouraging them to use energy and natural resources efficiently with higher added values; ii) conduct research and enhance application of appropriate advanced technologies to more efficient use of natural resources, reduce GHG emissions intensity and contribute to an effective response to climate change; and iii) improve living standards of the people, creating an environment friendly lifestyle through employment generation from green industry, agriculture, and services; investment in natural capital; and development of green infrastructure (VGGS, Section I.2.b). To achieve the three objectives, the VGGS defines "strategic tasks" and "targets" and lays out 17 "policy solutions", while the VGGAP sets out 66 "activities" corresponding to the 17 policy solutions. Each activity in the VGGAP, in turn, also defines timeframes, a lead government institution and supporting institutions. Out of the 66 activities, 42 are labelled as priorities, which are to be delivered from 2014-2020. Based on the VGGAP, ministries and provinces have also developed their own Green Growth Action Plans.

Table 3.1 lists the strategic tasks and targets for urban areas in the VGGS. Table 3.2 summarises the policy solutions for urban areas and their corresponding activities in the VGGAP. Urban green growth cuts across a number of policy solutions in the VGGS and is given prominence, for example within "sustainable urbanisation", one of the 17 solutions in the VGGS (Table 3.2).

Table 3.1. Strategic tasks and targets in the VGGS related to urban areas

Strategic tasks	Targets
Reduce the intensity of GHG emissions and promote the use of clean and renewable energy	Reduce intensity of GHG emissions by 8-10% compared to 2010 level
	Reduce energy consumption per unit of GDP by 1-1.5% per year
	Reduce GHG emissions by at least 1.5-2% per year[1]
	Reduce GHG emissions by energy activities by 20-30% compared to BAU[1]
Greening lifestyle and promoting sustainable consumption	60% of Class III cities will have wastewater collection and treatment systems that meet regulatory standards
	40% of Class IV and V cities will have wastewater collection and treatment systems that meet regulatory standards
	100% environmental improvement in severely polluted areas
	The rate of urban solid waste collected and treated will meet regulatory standards according to PM's decision No 2149/2009/QD-TTg
	35-45% shared public transportation in large and medium cities
	50% of large and medium-sized cities attain green urban standards

1. Indicates targets oriented to 2030.

Source: VGGS.

Although sustainable urbanisation is included as one of the 17 policy solutions, this policy review found that the role of cities in achieving green growth for the whole country is not explicitly defined in the current VGGS and VGGAP. Given the rapid pace of urbanisation, the VGGS and VGGAP could be further strengthened by clearly defining urban green growth. "Sustainable urbanisation" and corresponding activities in the VGGS and VGGAP could also be fine-tuned to reflect the increasing role of cities.

Table 3.2. Policy solutions and activities within the VGGS and VGGAP relevant to urban green growth

Policy solutions in the VGGS	Corresponding activities in the VGGAP
1. Communication, awareness raising and encouragement of support to implementation	#4: Raise awareness and involving wide participation of all the people in VGGS implementation #11: Improve the people's awareness of efficient and effective use of energy #61: Implement the campaign of "green lifestyle" #62: Implement the campaign on building a model of "energy saving in each household"
2. Improve effectiveness and efficiency of energy use, reduce energy consumption in production activities, transportation and trade	#12: Develop technology for saving energy #13: Promulgate minimum energy efficiency standards and energy labeling for products #14: Improve energy efficiency in enterprises in the most energy-intensive sectors #15: Improve energy efficiency in small and medium enterprises (SMEs) #16: Improve energy management capacity in industries and constructions #17: Change the structure for energy efficiency and effectiveness in transport #18: Innovative technology to use energy efficiently and effectively in transport #58: Efficient and effective use of energy in constructions and buildings
4. Promote new and renewable energy sources in energy production and consumption	#26: Formulate and implement policies that give priority to develop clean energy sources
6. Review and adjust master plans for the production sectors and gradually limit the development of economic sectors that generate large amount of waste, significant environmental pollution and degradation of natural resources, while creating favourable conditions for the development of new green production sectors	#29: Review the SEDP in the light of sustainable development and formulate the project to restructure the economy towards green growth for the period 2014 – 2020 #30: Review sectoral development plans in the light of sustainable development and formulate policy framework as well as green growth action plan for the industry sector in the period 2014 – 2020 #32: Review sectoral development plans in the light of sustainable development and formulate policy framework as well as green growth action plan for the transport sector in the period 2014 – 2020 #33: Review sectoral development plans in the light of sustainable development and formulate policy framework as well as green growth action plan for the construction sector in the period 2014 – 2020 #34: Review sectoral development plans in the light of sustainable development and formulate policy framework as well as green growth action plan for the natural resources and environment sectors in the period 2014 – 2020 #35: Review development strategy and master plans for science and technology in the light of sustainable development and formulate policy framework and green growth action plan for science and technology in the period 2014 – 2020 #54: Review urban master plans and formulate urban innovation plans according to sustainable standards
7. Economic and efficient utilisation of natural resources	#39: Prevent land degradation and promote efficient use of land resources #40: Promote efficient use of water resources #46: Promote the production of environment goods and services #47: Restore and develop natural capital resources
8. Promote fast development of green economic sectors to create jobs, increase income and enrich natural capital	#36: Support and encourage R&D for applying green technology #56: Encourage technology innovation in construction towards greening orientation #57: Encourage the development of green building and construction material industries

Table 3.2. Policy solutions and activities within the VGGS and VGGAP relevant to urban green growth (*cont.*)

Policy solutions in the VGGS	Corresponding activities in the VGGAP
9. Develop key sustainable infrastructure including: transportation, energy, irrigation and urban works	#19: Develop public transport #48: Improve transport infrastructure #49: Improve energy infrastructure #50: Improve and develop irrigation infrastructure #51: Widely implement the campaign: "enterprises achieving sustainable development standards"
11. Sustainable urbanisation	#6: Formulate local GGAP in some provinces and cities, synthesise and disseminate best practices #55: Improve technical infrastructure in some selected urban areas #59: Improve transport in municipalities #60: Green urban landscape #66: Expand the modern information technology application in management and social life
13. Promote sustainable consumption and building green lifestyles	#45: Promote reuse and recycle waste in the country #65: Guide and encourage sustainable consumption initiatives by the people
14. Mobilise resources to implement the Green Growth Strategy	#3: Formulate green growth financial policy framework
15. Human resource training and development	#38: Support development of human resources for green jobs

Source: VGGS and VGGAP.

Subnational governments face capacity challenges

While VGGS and VGGAP frameworks count on subnational actions, most subnational governments face capacity challenges. While the VGGAP requires all provinces to develop a Provincial Green Growth Action Plan (PGGAP), only 23 provinces out of 63 (including the City of Hai Phong as a centrally-administered city) have completed their PGGAPs, 13 are in the process of doing so (including Ha Noi and Ho Chi Minh City), and 27 are yet to begin the process (Figure 3.3).[1]

Figure 3.3. Current status of the development of PGGAPs in Viet Nam

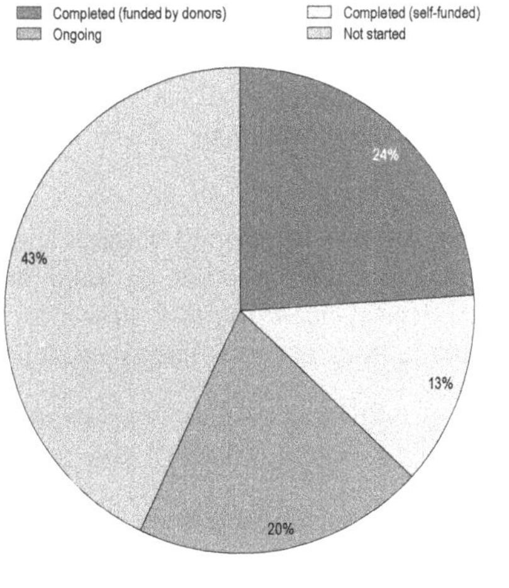

Source: Authors.

The Ministry of Planning and Investment (MPI) has issued guidance on how to implement the VGGS and VGGAP at the provincial level. All the PGGAPs examined for this report have a focus on urban areas and include concrete projects that encompass issues from urban planning to capacity building or urban infrastructure investment (wastewater treatment, public transport, renewable energy such as rooftop solar panels, etc.). However, there are significant variations in scope and levels of analysis in the PGGAPs across provinces, mainly due to capacity. For example, some provinces which have received support of international donors were able to carry out a greenhouse gas (GHG) inventory and GHG reduction targets at the provincial level, which requires significant resources and skills. In contrast, self-funded provinces have often ended up with PGGAPs with much simpler contents, and with targets that were taken from other existing policy documents, instead of developing their own. Some PGGAPs remain very vague in their objectives, with no baseline data developed, which makes it difficult to measure progress and evaluate results (Box 3.2).

Box 3.2. Examples of PGGAPs

To date, 23 provinces (including the City of Hai Phong) have completed their PGGAPs. However, there are significant variations in scope and levels of analysis across provinces, mainly due to capacity.

- Provinces with support of international donors have often developed PGGAPs with a GHG inventory and more tailored green growth targets. For example, Thanh Hoa Province's PGGAP was supported by the United States Agency for International Development (USAID). It includes the calculation of GHG emissions using various estimation tools. The steps involved were as follows:
  1. Establishment of the Green Growth Task Force. The USAID provided technical support to develop a vision and an outline for the PGGAP.
  2. Development of GHG inventory. The GHG emissions between 2010 and 2014 were calculated in the selected sectors (energy, industry, agriculture, forestry, land use, and waste) and an inventory was developed.
  3. Development of emission baseline and targets. The GHG reduction target was set at 14% by 2020 and 23% by 2030.
  4. Selection of priority intervention actions.
- Ben Tre Province's PGGAP includes the Marginal Abatement Cost Curve (MACC) analysis with detailed emission calculations for each socio-economic scenario. This approach is applied to another 20 provinces, most of which are supported by international donors such as United Nations Development Programme (UNDP), the Deutsche Gesellschaft für Internationale Zusammenarbeit (GIZ) or the Belgian Technical Cooperation (BTC).
- Dak Lak Province's PGGAP was developed without support from international donors. It uses the targets that are stated in other national decisions such as *the National Strategy on Solid Waste Management to 2025, vision to 2050* (Decision 2149/QĐ-TTg) and the city classification ranking criteria. They include:
  - Percentages of cities with a system of wastewater collection and treatment that meets national standard are100% (Class III cities) and 15% (Class IV and V cities);
  - Solid waste collection and treatment that meets national standard is 90%;

Box 3.2. Examples of PGGAPs (*cont.*)

  - Share of public transportation increases to 40%;
  - Area of urban green space per person is 10-15m^2 (Class I cities), 7-10m^2 (Class III cities) and 5-7m^2 (Class IV and V cities); and
  - Percentage of manufacturing factories/companies that follow environmental regulations is 90%.
- Kon Tum Province's PGGAP's was developed also without support from international donors. Its objectives include:
  - Green the current sectors and encourage development of industries that use energy efficiency and natural resources with high value added;
  - Improve quality of life, establish a way of life that is environmental friendly through green jobs in industries, agriculture, and services;
  - Develop green infrastructure;
  - Encourage R&D for energy efficiency technology, with the highest benefit to the natural resources; and
  - Reduce GHG emission, contributing to effective climate change adaptation and mitigation.

Source: PGGAPs from Thanh Hoa, Ben Tre, Dak Lak and Kon Tum Provinces.

In order to address the capacity challenge, the Ministry of Planning and Investment (MPI) and other relevant ministries could expand their support towards provinces. For example, MPI's guidance document could further articulate the elements to be included in PGGAPs and encourage provinces to secure the necessary budget. It is also recommended for MPI to establish a knowledge sharing platform where provinces can share their PPGAP experience (e.g., methodology, development processes) with other provinces, so that they can efficiently develop their PGGAPs with less external resources. A central support team could be organised with the involvement of relevant ministries (for example, the Ministry of Construction for urban green growth) which provides training as well as some hands-on support to develop PGGAPs. The central support team, together with the knowledge sharing platform, can ensure effective knowledge exchange and capacity building at the provincial level. These capacity building strategies are crucial, given the role of provinces and cities in achieving the national green growth objectives. Finally, MPI could consider providing financial support for developing a PGGAP for provinces with limited resource.

National level climate change policies

Since 2008, Viet Nam has produced a series of policy documents that set the landscape for climate change response and green growth development in the country. Among them, the following four documents form the basis of current national climate policies:

- The National Target Program to Respond to Climate Change (NTP-RCC) sets out comprehensive effort to assess, measure and combat climate change during five years (2008-2012). The programme requires relevant ministries and agencies, provinces, and cities to develop their own action plans. It also plays an important role in assigning international and domestic resources to concrete projects (MPI, 2015).

- The National Climate Change Strategy (NCCS), developed in 2011, provides an overarching policy framework that sets out a clear direction for climate change responses in the country. An important addition to the NTP-RCC is that the NCCS promotes climate resilience through early warning systems, better disaster response, water security and transport (Office of Prime Minister, 2011).
- The National Action Plan on Climate Change (NAPCC), developed in 2012, identifies 65 actions to be taken between 2012 and 2020 with 10 priorities. The NAPCC underlines the importance of mitigating GHG emissions and directing the economy towards low-carbon development.
- Viet Nam's Nationally Determined Contribution (NDC), developed in 2015, sets an unconditional target of 8% reduction of greenhouse gas emission and a conditional target of 20%. It also highlights sustainable urban development and urban infrastructure as a priority action.

These policy documents include specific targets and actions for urban areas, and thus provide a clear direction for urban green growth. Of the 65 actions stipulated in the NAPCC, the urban dimension is well addressed in at least 18 actions (Table 3.3). Rather, the challenge for these climate policies lies in their implementation, especially how to ensure local actions. As discussed earlier, provincial and city governments in general lack resources to implement the identified climate policy actions. Another important caveat is a lack of clarity in terms of responsibility of subnational governments. While the NAPCC assigns responsibilities for urban-related actions across different national ministries and agencies, the role of provincial and city governments is not clearly mentioned. The central government thus has an important role in providing technical and financial support, as well as a clear legal basis in order to engage subnational governments.

Table 3.3. Actions for urban areas in the NAPCC and the lead agencies

	Actions	Lead agencies
1.	Develop a monitoring system for climate change and sea level rise	MONRE
5.	Deploy a lockout alarm system of tsunami warning for high risk areas (integrated into the coastal disaster alarming tower system)	MARD
10.	Develop Mekong Delta program on management of water resources and adaptation to climate change	MONRE
11.	Develop Red River program on management of water resources and adaptation to climate change	MONRE
13.	Review regulations on construction and guidance on construction techniques in disaster prone areas	MOC
14.	Improve safety conditions of housing for poor households in disaster prone areas (i.e. Mekong Delta and Central Region)	MOC
15.	Identify residents in areas frequently affected by natural disasters and proactively relocate them out of the dangerous areas	MARD
22.	Implement projects under the irrigation plan against flooding for Ho Chi Minh City, Hanoi and Can Tho	MARD
24.	Prevent river bank and coastal erosion (priority is given to protection of dikes, concentrated residential areas and critical infrastructure) and enhance drainage dredging	MARD
30.	Develop a plan for eliminating ineffective and climate unfriendly technology in the agriculture, industry, energy and transport sectors and develop a list of alternative technologies with appropriate emission criteria	MARD

Table 3.3. Actions for urban areas in the NAPCC and the lead agencies (*cont.*)

	Actions	Lead agencies
33.	Experiment models of green urban areas, green residential areas which consume less energy and raw materials and are climate-friendly	MOC
36.	National target program on energy use and efficiency	MOIT
38.	Develop mechanisms and policies to encourage the use of energy-saving means of transport energy, remove energy-consuming means of transport, develop public transport in urban areas, control the increase in individual transport modes and transform buses and taxis to use compressed natural gas fuel and liquefied petroleum gas	MOT
39.	Apply new technologies which emit less greenhouse gas in industrial production, promote research on innovation and high-tech applications in key industries, develop and apply technical standards and regulations for equipment with efficient use of energy in production of materials and construction works	MOIT
40.	Develop waste management plans and enhance management capacity for waste reduction, reuse and recycle	MOC
41.	Apply advanced technology in waste treatment and landfills to recover methane gas, and apply modern technology for waste disposal in urban and rural areas.	MOC
47.	Adjust technical standards and regulations on construction works and infrastructure design based on climate change scenarios	MOC
59.	Update scenarios of climate change and sea level rise (to be published in 2015 and 2020)	MONRE

Source: NCCAP.

Mainstreaming green growth into key urban policies

As discussed in Chapter 2, Viet Nam's urban development policies are laid out mainly in four key documents: Law on Urban Planning (National Assembly, Law No. 30/2009/QH12); Decree on the Formulation, Evaluation, Approval and Management of Urban Planning (Government Decree No.37/2010/ND-CP); Development of Vietnamese Cities in Response to Climate Change (Decision 2623/QĐ-TTg) and the Resolution on City Classification in Viet Nam (Resolution No. 1210/2016/UBTVQH13). However, these documents lack a green growth perspective. The first two documents focus on the process rather than the outcomes of urban development, such as the procedures for developing urban masterplans and for obtaining development permits. Green growth is not clearly mentioned in the objectives, and the only links to green growth are policy targets on green spaces, number of trees and environmental impact assessments. Whereas Decision 2623/QĐ-TTg focuses on urban infrastructure from a climate change adaptation point of view, it has not fully addressed climate change mitigation. The city classification system in Viet Nam has placed little regard for the development of green and compact cities (as previously discussed in Chapter 2). It has serious ramifications, as city leaders currently tend to consider urban green growth as just another sectoral policy and prioritise other policy objectives such as increasing urban population and building infrastructure. Finally, urban masterplans often focus only on land use zoning and infrastructure planning, primarily trying to meet the objective of moving up in the city classification system. Put differently, current urban masterplans function as construction plans rather than envisioning a holistic sustainable development pathway for the city.

As already discussed, the VGGS presents five key policy areas necessary for "sustainable urbanisation": i) urban planning and management; ii) technical infrastructure; iii) green cities, ecological urban areas and green works; iv) urban transport; and v) greening of urban landscape. It is crucial for the ministries responsible for the five areas to ensure that green growth objectives are appropriately incorporated in all their policy frameworks, so that urban masterplans and other urban development mechanisms become useful policy instruments to achieve green growth. To this end, five concrete actions could be considered:

- Include urban green growth and climate change actions as an annex to *the Law on Urban Planning* (for example in Articles 22, 23 and 43). These actions should outline how MOC will address the aims of the VGGS, VGGAP and NDC.
- Include reference to urban green growth into the "planning tasks" in *the Law on Urban Planning* and require all urban development plans (General Plans, Zoning Plans and Detailed Plans) to reflect this. This will significantly increase the importance of urban green growth in cities' planning tasks, and will require an expanded research process (e.g., green growth status quo assessment) in terms of how to address the goals set by the VGGS, VGGAP and NDC.
- Provide technical guidance for local policy makers so that they can incorporate green growth into urban development. Developing a mechanism to prioritise urban green growth actions would be key, as seen in an example of Cambodia (Box 3.3).
- Incentivise smart, resilient and compact cities into the city classification system. A simple "quick win" would be to give more weight to the population density in built-up areas. Giving points for better co-ordination with surrounding cities on urban infrastructure investment could also be considered. A longer-term option would be to develop a more complete set of urban green growth indicators (discussed later in this Chapter) and incorporate it into the city classification system.
- Integrate local green growth action plans (GGAPs) and climate change action plans (CCAPs) with urban masterplans. Cities should no longer have to produce a GGAP or CCAP as a separate policy document but instead focus their efforts on producing a green climate resilient urban master plan, a single key document that incorporates urban green growth and climate change. The urban masterplan will become an official document to be approved by MOC and MPI, at the same time as a legal document required by *the Law on Urban Planning*. This would reduce the burden on local governments, while making sure to address urban green growth and climate change.

Box 3.3. Green city planning in Cambodia: from a vision to prioritised actions

As rapid urbanisation takes place in Cambodia together with increasing demand for and consumption of natural resources, in 2015 the Government of Cambodia has developed a strategic green city planning methodology for CambodianPhnom Penh and other cities. The methodology will serve as guidance for policy makers at national and subnational levels, covering broad areas of intervention such as urban planning, energy, transport, manufacturing and solid waste management. The methodology proposes a holistic approach that directly targets multiple benefits of green growth, including climate resilience, job creation and urban economic development, environment sustainability, and inclusiveness. It also proposes steps to be undertaken to develop a green city, including:

Box 3.3. Green city planning in Cambodia: from a vision to prioritised actions (*cont.*)

- Establishing green city strategic planning governance arrangements;
- Designing a green city shared vision and green urban goals for the city;
- Assessing the urbanisation context;
- Identifying actions to be taken to green the urban sectors (e.g., setting green growth goals for each sector; determining short-term investments, comprehensive sector reforms and measures to reinforce knowledge base);
- Planning scenarios for the city: *i)* setting a business-as-usual scenario; *ii)* piloting a green growth scenario; and *iii)* mainstreaming an urban green growth scenario;
- Short-listing and prioritising from the identified green growth actions (approximately 8 to 15) through carrying out a multi-criteria analysis;
- Performing an economic analysis of short-listed proposed priority green actions and investigating financing and partnership opportunities; and
- Developing implementation arrangements, including focal points, a monitoring and evaluation plan, and a project pipeline review process.

The methodology has already been applied in the city of Phnom Penh and is expected to support other cities' effort towards green city planning.

Source: GGGI (2016a), "Green City Development Guidelines", Hanoi.

Cities present opportunities for renewable energy and energy efficiency

Energy is key to climate change mitigation. Urban areas in Viet Nam present opportunities for renewable energy (RE) and energy efficiency (EE) investment. RE has been recognised as a key energy source of the country since the 2000s. The Viet Nam National Energy Development Strategy to 2020, issued in 2007, highlights RE as one of the key development objectives. Viet Nam's revised Power Development Plan VII (PDP 7), issued in 2016, set the RE target to 6.5% by 2020 and to 10.7% by 2030. It also includes sub-targets for wind, biomass and solar energy. The Strategy for the Development of Renewable Energy by 2030, issued in 2015, defines targets for each RE source including hydro, biomass, solar and wind for 2050. The strategy also proposes policy solutions to achieve these targets that include electricity prices, net metering, tax incentives, and land-use incentives, among others. The Ministry of Industry and Trade (MOIT) is primarily responsible for RE policies.

Urban areas can be a driver for solar energy provision in Viet Nam

Currently, the most common RE technology in Viet Nam is photovoltaic (PV) solar systems. Since Viet Nam is a mountainous country with limited flat land, urban areas are important not only as space for living and economic activities but also for energy generation. In fact, increasing electricity demand and high population density in urban areas poses strong opportunities for RE investment, rooftop solar systems in particular. Two types of rooftop solar systems exist: grid-connected and off-grid. Both are sold and installed by private companies. Ho Chi Minh City is the first and only city in Viet Nam which operates a pilot programme promoting a grid-connected PV system. Households receive a compensation of VND 2 000 (USD 9 cent) per KW (Ho Chi Minh City, 2016). However, a grid-connected PV system is not economically viable for households without such financial incentives, partly because the installation cost is still significant.[2] Even with the current compensation scheme, it will take households 10 years to recover their initial investment, without mentioning the maintenance cost. Therefore, solar energy is currently most often used by households in the form of solar water heaters. Their cost is minimal, although the impact on reducing GHG emissions may be limited.

In order to attract more private investment into solar energy in Vietnamese urban areas, the following policy options could be considered:

- Include the role of subnational governments in promoting RE in key national strategies, namely the Viet Nam National Energy Development Strategy to 2020, the PDP 7 and the Strategy for the Development of Renewable Energy by 2030, so that they are given clear mandates for promoting RE in their capacity.
- Require subnational governments to develop a local strategy for RE. The Ministry of Industry and Trade (MOIT) could support this initiative with technical capacity to enable them to contribute to the overall RE target of the country.
- Mandate solar installations in certain residential and commercial rooftops. Such a regulatory scheme has been proven effective in some OECD cities (Box 3.4).
- Promote grid-connected PV systems, by supporting local governments' pilot programmes. Ho Chi Minh City's programme could be replicated countrywide.
- Provide more incentive for households and companies to invest into solar energy in urban areas, for example by revising the feed-in-tariff system.
- Invest in upgrading electricity grids in urban areas to allow more solar PVs to be connected to the grids with stability.
- Provide training for workers to develop skills for installing and maintaining PV systems. Develop collaboration among local governments, business communities as well as universities to create effective policies and programmes to develop a skilled labour market for RE.

While rooftop solar panels can effectively increase land use efficiency in urban areas, green-field solar farm development should be given some attention. In Cebu (Philippines), some controversy was created when about 1 000 trees were cut down in attempts to construct a solar farm, leading to the loss of premium and native tree species (Mangubat, 2015). Due to the competing needs for scarce land resources, trade-offs between RE supply and the environmental cost of developing in green areas have to be carefully examined. One pertinent issue to be taken into consideration is site selection. Compensation mechanisms such as afforestation and reforestation responsibilities could also be considered as a prerequisite for permits.

Box 3.4. Policies to promote solar energy in selected OECD cities

Cities governments are increasingly playing a leading role in promoting solar energy through their regulatory and planning powers. In some OECD cities, solar ordinances mandating installation of rooftop solar panels or solar water heaters have led to increases in the area of collectors. This has often been combined with financial and information instruments. Solar obligations have been useful in providing a minimum share of solar powered energy in new constructions as well as renovated buildings.

Box 3.4. Policies to promote solar energy in selected OECD cities (*cont.*)

- Barcelona (Spain) is seen as the pioneer of solar regulation in Europe (ESTIF, 2017). As of 2008, solar thermal energy associated with the solar ordinance had seen drastic improvements. Solar collectors to heat water had risen from 2 500m^2 in 1999 to 65 506 m^2 (OECD, 2016a).
- Los Angeles (United States), by the end of 2014, had the highest total solar PV installed in the United States with a capacity of 215 MW direct current (ECRPC, 2016). Realising that residential rooftop solar systems could help meet RE goals, Los Angeles County has streamlined the permit process for small residential rooftop solar energy systems (CSE, 2016). Furthermore, the CLEAN LA Solar programme allows businesses and property owners to generate power for the city's grid by taking advantage of the vast unutilised rooftop spaces to install rooftop solar panels (Clean LA Solar, u.d). The programme has led to the production of RE within cities, as opposed to generating and transmitting it from outside the city. It has also contributed to creating jobs (e.g. solar panel installation and maintenance) and encouraging private investment in clean energy. What has made Clean LA Solar successful is the strong support from the Los Angeles City Council, the mayor, businesses, civic community as well as knowledge/academic partners such as the UCLA Luskin School of Public Policy.

Source: European Solar Thermal Industry Federation (2017), "Solar Ordinances", www.estif.org/policies/solar_ordinances/; OECD (2016a), *Urban Green Growth in Dynamic Asia*, OECD Publishing, Paris, http://dx.doi.org/10.1787/9789264266360-en; Norman, K., R. Sargent and B. Fanshaw (2016), "Shining Cities 2016, How Smart Local Policies Are Expanding Solar Power in America", Environment America Research and Policy Center, www.environmentamerica.org/sites/environment/files/reports/EA_shiningcities2016_scrn.pdf; Center for Sustainable Energy (2016), "Los Angeles County Solar PV Permitting Case Study", https://energycenter.org/permitting/guidebook/los-angeles-county-solar-pv-permitting-case-study#_edn1; Clean LA Solar (n.d), http://cleanlasolar.com/The-First-Project.

Energy efficiency also presents strong potential of subnational action

EE is crucial for Viet Nam's industry to become more competitive and environmentally friendly. Energy-efficient production systems can cut the cost per unit of production and increase price competitiveness, in addition to consuming less energy. EE is enshrined in *the 2010 Law on Energy Efficiency and Conservation (No. 50/2010/QH12)*. Subsequently, two decrees (*No. 21/2011/ND-CP* and *No. 73/2011/ND-CP*) provide detailed regulations and policy measures for the implementation, including EE labelling, EE in public buildings and equipment, EE examination and inspection, and financial support on EE. In addition, *the National Target Program on Energy Efficiency and Conservation for the period 2006-2015 (VNEEP)* is the main driver behind energy efficiency in Viet Nam, including for urban areas (Box 3.5).

Box 3.5. Viet Nam's National Target Program on Energy Efficiency and Conservation (VNEEP)

Following *the Decision No. 1427/QD-TTg*, approved in 2012, *the National Target Program on Energy Efficiency and Conservation for the period 2006-2015* (VNEEP) is the main driver behind energy efficiency in Viet Nam. It includes six components (state management, education and information dissemination, equipment, industry, buildings, and transportation) and sets specific targets:

Box 3.5. Viet Nam's National Target Program on Energy Efficiency and Conservation (VNEEP) *(cont.)*

- achieve 5-8% savings on total national energy consumption for the period 2012-2015;
- set up a network for the implementation of the Law on Energy Efficiency and Conservation at central and local levels;
- widely use high efficient equipment, removing backward technologies and equipment, reducing 10% of energy intensity in energy intensive industries;
- ensure that all of new or renovated buildings have EE management in accordance to Viet Nam Building code; and
- increase the modal share of public transport in big cities to 10-15 percent.

The VNEEP includes 11 projects to achieve the targets (World Bank, 2010). For example, it runs extensive awareness campaigns, which has resulted that more than 80 percent of the Vietnamese population are aware of energy efficiency and conservation (RCEE-NIRAS JSC, 2016). The energy saving effect is estimated more than 5%, which is equivalent to 13.3 million TOE for the period of 2011-15 (RCEE-NIRAS JSC, 2016). The EE labelling campaign has also been highly successful in changing consumer behaviour. The market share of inverter air conditioners increased from less than 1% in 2008 to almost 30% in 2014. Similarly, incandescent light bulbs with capacity of 60W or above have been almost completely replaced by compact fluorescent lamps (CFLs) or LED bulbs (MOIT, 2015). The VNEEP also trained and accredited 2 599 energy managers on building codes and 320 energy auditors in order to address the lack of skilled professionals on energy performance and audit systems.

Source: Ministry of Industry and Trade (MOIT) (2015), "Chương trình dán nhãn năng lượng, phát huy hiệu quả, đi đúng lộ trình", http://tietkiemnangluong.com.vn/tin-tuc/nhan-nang-luong/t17977/chuong-trinh-dan-nhan-nang-luong-phat-huy-hieu-qua-di-dung-lo-trinh.html; RCEE-NIRAS JSC (2016), "Evaluation of Viet Nam Energy Efficiency Programme Phase II, Final Evaluation Report" (unpublished), Hanoi; World Bank (2010), "Viet Nam Expanding Opportunities for Energy Efficiency", Asia Sustainable and Alternative Energy Program, March, http://documents.worldbank.org/curated/en/792971468320734217/pdf/611530WP0P10581or0Energy0Efficiency.pdf.

While the central government has made extensive efforts to promote EE, it has not fully mobilised subnational governments. In fact, there is a strong potential to enhance EE by them. In order to unleash the potential of subnational governments, the following central government actions could be considered:

- Include the role of subnational governments in promoting EE in key national strategies, including the 2010 Law on Energy Efficiency and Conservation and the VNEEP, so that they are given clear mandates for promoting EE.
- Require local governments to develop a local strategy for EE. In Hai Phong, the Hai Phong Green Growth Strategy for Industry in 2020 formulates a vision for modernising industry and encourages energy-effective production. Based on the strategy, the city helps 120 casting companies that use coal to modernise their manufacturing process. The city also supports firms in energy auditing and has provided consulting solutions to save energy, which has resulted in remarkable energy consumption reduction (OECD, 2016b).[3] Such initiatives should be accelerated and supported by the central government.

- Allow subnational governments to set higher EE standards within their local jurisdictions. For example, while MOC's circular on Energy Efficiency Building Code (No. 15/2013/TT-BXD) sets EE standards for all new and renovated buildings with total floor area of 2 500m^2 or larger, local government could extend the regulation to smaller buildings of certain types, or apply stricter EE standards to certain types or sizes of buildings, reflecting their local needs.
- Set up an EE central fund that can be used to leverage public and private investment in EE. The fund could be used to guarantee bank loans for EE investment in small and medium enterprises (SMEs) and provide technical assistance on developing EE performance and audit systems. Subnational governments could also access the fund to accelerate their EE investment in public buildings, for example.
- Establish a knowledge sharing platform where different levels of governments, the private sector and other key actors can share their EE policies and experience.

Urgent need for accelerating wastewater treatment

Wastewater collection and treatment is a fundamental public service to sustain economic activities and quality of life. However, due to rapid urban expansion, many cities and towns face difficulties in providing adequate levels of drainage systems, wastewater collection and treatment services. Water quality in groundwater aquifers and rivers in urban areas is often poor, creating "black rivers" flowing throughout urban agglomerations and industrial zones (ADB, 2014). Poor wastewater collection and treatment has also caused serious health problems. The costs of pollution from untreated wastewater were estimated as equivalent to 5% of Viet Nam's GDP (GIZ, 2013).

Urban wastewater collection and treatment is primarily a responsibility of MOC. The current national policy framework includes the following documents:

- Decree 80/2014/ND-CP, issued in 2014, provides regulations for drainage and sewerage systems in urban and industrial areas. It designates Provincial People's Committees (PPCs) as "owners" of these infrastructures. It also includes a framework for wastewater charges. Supporting circulars, which are currently under preparation, are supposed to provide water quality requirements, decentralised wastewater treatment, sludge and septage management,[4] and reuse of treated effluent.
- Decree 154/2016/NĐ-CP, signed by the Prime Minister in 2016, defines penalties regarding environmental pollution, including environmental protection (EP) fees. EP fees are charged against wastewater discharge violations and work as a means of incentivising polluters (essentially industries and craft villages) to treat wastewater at source.
- Prime Minister's Decision 589/QD-TT, approved in April 2016, provides targets for drainage and wastewater collection networks as well as wastewater treatment plants in urban centres and industrial parks up to 2025 (with a vision towards 2050). It aims to have rainwater drainage systems installed in all urban roads and residential streets by 2020.[5] It also aims to expand the service capacity of rainwater drainage systems in urban areas to more than 70% by 2020 and to over 80% by 2025. On wastewater, the Decision envisages that 50% of wastewater from Class I and Class II cities and 20% of wastewater from Class III, IV and V

cities should be collected and treated by 2025. A longer-term objective is to stop flooding and achieve 100% of domestic wastewater treatment in all cities by 2050.

While the main constraint is insufficient resources to build adequate levels of wastewater management systems, a challenge may also lie in public awareness and consensus building. For example, many urban households are reluctant to be connected to sewerage systems. In Viet Nam, whether or not a sewerage system is available, septic tanks continue to be the norm for individual households. Although households are obliged to connect their septic tanks to the sewerage network, connections are sometimes extremely difficult in cramped urban centres and residents are naturally reluctant to undergo the inconvenience of intrusive works within their properties. Moreover, not being convinced of the benefit of the sewerage system, they often object to paying for the connection. The obligation to pay for municipally-managed wastewater treatment is also perceived as an unnecessary additional burden.

A related large problem is enforcement of wastewater related regulations. For example, the EP fee for the households which are not connected to their sewerage system is only 10% of the water tariff, which provides no financial incentive for them to connect to the piped sewerage system. As a result, cities have tended to postpone the costly and unpopular sewerage construction process which also comes with street closure. Very little progress has been made towards universal connection of individual houses to sewerage systems (GGGI, 2016b). Another key problem is the poor maintenance of existing septic tanks, which is not properly regulated or enforced. Industrial wastewater is not effectively regulated or enforced, either. According to the Viet Nam Union of Friendship Organizations – NGO Resource Centre, only 60% of industrial parks in Viet Nam are equipped with wastewater treatment systems, due to legal loopholes, weak regulations and ineffective enforcement.

It is critical for Viet Nam to allocate more resources to wastewater treatment for safeguarding the country's urban eco-systems and people's health. The government should urgently consider the following policy options:

- Strengthen inspection on wastewater discharge in residential and industrial zones. More manpower (staff or outsourced) needs to be allocated at the city level. Inspection at the completion of new urban development should be mandated in order to ensure proper sewage connection and septic tank installation. Incentives such as staff awards could be given to officials who report abuses or successfully enforce regulations.
- Deregulate the septic tank requirement and allow households to connect directly to their sewage system, where sewerage system is available. The capacity of wastewater treatment plants need to be revised accordingly.
- Provide a discount, a loan or other forms of financial support for households for sewerage connection in a targeted period, in order to accelerate the process.
- Increase the EP fee for wastewater related violations and make it progressive, so that households are encouraged to connect to the sewerage networks. Allocate the fee for accelerating wastewater treatment.
- Increase wastewater tariffs and allocate it for financing operation and management of wastewater treatment. Such cost recovery tariff needs to carefully take into account the affordability of households (ADB, 2015).

- Implement interim decentralised solutions such as decentralised wastewater treatment system (DEWATS) that can provide safe and efficient collection services with affordable costs.
- Improve data systems to measure the amount and content of wastewater discharged both from households and industries, in order to give more accurate estimates, which in turn can be used to calculate appropriate EP fees as well as wastewater tariffs.
- Shift national and subnational government's budget priorities for wastewater treatment to accelerate the investment.

Solid waste management presents another untapped opportunity for green growth

Solid waste management is another persistent policy challenge, but at the same time presents an untapped green growth opportunity for Viet Nam. As presented in Chapter 1, the challenge is two-fold: one is a relatively large volume of waste per capita, and the other is poor waste collection and treatment with great disparity across cities (Figure 1.18 and 1.19). Currently, only 84.5% of urban solid waste is collected and treated in the whole country (Ministry of Construction, 2015). Moreover, the current trend indicates that waste production in cities is likely to further increase in the future. In Hai Phong, for example, annual waste generated in 2025 is expected to be quadruple the levels produced by the city in 2015 (OECD, 2016b).

Viet Nam's current major national policies for solid waste management are as follows:

- Decision No.2149/2009/QD-TTg, approved by the Prime Minister in 2009, sets a comprehensive national strategy for integrated management of solid waste up to 2025, with a vision to 2050. It includes specific targets for the collection and treatment of solid waste in urban and rural areas for industrial, hazardous and non-hazardous wastes, towards 2015, 2020, and 2025. For example, by 2020, 90% of municipal solid waste is to be collected and treated in all cities and 85% of the collected waste is to be recycled, reused or used for energy recovery and organic fertiliser production.
- Decision No.1440/QD-TTg, approved by the Prime Minister in 2008, sets a plan on the construction of solid waste treatment facilities in three key economic regions (northern, central and southern) up to 2020.
- Decision 1216/QD-TTg, approved in 2012, provides the National Strategy on Environment Protection to 2020, with Visions to 2030. It supplements the 2008 Decision to enable and strengthen the implementation of solid waste collection and treatment facilities.

Despite the ambitious targets set by these decisions, effective policies have not been introduced to promote waste separation at source or waste-to-energy incinerators, which has significant growth potential by recycling and generating energy. Furthermore, limited financial and technical support has been given to provincial and local governments for the construction of sanitary landfills. As a result, governments continue to suffer from the problems of existing sub-quality landfills and illegal dumping. Out of 660 landfills in operation in Viet Nam, only 203 (30%) meet the environmental standards set by the government. GHG emissions from landfills account for 32.2% of the emission from the waste sector and 1.9% of the total emission (MONRE, 2014).

Green growth policies and effective governance of circular economy in cities can shift the paradigm to regard solid waste as sources of revenue rather than as a source of problems. The following are among many policy options to be considered:

- Continue vigorous campaigns to raise awareness about waste separation, recycling as well as waste reduction.
- Retrofit existing landfills to minimise negative environmental impacts and to generate energy. With relatively small investment, some of them could be much more effectively managed. For example, Hai Phong city has piloted the Fukuoka semi-aerobic technology at the Dinh Vu dumpsite.[6] Applying this low-cost technology, the carbon dioxide index has dropped from 30.4% to 8%, while the methane gas index dropped from 67% to 6% (Ngoc, 2014).
- Encourage co-operation and partnership to share knowledge and expertise at the provincial and city level.
- Introduce effective waste pricing, reflecting the volume and the environmental cost. It can make the costs of waste more visible to the consumer, thereby creating the economic incentives for households and businesses to change waste disposal behaviour. It can also provide the financial resources needed for service improvement and shift the financial burden away from municipalities. In OECD metropolitan areas, waste pricing systems are centred on a flat rate or a variable fee based on either unit pricing (pay as you throw, or PAYT) or on municipal waste management cost. In Japan, Korea and Switzerland, a number of households are subject to PAYT and significant waste decrease has been observed. It is estimated that PAYT could reduce waste generation between 16% and 20% (OECD, 2014). PAYT is more suitable for a door to door collection service and achieves its objective of waste reduction best if combined with an effective recycling programme.

Strengthening governance to deliver urban green growth

Improving the governance structure may drastically improve the performance of green growth policies in urban areas in Viet Nam. This section first presents the current challenges around urban green growth governance and the importance of co-ordination among ministries and government agencies. Secondly, it highlights the need for more extensive and systematic data collection and better reporting mechanisms, in order to monitor progress for urban green growth.

Improve inter-governmental co-ordination at the national and local levels

Unclear allocation of responsibility for urban green growth has resulted in co-ordination challenges

In Viet Nam, green growth policies are primarily the responsibility of the Ministry of Planning and Investment (MPI) at the national level. However, since green growth policies cannot be separated from related sectoral policies, co-ordination among relevant national ministries is critical to the successful implementation. The current unclear allocation of responsibility in urban green growth has resulted in co-ordination challenges. The following are examples of co-ordination challenges at national and local levels:

- The Ministry of Natural Resources and Environment (MONRE) is responsible for monitoring air pollution of the whole country. However, other ministries are also responsible for monitoring air pollution based on the economic activities under their supervision. For example, Ministry of Transportation (MOT) is responsible for monitoring emissions from cars and other transport modes. This has created overlapping mandates. In addition, air pollution monitoring per se is not clearly mentioned in MOT's mandate; the mandate only includes establishing vehicle standards and energy efficiency labels. This also creates some confusion about which actual policies can be decided by MOT.
- At the city level, no departments/agencies are clearly mandated to monitor air pollution from transport in cities. Department of Transport (DOT) under MOT is not in charge of urban transport. While urban transport is under the management of DOC or Office of Urban Management and Provincial People's Committee (PPC), they are not given clear mandates. Since they can easily put the responsibility upon other agencies, it is equally easy for the task to not be undertaken.
- Overlapping responsibilities arise with emissions from industrial activities. According to the government's mandate, MOIT, PPC, and Department of Industry and Trade (DOIT) are all responsible. If the industrial zone is within the city, DOC and PPC are involved as well. The overlapping of mandates, coupled with the lack of co-ordination has crippled effective implementation.
- In June 2016, the Prime Minister issued Decision 985a/QĐ-TTg on the National Action Plan on Managing Air Quality until 2020, vision to 2025. The Decision has assigned each ministry to be responsible for the air quality resulting from the economic activities that they manage, and all ministries to be equally responsible for the implementation of this decision. However, no co-ordination mechanism across ministries such as an appointed focal point has been proposed, which tends to make the implementation more difficult.
- On solid waste, the Office of Natural Resources and Environment (or DONRE at the provincial level and MONRE at the national level) sets environmental and technical standards on waste collection and treatment. It also issues licenses to companies that provide waste collection and treatment services. Yet, they are not responsible for waste collection and treatment activity; it is under the management of the Office of Urban Management (or DOC at the provincial level and MOC at the national level). In fact, it is a very common practice in Viet Nam that an agency sets standards and others are responsible to implement. When there is a lack of co-ordination, the result is poor implementation and limited results, as observed in the case of solid waste management performance. Furthermore, it is often hard to ensure that the operation process meets the standards required.

Develop an institutional mechanism for inter-sectoral and multi-level co-ordination for urban green growth

A potential solution for Viet Nam to address these complex co-ordination challenges at the national and local levels is to create an institutional mechanism which allows inter-sectoral and multi-level co-ordination in the light of the nationwide objective of green growth. On climate change, such an institutional mechanism for inter-ministerial co-ordination exists. The Viet Nam National Commission on Climate Change (NCCC), chaired by MONRE, consists of all ministries to co-ordinate all activities related to climate change. In contrast, on green growth, to date there is no such institutional mechanism for co-ordination. The NCCC does not have any mandate over green growth and any matter labelled as green growth is out of its responsibility.

In fact, the VGGS has assigned MPI to set up an Inter-ministerial Coordination Board (ICB) for green growth that sits under the National Committee on Climate Change (NCCC). If implemented properly, the ICB may drastically improve the performance of green growth policies. According to the Prime Minister's Decision, the ICB will be headed by the Deputy Prime Minister, who will report to the Prime Minister. The Deputy Prime Minister will be supported by four vice-heads: Minister of Planning and Investment, Minister of Industry and Trade, Minister of Agriculture and Rural Development, and Minister of Finance. The Deputy Prime Minister will report both CC and GG activities to the Minister (Figure 3.4).

With the view to placing stronger focus on policy co-ordination in urban areas, the ICB structure could also be revisited. For example, given the crucial role of MOC in urban green growth, MOC could be added to one of the vice-heads of the ICB. As outlined in the previous section, out of VGGAP's 42 actions which are relevant to urban areas, only five actions have been allocated to MOC to lead on. In this regard, it is important to engage MOC more actively in the co-ordination process, to ensure that MOC's policies and programmes in urban areas are aligned with VGGAP's actions.

At the subnational level, a similar co-ordination structure could be developed across departments and offices in provinces and cities. Currently, while green growth is assigned to DPI and climate change is assigned to DONRE, no inter-sectoral co-ordination mechanisms are institutionalised.

Figure 3.4. The future NCCC structure, with ICB under its wing (according to the Prime Minister's decision)

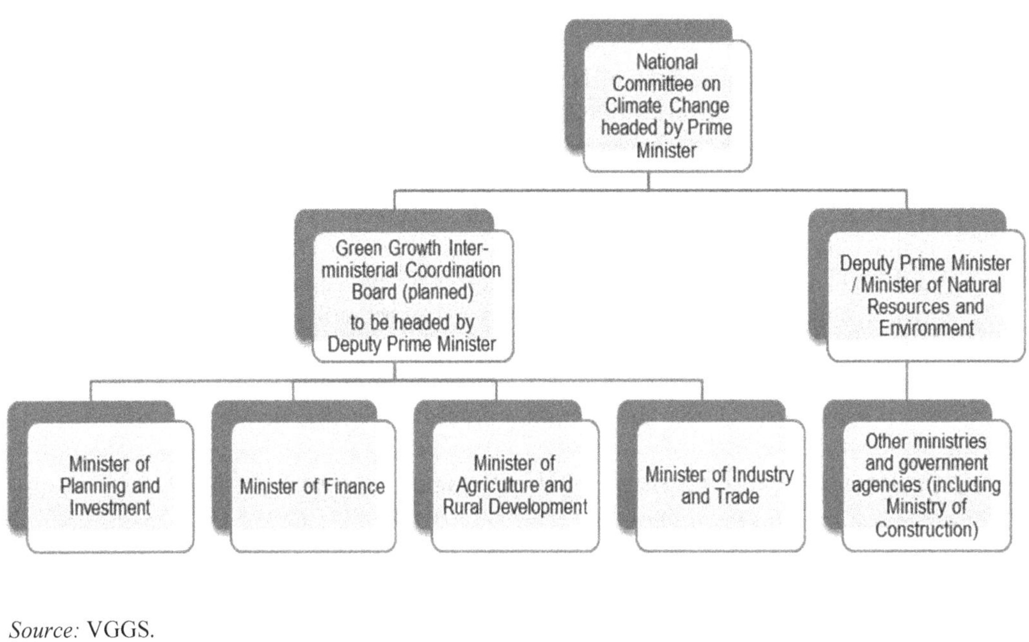

Source: VGGS.

Stronger legal framework may ensure engaging subnational government and other urban stakeholders

Effective implementation of green growth policies at the subnational level will require clear allocation of responsibility and effective working relationships across central, provincial and local governments. This study found that the current national green growth policy frameworks, such as VGGS and VGGAP, fall short of providing clear direction for subnational governments to do so. This has kept subnational green growth actions 'optional' for some subnational governments, leaving them dependent on local political will. Moreover, Vietnamese cities vary to a great extent in terms of administrative and financial capacity, which has considerable implications on their ability to implement green growth within the urban areas that they manage. With competing interests and stringent resources, it would be extremely difficult for them to justify allocating resources to tasks that are vaguely mandated.

As previously discussed, stronger urban legal frameworks can effectively support Viet Nam's green growth implementation at subnational level. Currently, national green growth policies and strategies are neither legally founded nor mainstreamed into sectoral legal frameworks such as *the Law on Urban Development*. An important option would be to clearly state in a legally binding document that subnational governments are responsible for fostering green growth within their administrative areas. Providing clearer mandates and specific actions for subnational governments will actively steer them toward allocating their manpower and budget to green growth actions.

Engaging non-governmental stakeholders such as community groups and the private sector is another important element which lacks in the current VGGS and VGGAP framework. Engaging them at the local level would assist the implementation process. Recognising their roles and responsibilities in a legally binding framework and providing a mechanism as to how they can contribute to the overall national and local targets would be highly effective to ensure their engagement.

Strengthen training and skill development

Both the VGGS and VGGAP include policy solutions and activities for training and human resource development. However, one of the prominent feedback provided from local governments was a lack of training programmes on green growth. While both MPI and MOC have conducted trainings on green growth, the target audience has been mostly high-level officials from provincial governments. It appears that city government officials, especially those working in smaller cities, have received much less training. Mid-level and technical officials, who are central to the implementation, are often not given such an opportunity. As a result, there is a large knowledge gap between levels of the government on green growth. The central government needs to recognise this and take action to close the gap. Making all information and references about green growth freely available among all public government officials would be an important first step. Offering more training opportunities for young, mid-level and technical officials in cities would also be an effective option. Training programmes specifically tailored to these targeted officials should also be developed.

Improve data and reporting mechanisms for green growth at the city level

Develop urban green growth indicators

Viet Nam, as many other developing countries, presents an urgent need for improving its data and reporting mechanisms for green growth, especially at the city level. In Viet Nam, General Statistics Office (GSO) is the central government's agency responsible for the national census and official statistics for all cities and provinces.[7] While the Vietnamese official statistics currently measures 11 sectors, consisting of more than 200 indicators,[8] these indicators measure mostly the economic performance of the sectors, with less regards to its environmental or social impacts. For example, the agriculture sector has 46 indicators that measure area of farming, quantity of outputs, and crop yield, but they do not contain indicators that measure agriculture waste, energy consumption or GHG emissions. Energy and water input to the agriculture sector is often measured by MONRE and MOIT, and forests being converted to agriculture activities are measured by the Ministry of Agriculture and Rural Development (MARD). However, having these data measured outside GSO using different methodologies creates a fragmented picture of green growth, making it difficult for the national and local governments to set reliable green growth targets and to monitor the progress. More generally, this is a governance challenge due to lack of capacities in national and local administrations to collect and produce the data. The lack of acknowledgement of the importance of green growth also creates difficulties in unlocking resources to produce such statistics. The causes of such issues are therefore both institutional and political (OECD, 2016a).

In an effort to fill the data gap, the government has been developing standardised sets of green growth indicators for cities, supported by international partners (Table 3.4). For example, in 2015, MOC worked with the Global Green Growth Institute (GGGI) to develop a comprehensive set of Urban Green Growth Indicators, with 40 indicators under four categories: environmental sustainability; economic sustainability; social inclusion; and institutional responsiveness. The indicators span across key green growth sectors including energy, water, air quality, waste and transport (Table 3.5). Most of them are already required by existing national policy documents, thus making it easier for cities to collect them without requiring additional resources.

Table 3.4. Urban green growth indicators developed for Viet Nam

	Year	Institutions	Government counterpart	Number of indicators
Urban Green Growth Indicators	Completed – 2016	GGGI	MOC	40
City's Resilience Index	Ongoing	The Asia Foundation and ISET	MOC	Over 50
City's Prosperity Index	Ongoing	UN Habitat	MOC	62
Green City Indicators	Ongoing	Korea International Cooperation Agency (KOICA)	MOC	177

Source: Author.

Table 3.5. Urban Green Growth Indicators developed by MOC and GGGI

Environmental sustainability	Economic sustainability	Social inclusion	Institutional responsiveness
RE % of overall consumption Energy consumption/GDP Energy intensity (per capita) Grid connectivity Carbon emission per person Carbon emission per GDP PM10/PM2.5 daily concentrations Population density Green spaces per person Area of livable space Number of green building rated Public transportation networks per capita	Urban vulnerability resilience index Number of households inundated at least once per year Water consumption per person Water consumption per GDP Water recycling per capita Share of wastewater treated Waste generated per person Share of solid waste collected and adequately disposed Households having access to clean water Access to improved sanitation Number of jobs requiring higher education Number of green job created Share of high tech sector of GDP	Average income per person Percentage of poor households Percentage of households having durable house Number of community forums Mobile phone coverage Internet connection	Urban Master Plan Climate Change Action Plan Disaster Risk Reduction Plan Policies to implement VGGAP or PGGAP Source of funds for green growth investments (e.g. environmental tax) Green growth investment forums Green growth training and capacity building programmes Green growth monitoring and evaluation framework

Source: GGGI (2015), Urban Green Growth Index Report, (unpublished), Hanoi.

An important fact to highlight is that none of these indicators developed for Viet Nam has been officially recognised or implemented by the central government, leaving cities little incentives to invest resources to achieve these goals. MOC is currently preparing a Circular on Urban Green Growth Indicators and Guideline for Implementation, in which the MOC-GGGI Urban Green Growth Indicators will be incorporated. At the time of writing this report, the Circular was still in the process of approval. However, once it is issued, it will be an important step to engage cities and to make the reporting process across cities more standardised and systematic. It is further recommended to make the most use of all the existing indicator-related work conducted by different development partners, when developing the Circular and the Guideline. A set of urban green growth indicators proposed by the OECD for Southeast Asian cities could also be considered. A total of 39 indicators, grouped into 10 categories, have been developed by adapting two sets of existing OECD green growth indicators to fit the context of Southeast Asian cities (OECD, 2016a).

In a longer term, it is important for Viet Nam to go one step further and incorporate urban green growth data into GSO's official statistics, both sector-wise and city-wise. This will enable a sector or a city to measure its performance from sustainable growth perspectives (as opposed to just economic growth). It will also affect policy makers' mind set and encourage them to develop cities in a more sustainable way.

Improve the reporting mechanism under VGGS and VGGAP

The VGGS currently assigns MPI to review progress in three timelines: a review every five years, a mid-term review in 2020 and the final review in 2030. In addition, the VGGAP assigns relevant ministries and provinces to submit an implementation report to MPI every year. However, the VGGS and VGGAP do not mention how to measure progress; there is no clear instruction on what information these reports should entail and what data should be collected and reported. At the subnational level, some PGGAPs, such as those in Can Tho and Phu Tho provinces, require the Department of Planning and Investment (DPI) to consolidate inputs from other departments and submit implementation reports to the Provincial People's Committee. However, the reporting mechanisms are not clearly defined, either.

In order to improve the reporting mechanism based on the VGGAP, providing more detailed instructions would be useful. For example, MPI could require standardised reporting for each sector through an easy-to-understand template. The VGGAP implementation reports should at least include the actions taken during the given period, what has been achieved and the impacts (by using indicators), assessments of the results, and propose future actions. Online reporting is encouraged in order to reduce paper work and make the process more efficient, transparent and accountable. It is also important to make the implementation reports and their data publicly available. This will allow citizens to evaluate government's actions and provide feedbacks that are critical to improve policies. Moreover, by being scrutinised, national and local governments are more motivated to perform better and restrain from window-dressing actions.

Furthermore, the VGGAP process could further benefit by introducing measures to ensure compliance to some key targets. For example, the proposed Inter-ministerial Coordination Board (ICB) for green growth could be used to request ministries to submit an action plan to improve their performance if they are proven underperformers according to implementation reports. MPI could consider choosing several provinces every year and audit their PGGAPs and actions being taken to ensure their compliance. In addition, MPI could also consider a reward for some outperforming provinces.

Notes

1. Da Nang has completed a green growth strategy in 2014, as an early mover ahead of the national VGGAP. Although this is not counted as a PGGAP, the city is actively implementing urban green growth based on their own strategy.

2. The installation cost is typically VND 120 to 200 million (approximately USD 5 000 to 8 800). To put into perspective, Viet Nam's GDP per capita is USD 2 185 in 2016 (World Bank data). http://thuongmaisaigon.vn/tin-tuc-su-kien/he-thong-nang-luong-mat-troi-tiet-kiem-cho-cac-ho-gia-dinh.html.

3. According to the Energy Conservation and Cleaner Production Centre of Hai Phong City (ECCH), the energy audit activities have saved a total of 50.3 million kWh per year, equivalent in monetary terms to more than USD 3.03 million (VDN 64 billion) and a reduction in carbon emissions of 42 000 tons per year (ECCH, 2014a).

4. Septage is the fecal sludge that builds up in septic tanks as a by-product of the pretreatment of household wastewater in septic tanks.

5. In Viet Nam, most of the existing rainwater drainage systems have been (or are being) transformed into combined sewerage systems. Separated sewerage systems are limited, often to some new urban development.

6. The Fukuoka semi-aerobic technology (Fukuoka Method) collects and recirculates leachate by a perforated drain pipe system simply installed at the bottom of a landfill site. The surface of the landfill has aerobic systems to facilitate microbial decomposition and reduce methane gas concentration in the landfill up to 45 percent.

7. GSO is under MPI and has a branch office in each city and province. Apart from GSO, other ministries, governmental agencies and subnational governments collect their own statistics and develop their own system of data.

8. The 11 sectors are: 1) Administrative unit, land use and climate; 2) Population and employment; 3) National accounts and State budgets; 4) Investment and Construction; 5) Agriculture, forestry and aquaculture; 6) Industry; 7) Commerce, price index; 8) Transportation and postal services; 9) Education; 10) Health care, Culture and lifestyle; 11) International statistics.

References

Asian Development Bank (ADB) (2015), "Financing Urban Wastewater in Sa Dec, Vinh Long, and Vi Thanh", presented at the workshop in Can Tho.

ADB (2014), "Country Water Assessment Viet Nam", Summary (unpublished), Hanoi.

ADB (2013), "Viet Nam Environment and Climate Change Assessment", Institutional document, https://www.adb.org/sites/default/files/institutional-document/33916/files/viet-nam-environment-climate-change.pdf.

Center for Sustainable Energy (2016), "Los Angeles County Solar PV Permitting Case Study", https://energycenter.org/permitting/guidebook/los-angeles-county-solar-pv-permitting-case-study#_edn1 (accessed 31 August 2017).

Clean La Solar (n.d), http://cleanlasolar.com/The-First-Project (accessed 31 August 2017).

Energy Conservation and Cleaner Production Center of Hai Phong City (ECCH) (2014), "Activities of Hai Phong Energy Conservation and Cleaner production Centre associated with green growth and sustainable development", Energy Conservation and Cleaner Production Centre, http://ecchaiphong.gov.vn/defaulte.aspx?pageid=newsdetailsE&catID=6&id=131 (accessed 31 August 2017).

European Solar Thermal Industry Federation (2017), "Solar Ordinances", www.estif.org/policies/solar_ordinances/ (accessed 31 August 2017).

Gesellschaft für Internationale Zusammenarbeit (GIZ) (2013), "Economic impact of the development of wastewater collection and treatment in nine provinces/cities", Wastewater and Solid Waste Management Project, Hanoi.

Global Green Growth Institute (GGGI) (2017), "GGGI Refreshed Strategic Plan 2015-2020: Accelerating the Transition to a New Model of Growth", Seoul.

GGGI (2016a), "Green City Development Guidelines", Hanoi.

GGGI (2016b), "Urban Wastewater Sector in Viet Nam", Hanoi, unpublished.

GGGI (2015), "Urban Green Growth Index Report", Hanoi, unpublished.

Ho Chi Minh City (2016), "Tp. Hồ Chí Minh hỗ trợ 2 000 VND trên mỗi kWh điện mặt trời nối lưới", http://ecc-hcm.gov.vn/index.php/vi/news/tin-tuc/tp-hcm-ho-tro-2-000d-tren-moi-kwh-dien-mat-troi-noi-luoi-375/ (accessed 18 August 2017).

Mangubat, E.G. (2015), "982 Trees Cut", *Cebu Daily News*, http://cebudailynews.inquirer.net/73683/982-trees-cut-2 (accessed 31 August 2017).

Ministry of Construction (MOC) (2015), "Xã hội hóa trong xử lý chất thải rắn", www.moc.gov.vn/web/guest/56/-/tin-chi-tiet/1Lu9/28112/252749/xa-hoi-hoa-trong-xu-ly-chat-thai-ran.html (accessed 18 August 2017).

Ministry of Industry and Trade (MOIT) (2015), "Chương trình dán nhãn năng lượng, phát huy hiệu quả, đi đúng lộ trình", http://tietkiemnangluong.com.vn/tin-tuc/nhan-nang-luong/t17977/chuong-trinh-dan-nhan-nang-luong-phat-huy-hieu-qua-di-dung-lo-trinh.html (accessed 24 August 2017).

Ministry of Planning and Investment (MPI), the World Bank (WB) and the United Nations Development Programme (UNDP) (2015), "Financing Vietnam's Response to Climate Change: Smart Investment for a Sustainable Future: The Climate Public Expenditure and Investment Review", http://documents.worldbank.org/curated/en/260881468185041568/pdf/96580-wp-p149247-public-box391458b-vietnam-cpeir-report-eng.pdf.

Ministry of Natural Resource and Environment (MONRE) (2014), "The Initial Biennial Updated Report of Viet Nam to the United Nations Framework Convention on Climate Change", Hanoi, http://unfccc.int/resource/docs/natc/vnmbur1.pdf.

MONRE (2010), "Viet Nam's Second National Communication to the United Nations Framework Convention on Climate Change", Hanoi, http://unfccc.int/resource/docs/natc/vnmnc02.pdf.

Ngoc, T. (2014), "Effectively Applying Japanese Waste Treatment Technology", Viet Nam Chamber of Commerce and Industry, Viet Nam Business Forum, http://vccinews.com/news_detail.asp?news_id=30704 (accessed 31 August 2017).

Norman, K., R. Sargent and B. Fanshaw (2016), "Shining Cities 2016, How Smart Local Policies Are Expanding Solar Power in America", Environment America Research and Policy Center, www.environmentamerica.org/sites/environment/files/reports/EA_shiningcities2016_scrn.pdf (accessed 31 August 2017).

OECD (2016a), *Urban Green Growth in Dynamic Asia*, OECD Publishing, Paris, http://dx.doi.org/10.1787/9789264266360-en

OECD (2016b), *Green Growth in Hai Phong, Viet Nam*, OECD Publishing, Paris, http://dx.doi.org/10.1787/9789264260207-en.

OECD (2014), *Greening Household Behaviour: Overview from the 2011 Survey – Revised edition*, OECD Publishing, Paris, http://dx.doi.org/10.1787/9789264214651-en.

OECD (2013), *Green Growth in Cities*, OECD Publishing, Paris, http://dx.doi.org/10.1787/9789264195325-en.

OECD (2011), *Towards Green Growth*, OECD Publishing, Paris, http://dx.doi.org/10.1787/9789264111318-en.

OECD (2010), *Cities and Climate Change*, OECD Publishing, Paris. http://dx.doi.org/10.1787/9789264091375-en.

Office of Prime Minister (2011), Decision No. 2139/QD-TTg on the approval of the National Strategy on Climate Change, issued by the Prime Minister on December 5.

Smajgl, A. et al. (2015), "Responding to rising sea levels in the Mekong Delta", *Nature Climate Change*, Vol. 5, pp. 167–174.

Dasgupta, S. et al. (2007), "The Impact of Sea Level Rise on Developing Countries: A Comparative Analysis", *World Bank Policy Research Working Paper*, No. 4136, February, https://openknowledge.worldbank.org/bitstream/handle/10986/7174/wps4136.pdf.

RCEE-NIRAS JSC (2016), "Evaluation of Viet Nam Energy Efficiency Programme Phase II, Final Evaluation Report", Hanoi, unpublished.

Yale University (2016), "Global Metrics for the Environment: The Environmental Performance Index rank countries' performance on high-priority environmental issues" http://epi.yale.edu/sites/default/files/2016EPI_Full_Report_opt.pdf.

World Bank (2017), CO2 emissions (kg per 2010 US$ of GDP) database, Carbon Dioxide Information Analysis Center, Environmental Sciences Division, Oak Ridge National Laboratory, Tennessee, https://data.worldbank.org/indicator/en.atm.co2e.kd.gd.

World Bank (2010), "Viet Nam Expanding Opportunities for Energy Efficiency", Asia Sustainable and Alternative Energy Program, March, http://documents.worldbank.org/curated/en/792971468320734217/pdf/611530wp0p10581or0energy0efficiency.pdf.

Chapter 4

Governing urbanisation in Viet Nam

This chapter is dedicated to evaluating Viet Nam's urban governance architecture and institutions. It begins with an assessment of the current local government systems and inter-governmental relations and offers possible alternatives to improve co-ordination across levels of government. It also analyses urban governance system with a focus on horizontal co-ordination at the central level among national policy actors. It then explores local government finance, inter-governmental fiscal relations and overseas development aid and discusses how cities can make resources available to pay for urbanisation. Finally, it concludes with recommendations to strengthen civil service reform with a particular focus on subnational levels of government.

Viet Nam is urbanising rapidly. As urban population grows, city governments need to meet demands for more and better public services while meeting the challenges brought about by urbanisation such as environmental pollution and inequality. If Viet Nam's path to economic development is to be sustained, if environmental degradation is to be avoided – and reversed in many places- and if well-being levels are to be increased, the process of urbanisation must be well managed and the pressures on local public services engendered by urbanisation must be ameliorated. For this to be possible, the Vietnamese government should strengthen the capacity of national and local public institutions. Moreover, Viet Nam requires modernising its public governance arrangements and its decision-making processes which are currently at odds with the ongoing transition to a more urbanised country. The Vietnamese national government must provide clear leadership and a vision for the long term. Like many governments of OECD countries, it may also need to relearn the art of strategic planning if it is to use the full potential of cities as the engines of national economic development.

The local government structure

To manage urbanisation effectively, it is necessary to have a local government structure that acts in a co-ordinated and collaborative fashion guided by national objectives but able to meet local needs.

The local government system is highly fragmented and complex…

As discussed in Chapter 1, Viet Nam's local government system comprises three levels of government: provincial (including centrally-administered cities); district; and communal (Figure 1.1). This system was established in 1945 when the Democratic Republic of Viet Nam was founded. The local government system is organised and operates under the principle of "democratic centralism" which creates a hierarchical top-down administrative system. This means that local governments obey central government's commands. Every local government is an 'administrative unit' of the central government. According to the Law on Organizing the Local Government, they are classified in three different grades based on criteria such as population scale, natural area, the number of subordinated units, socio-economic development level and particular elements of each administrative unit in rural, urban areas and islands. Ha Noi and Ho Chi Minh City are special-grade province-level administrative units (see Chapter 2 for more details).

… and characterised by its hierarchical organisation and limited autonomy

Central control over local decisions is considerable. A key feature of the Vietnamese system of local government is the subordination of lower levels of government to the level immediately above. Local authorities can only carry out administrative functions that are assigned by national legislation. The Budget Law formalises the fiscal arrangements between the different levels of government, assigning important budget responsibilities to local authorities, especially at the provincial level.

Sub-national governments in Viet Nam, particularly the provincial governments including the cities of Ha Noi and Ho Chi Minh City, have considerable decision-making powers related to public investment, but districts and communes have much less decision-making power. Their investment plans must be approved by the upper levels of government. Moreover, most of their funds come from central grants and their tasks are essentially linked to supervision and control. In fact, one of the reasons why cities apply for reclassification is to enjoy more autonomy and obtain more resources. For example, Da Lat aims to be a first level city and Tan An a second level city to attract investors and improve their level of autonomy (see Chapter 2).

The key question for the provinces are related to: i) the way they interrelate with districts and communes for their investment decisions; ii) whether they develop integrated territorial approaches for development, rather than segmented policies; and iii) how they support the particular needs of some cities in the view of national priorities. Responsibility for planning, implementation and operation of facilities is split, although the implications for each province depend on the importance of the province. Large urban centres under the central administration such as Ho Chi Minh City, Hai Phong, Da Nang, Can Tho, and Ha Noi and several provincial governments enjoy a high degree of autonomy. They are authorised, for instance, to license foreign investments up to a certain value, approve local development plans of the urban districts within their territory, manage the urban land reserve, manage urban housing and use the reserve of state-owned houses of the city to develop houses for city dwellers, decide on the budget distribution across the local governments under their supervision, decide on the decentralisation of the revenue sources and expenditure tasks to the local administration's budget of each level of government, and formulate their own budgets.

Local executive authorities are appointed by elected people's representatives

The local government system includes the People's Council (a representative body) and the People's Committee (the executive body). The people's committees and people's councils often have overlapping membership. But members of the standing People's Council cannot be at the same time members of the People's committee at the same level. The local people elect the people's council; the candidates must be approved by the higher-level administrative unit. The people's council selects the chairman and vice-chairman of the people's committee. The people's committee is the executive organ of the people's council as well as the State administrative agency within localities, and is accountable to the local people, the people's council at the same level and the State administrative agency at the higher level. Indeed, provincial and local departments have dual reporting responsibility to the local people's committee and assembly, and to the central line ministries. The people's committee has both budgetary and administrative responsibilities. The people's council, on the other hand, is the local organ of the State power; however, it often has inadequate resources, skills and infrastructure to carry out its growing volumes of work. It only meets twice a year and has a limited contribution to the policy discussions at the national level.

Viet Nam lacks mechanisms of collaboration among subnational governments…

Viet Nam does not appear to have effective co-ordination mechanisms that facilitate and encourage a more integrated approach to urban development across levels of government. Collaboration among provinces is limited to technical issues. Departments of Construction from provinces and cities under central government have regular meetings on technical issues, but for joint investment projects or shared vision etc., collaboration becomes complicated. Interviews for this review revealed that most of the times co-operation among provinces is due to good will but there is no obligation to do so. Provincial governments organise conferences attended by district and communal level cities within their territory on the co-operation with other provinces; for example, Long An province organises conferences on the co-operation with Ho Chi Minh City on railway connection and with Tien Giang province on anti-salinity water management and hi-tech agriculture. But these meetings lack pragmatism, and are insufficient to allow co-operation among cities at the same level even within the same province. The lack of collaboration mechanisms among subnational governments at district and communal levels, for instance, reflects the absence of metropolitan thinking. District level governments plan without reference to the functional urban area. Part of the problem is rooted in the organisation of local government. For example, the Law on the Organisation of Local Government states that issues involving more than two district-level administrative units shall be tackled under the authority of the province-level local governments. The same apply for other levels of government either provincial or communal level. This means that subnational governments do not work together for public investment and service delivery to create economies of scale as that issue is addressed by the upper level government. These arrangements blurred even more accountability for urban development. Since the issues are taken over by the upper level of government it is unclear what the role of lower level governments should play.

…and there is no comprehensive regional nor metropolitan planning

In Viet Nam, regional co-ordination and planning is also crucial for the success of urban development projects that are too large or complex for any one unit of government to address. Issues such as land use, housing development, transport, solid waste disposal, groundwater management, and the quality of the urban environment are issues that require regional or metropolitan co-ordination. However, although some national plans exist for infrastructure investment and socio-economic development at the regional scale,[1] there is no master plan per region or metropolitan area to deal with these urban issues comprehensively both in term of spatial planning and actual investment strategies including investment priorities. As a result, Vietnamese cities tend to compete against each other for investment and resources with little synergy-building. For example, the cities of Hue and Da Nang have an international airport each at a 100 km distance from each other, when they could have a larger regional airport serving the two or even more cities in a more cost efficient manner. Moreover, when working towards a reclassification, cities tend to focus more on the requirements to be upgraded than on building synergies with neighbouring cities and rural communities. By adopting regional or even a functional urban area approach to planning and co-ordination Viet Nam could benefit from the effectiveness and efficiency of pooling resources, the use of the available structure and capacity within provinces, and prevent competition among cities which sometimes leads to duplication of investment.

Fostering collaboration in metropolitan areas could contribute to higher productivity levels…

Organisational arrangements of local government in Viet Nam are acting in detriment of economic development of the cities and in particular of the metropolitan areas. Thus, Viet Nam requires adopting mechanisms that facilitate urban co-ordination and collaboration for urban development investment projects at metropolitan level. The fact that when issues are related to two or more subnational governments at the same level they are taken over by the upper level government contributes to blur the distribution of responsibilities (discussed below) and even budget allocation and management. This arrangement also prevents the development of negotiation and technical skills at subnational governments as for important projects the upper level conducts the job.

As it was explained in Chapter 1, the two main metropolitan areas of the country contribute one-third of the national GDP. OECD studies have shown that metropolitan areas with fragmented governance tend to have lower levels of productivity (for example, see OECD, 2015b). Administrative fragmentation is most of the times unavoidable but the way to overcome it is through co-ordination mechanisms and multi-level governance arrangements that reduce transaction costs and asymmetries of information across levels of government. This suggests that municipalities in Viet Nam could improve their economic output if they were allowed to assume their own responsibilities in co-ordination with neighbouring provinces, districts or communes depending on the level of government. Co-ordination between municipalities also helps to provide services at the right scale. The experience of Germany may be useful in that metropolitan regions created by bottom-up processes can address local needs more effectively (Box 4.1). Allowing municipalities to conduct investment directly rather than upper levels of government when they are better placed to do so would help to improve cąpacity and spur public sector innovation in lower levels of government as most of the times lower level of government act under the "learning by doing" principle. Upper level governments should have a less direct intervention and focus on facilitating this collaboration and act merely as arbiters in cases of disagreements or conflict.

Box 4.1. Creation of metropolitan regions in Germany

Germany has eleven metropolitan regions. In 1995, the metropolitan regions of Rhein-Ruhr, Berlin/Brandenburg, München, Rhein-Main, Stuttgart and Hamburg were created, Mitteldeutschland followed in 1997, and further four regions, Hannover-Braunschweig-Göttingen-Wolfsburg, Nürnberg, Bremen/Oldenburg and Rhein-Neckar came into being in 2005.

These metropolitan regions were created by strong bottom-up processes, due to the awareness of regional stakeholders that larger urban cores could not manage many spatial development issues on their own. For example, housing needs for core cities cannot be managed only by themselves, as the increasing population also lives in the suburbs. Subsequently, the increasing traffic across administrative borders, whether by individual cars or by public transport, has to be managed. Furthermore, economic activities are also locating themselves at space outside core cities. The conclusion was: better solutions can be found when municipalities in a region work together instead of on their own. It is important to stress that the agendas of the metropolitan regions are decided by themselves, even if the main topics in all metropolitan regions are quite similar. Similarly, the types of governance structure were not given by the federal or State governments; on the contrary, each region chose its own structure through a process of negotiation between the stakeholders. Each metropolitan region also chose a financing model on their own (e.g., by a contribution of each municipality according to their number of inhabitants).

During the last two decades, the metropolitan regions have especially become a major player in regional development. This is mainly due to an increasing recognition that their policy is neither only for the urban cores nor merely for the rural areas, but that it is a mutual giving and taking for the benefit of a larger region. The federal government supported this idea and funded a wide variety of project in metropolitan regions on urban-rural partnerships, where more interaction and increase of flows (people and goods) between the municipalities of metropolitan regions can create win-win-situations and their conflicts can be avoided.

Source: Federal Ministry of Transport, Building and Urban Development (2012), "Urban-Rural Partnerships. Growth and innovation through cooperation", Berlin.

... and collaboration could make urbanisation more efficient

Allowing the metropolitan areas and their constituent lower levels of government to build economies of scale by allowing the co-ordination of investment and service delivery among governments at the same level would be a first start. There are different co-ordination mechanisms that Viet Nam could adopt. For instance, the experience of OECD countries suggests that contractual arrangements and financial transfers may always provide tools for co-operation and co-ordination. Contractual arrangements have been widely used as an instrument for carrying out joint action for regional development across levels of government, and OECD countries are also applying them at a metropolitan scale. The central government would need to commit to giving specific advantages to metropolitan areas in exchange for stronger co-operation among district-level governments. Financial transfers could be designed to incentivise co-operation. For example, Mexico established a "metropolitan fund", the national government's way of transferring resources to cities for joint investment projects (OECD, 2015c). France established the inter-communality grant to municipalities willing to levy a joint business tax with neighbouring municipalities (OECD, 2015a).

As part of the reclassification requirements of cities (see Chapter 2), Viet Nam's central government could demand that cities provide evidence that they have been working in collaboration with neighbouring districts and rural areas to ensure synergy-building. These urban-rural interactions can include linkages across space (i.e. flows of people, goods, money and information) and linkages between sectors, for instance between agriculture and services and manufacturing. In Viet Nam rural-urban linkages are not given priority. The experience of OECD countries suggests that effective rural-urban partnerships can help achieve economies of scale; attain economic development objectives for both urban and rural areas; can facilitate better access to jobs, amenities and different types of services; contribute to environmental protection by making better use of resources such as water and land; and rural areas would have more possibilities of attracting investment. Candidate cities to be classified as first level cities should also prove that they have the capacity to act as metropolitan city core by interacting with neighbouring municipalities and leading public investments as it occurs with the metropolitan cities in Italy (OECD, 2015a).

Platforms for dissemination of information and best practices are needed

It would be relevant for the chairmen and vice-chairmen of the People's Committees of different regional and district level governments to have the possibility of meeting regularly with their peers to discuss common challenges, create networks, exchange information and knowledge. The Association of Cities of Viet Nam (ACVN) can be leveraged for the exchange of information and best practices on urban development.

The ACVN groups cities to share opinions and experiences; it provides comments on government's urban policies and programmes, and collects opinions from its membership on urgent issues at the request of the national government. Its members are representatives of people's committees. The ACVN should do more than collecting opinions and providing comments on government's policies; it could be the platform where urban policies actually emanate through the experience of the different regions and districts. It would be important that the central government also takes part in the meetings of the ACVN. Working groups at technical level could be organised to discuss different urban challenges on housing, transport, environment protection etc. Meetings at more senior levels with the chairmen and vice-chairmen of the people's committees could take place twice every year to give direction to the working parties. The chairman and vice-chairman of the people's committee of any region or district should attend personally to those meetings as this would ensure political support and a clear mandate for the working groups.

The ACVN could also be the focal point for the creation of a seamless horizontal government through Information and Communication Technology (ICT). There is enormous potential for quality improvement and savings through the horizontal integration of policy execution through, for instance, e-government projects based on common portals. The Danish experience on horizontal integration initiatives could be a source of inspiration for the short term as the use of ICTs leaves the institutional arrangement as it is but guarantees easy communication across government bodies and easy access for citizens to government services (OECD, 2012). A good information system would contribute to the promotion of investment where the Ministry of Planning and Investment (MPI) should have a central role.

Centralisation still permeates Vietnamese public administration

Urban development takes place in a setting where responsibilities are distributed across different governments. An urban governance structure will be effective if cities can take decisions commensurate with the problems they face in their respective territories and in relation to other levels of government. Viet Nam is incrementally transferring greater administrative and, to a lesser extent, fiscal responsibilities to the provincial level of government. Figure 4.1 shows that subnational governments' expenditure as a percentage of GDP is higher than many OECD countries. It must be noted, however, that in Viet Nam, as it will be mentioned below, subnational governments have little influence in investment decisions as most of the expenditure is earmarked. The decentralisation process has transferred implementation responsibilities to subnational governments but it has not been fully matched with the possibility of subnational governments to decide on what to invest.

Figure 4.1. Vietnamese subnational governments' expenditure as % of GDP is similar to those of OECD countries but earmarked by central government

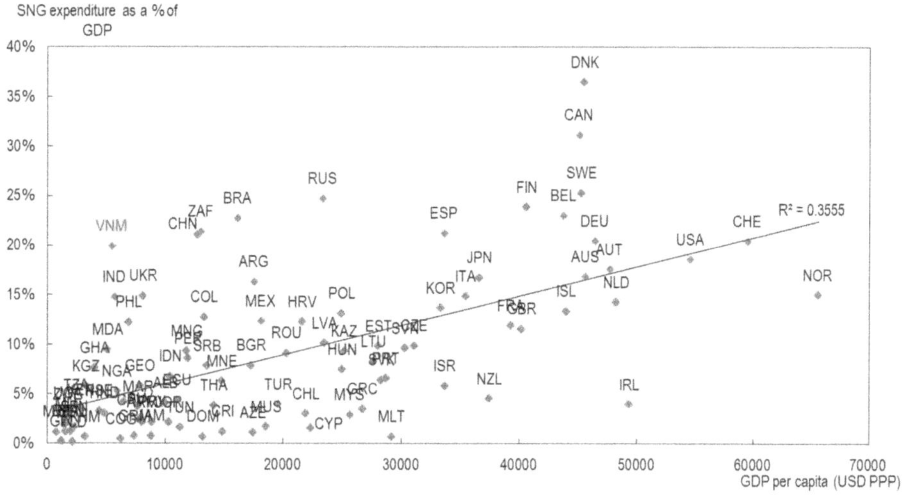

Source: OECD elaboration.

There are at least five important aspects to point out on Viet Nam's decentralisation process:

- Viet Nam is a unitary country where decentralisation is expressed in administrative terms. Sovereignty is not shared between central and subnational governments, local governments' organisation and reforms are decided by the central government and this has an impact on how power, responsibilities and resources are transferred from central to subnational governments. Indeed, *subnational governments do not have constitutionally mandated resources, responsibilities or legal statutes*, they are deconcentrated agents of the central government. Decentralisation in this context is being pursued incrementally by strengthening provincial-level management. The problem with administrative decentralisation is the resistance of powerful bureaucratic stakeholders to transferring control to the grassroots and the widening capacity gaps between local governments (Fritzen, 2006).
- *Urban management is not supported by a comprehensive decentralisation strategy.* In an attempt to improve efficiency and service quality, Viet Nam started a process of shifting the burden of service delivery to sub-national levels of government, but without the corresponding share of financial and human resources. The risk is that if the differences in capacity and capability of provinces and local governments across the country are not considered and addressed, the decentralisation process may only exacerbate the disparities among provinces and the urban-rural divide on issues such as poverty and inequality. For example, the increased urban demands for rural resources such as water and land without proper planning and rural-urban linkages have led to environmental pressures on agriculture production.
- The Law on Organizing the Local Government (Articles 12-14) differentiates between "delegation" and "decentralisation" of powers to local governments. Delegation of powers to local governments is stipulated by law according to the domain, within a specified period of time under specific terms and conditions. The Law gives central and locally-governed state organs to "decentralise" one or several duties and powers within their competence to inferior local governments in a continual or regular manner. It also states that superior-level state organs must ensure that the receiving authority in lower-levels of government be provided with the necessary resources to exercise the decentralised powers and be responsible for the results of their implementation. However, despite the rules for delegating and decentralising as stated in the law, *it is not clearly stipulated what kind of duties and powers can be transferred (delegated or decentralised) to lower levels of government,* which duties and powers should remain under the central government, and how the high-level authorities would ensure that local governments have the necessary resources to carry out their new tasks.
- Moreover, the fact that the transfer of responsibilities is unfolding concurrently with urbanisation makes *it necessary to bridge the information, skills, resources and competences gaps that currently exist at local level of government.* Failing to do so, any move for greater decentralisation, without careful management, may exacerbate the weak administrative and fiscal capacities of the poorer provinces and lower levels of government in the country reinforcing the gap between urban and rural areas and regional disparities.

- *Subnational governments have minimal discretion over the budget received from the centre*. Indeed, although over 50% of public expenditure is done by subnational governments, mostly provinces (the OECD average for unitary countries is 40.2%), it is largely covered by earmarked transfers for specific purposes. The Budget Law has pushed forward the boundaries of what provincial governments can do, notably in the management of regulation of infrastructure and the development of socio-economic development plans. However, as Fritzen (2006) points out, the high budget share indicators for subnational governments can be misleading, as it does not give any sense of how much discretion and control is actually wielded over such expenditure by each subnational level. The main problem seems to be the inadequacy of the intergovernmental transfer system that has failed to bridge the gap between poor and better-off regions. This is probably partly due to the lack of specific criteria and formulae to define the transfers and the almost full lack of obligation of higher levels of government to provide funds for "necessary important tasks" at lower levels of government. Moreover, such tasks are undefined in the Budget Law.

Enabling decentralisation to support the urbanisation process

To prepare the ground for urbanisation and to put cities on a solid, functioning basis, Viet Nam may wish to consider the following recommendations, based on the experience of OECD member countries:

Promote local self-government and participatory forms of urban policy-making

One key aspect for reinforcing the subnational governments in Viet Nam is to promote the *direct election of the chairman and vice-chairman of the People's Committee by citizens*. The chairman is the equivalent of a mayor in OECD countries and the direct election would help to direct accountability towards citizens and not only to upper levels of government. A reform of this kind would increase the responsiveness of local governments to their citizens through democratic institutions, since members of the People's Council are publicly elected. Since this would be a drastic political reform in Viet Nam, the election of the chairman and vice-chairman cold be done in some regions and/or districts as pilots from where lessons could be drawn before extending the practice to the rest of the country. Kazakhstan, a former Soviet country, has already introduced the direct election of rural mayors and other lower levels of government to promote local self-government and accountability (OECD, 2017b). The experiences of the United Kingdom and Chile may also be of relevance to Viet Nam in this respect. In the United Kingdom, city mayors are also indirectly elected, but there have been efforts to strengthen democratic practices and the mayors of, for example, Bristol, London and Liverpool are now directly elected by citizens. Mayors who are directly elected have been determined to be better at sharing power with their councils, have effectively had more authority, and given more direction and a better performance in terms of internal management and of the quality of services provided (Finding, 2015). The Chilean municipal reform shows that empowering municipal governments for urbanisation it is necessary to make them accountable to voters by pursuing a more inclusive policy-making process and strengthening their administrative capacities. Chile's reform is not intended to change the country's unitary system but aims to grant municipal governments more flexibility and autonomy to manage their own resources and priorities. Chile has recently approved the direct elections of city mayors and is now discussing the possibility to allow the direct election of heads of regional authorities who are still directly appointed by the president of the republic.

Administrative decentralisation should have a more strategic edge

To be effective, decentralisation in Viet Nam requires paying attention to at least four key issues. First, Viet Nam could allow cities at provincial and district level to decide on the investments projects they need to conduct to satisfy local people's needs for goods and services. Targeted public sector investment at subnational level would contribute to attract businesses to the cities. This would certainly imply that subnational governments are not seen as administrative units of the central government. It would also reduce administrative layers as district level cities have to get authorisation from upper levels of government to conduct investment or are being instructed on the investment projects they have to conduct.

Second, a public administrative reform focused on capacity-building at subnational levels is needed. It is essential to increase the capability and administrative capacity of local governments to make decentralisation work and facilitate urban management at the city level. This is because the burden of managing urban population growth and mitigating urbanisation's challenges in Vietnamese cities is largely born by subnational governments, mostly districts and communal level cities. This is problematic for many cities in Viet Nam as they struggle to provide at least a minimum level of services, let alone to expand service provision.

Third, as part of the decentralisation process, there should be closer attention to the rural-urban linkages for sustainable development. A functional urban area could include rural areas but there is no co-ordination or linkages between urban and rural zones. Rural areas even have somewhat different arrangements for their government and responsibilities according to the Law on the Organisation of Local Governments. Distinguishing between the various types of dynamic flows that exist between rural and urban spaces as well as the transaction costs between them are two aspects to consider in urban planning and decentralisation (von Braun, 2014). For instance, agriculture programmes should not be planned and evaluated in isolation from infrastructure such as roads that connect urban and rural areas. An important aspect to consider is to promote the income diversification of rural and urban communes by making their economies more interlinked as rural incomes tend to be less based only on agriculture. Viet Nam needs a better fit between national and sectoral policies and local development strategies that reflect the specific opportunities and challenges of rural and urban communes. For that, they need more financial autonomy and to be more accountable to their citizens. The formation of inter-communal partnerships (rural and urban) as it is done in municipalities in Austria, Estonia and Sweden, could be an option to foster rural-urban linkages (CEMR, 2013). These linkages could be helpful to define a functional area but an agreement on the distribution of wealth has to be reached beforehand. The urban-rural partnerships are a plus and should not replace policy interventions from the provincial governments.

And finally, Viet Nam should keep in mind that decentralisation is not a one-off policy change; it is an ongoing process where the end point of accountable and efficient local governments may well take many decades to achieve. In addition, in the process of institutional change, inertia and resistance can occur from those who have benefited from the previously centralised system, especially in terms of power, information and decision (Charbit, 2011). Decentralisation needs to be a flexible process, allowing the central/local dynamics to evolve and taking into consideration the potential instability of the political framework (Work, 2002).

The urban governance system

Urban development is approached from a siloed perspective…

One of Viet Nam's main management problems is the siloed approach to urban development. The origin seems to be in the way responsibilities for urban development have been allocated across the different ministries, and in the lack of co-ordination mechanisms across sectors to design and integrate policies. This distribution follows a purely siloed approach and there is no cross-cutting distribution of responsibilities. However, this is also a problem at subnational level. In general, departments conduct their planning specific to their sector without co-ordination and reference to one another. The OECD report on Green Growth in Hai Phong noted that a closer co-ordination between the ministries of finance and construction is essential to ensure that green growth projects are financially feasible in the city (OECD, 2017a). The local departments of finance and construction are not well involved in each other's activities, which makes the implementation of programmes difficult. The report recommended allowing the department of finance of Hai Phong to play a key role in the development of green growth initiatives, and making the department of construction's authorisation a prerequisite to finance any project or initiative that has an impact on green growth proposed by any other ministry.

The experience of OECD countries has shown that urban management requires the interaction of several domains to build up synergies and the seamless co-ordination across ministries and levels of government. However, multi-sectoral co-ordination at central and lower levels of government is posing particular difficulties to Viet Nam. These difficulties are rooted in the system of command and control (Fritzen, 2006). The governance arrangements in place seem to reinforce a system in which accountability is primarily directed towards the higher levels of government and is, at the same time, somewhat blurred by the overlapping spheres of authority and habits of intervention.

…and co-ordination among central agents for urban policy design and implementation is weak

In Viet Nam's central government, a number of ministries are responsible for urban development issues (Table 4.1). They all have implicit or explicit shared responsibility and authority for issues related to urban development. The Ministry of Construction (MOC) is the central public agency in charge of formulating, implementing and co-ordinating urban development policy at the national level. The Urban Development Agency (UDA), under the MoC, advises and assists the ministry in urban policy implementation and law enforcement.

Table 4.1. Central government bodies involved in urban development in Viet Nam

Government body	Responsibilities related to urban development
Ministry of Construction	Co-ordinate across ministries, branches and People's Committees of central-affiliated cities and provinces to hold implementation of National Programme on Urban Development in 2012-2020; to guide localities to make, appraise and approve their Urban Development Program; supervise the implementation of projects under the Urban Development Programme, and inform the Prime Minister on progress made.

Table 4.1. Central government bodies involved in urban development in Viet Nam (*cont.*)

Government body	Responsibilities related to urban development
Ministry of Home Affairs	Elaborate specific regulations on functions and duties of the new urban centre development management boards. Conduct research, propose models of urban authorities, urban system management.
Ministry of Finance	Provide guidance on the payment and settlement of funds for the formulation and implementation of urban planning; the rates and management and use of the fee for the grant of planning licenses. Allocate non-business funding for the implementation of tasks of the National Urban Development Programme of Ministries
Ministry of Natural Resources and Environment	Review the effectiveness of land use in the existing urban areas and areas expected for urban development; To guide localities to define boundaries, areas of land cultivating rice, especially land for water rice cultivation which need be strictly protected as basis of orientation of urban development
Ministry of Transport	Plan and develop the national, regional traffic system in connection with the central urban system and urban main traffic axes according to the approved regional construction plan, and the general urban plan.
Ministry of Planning and Investment	Balance the annual budget in order to ensure general expenditure of ministries and its branches in the implementation of the National Urban Development Programme and mobilisation to attract ODA capital source for activities of the Programme. Promote investment in urban development from domestic and international lawful capital sources. Guide the preferential mechanisms, encourage economic sectors to participate in investment in urban development construction.

Source: OECD research.

The large number of actors involved in urban policies poses a co-ordination challenge, as it is necessary to ensure policy consistency to obtain positive outcomes. Interviews for this review suggested that there are co-operation and collaboration problems across central ministries. Joint work across Vietnamese ministries is mainly issues-based rather than strategic. Some of the barriers for co-operation and collaboration are: i) restrictions on sharing information across ministries; ii) different organisational cultures; iii) the division of whole-of-government budget into separate ministerial allocations; iv) public managers who only have experience within a single ministry; and v) accountability structures that focus mainly on ministry-specific issues. The fragmented nature of the government may in turn inhibit resolution of problems and issues that cross ministerial boundaries. Once their strategic objectives have been set, ministries operate within sectoral silos, and there is little exchange of information at the level of policy implementation and monitoring. Viet Nam's co-ordination mechanisms at high levels such as the Inter-ministerial Coordinating Board for the implementation of the Green Growth Action Plan under the National Committee on Climate Change, appear to be too formal and insufficient to implement urban policy (Chapter 3).

Positive steps have been undertaken in the design and implementation of the National Green Growth Action Plan to improve cross-ministerial co-ordination. The Action Plan identifies the Ministry of Planning and Investment (MPI) as the focal point for green growth whereas the ministries of finance, and natural resources and environment are given specific tasks in the promotion of green growth and adaptation to climate change. Annex 1 of the Action Plan describes 66 implementation activities specifying the ministries responsible for each one of them. Nonetheless, there are no accountability structures specified in the Action Plan (Chapter 3).

Viet Nam requires pragmatism and a diversity of mechanisms for horizontal co-ordination at the central level…

Collaboration and co-ordination among central ministries and agencies could be strengthened through the systematic sharing of data, joint analysis and collaborative use of a variety of levers to enable government-wide implementation of urban policy. Encouraging working level contacts among ministries in urban related issues would be a pragmatic way to unleash collaboration. Streamlining bureaucratic formalities for exchanging information should be part of these efforts. All ministries and central agencies involved in urban policy should improve their understanding of the contribution of each central agency to advancing the urban development agenda. This should involve strengthening formal channels and informal networks of co-operation between ministries at the decision-making, managerial and technical level.

Vietnamese central government could take advantage of the Viet Nam Urban Forum (VUF) to assist with the works towards better collaboration and better understanding of the urban work across government. The VUF is a platform for discussion between all its stakeholders for sharing practices, information, and to facilitate discussion. Its mandate could be revised to ensure that it has a more active role in policy-making and monitoring, and providing feedback to government. The VUF is in a position to facilitate horizontal integration across ministries at national level (Box 4.2). It is worth pointing out that Ha Noi and Ho Chi Minh City governments are not involved in the activities of the VUF. These are two important absences as they are the largest cities in the country. The MoC, through the Urban Development Agency, should continue motivating the participation of these two cities in the activities of the Forum.

Viet Nam could also set up high-level committees, working groups and bilateral partnerships to supervise co-ordination of urban policy. The Urban Development Agency could be given the responsibility of co-ordinating urban development across ministries and levels of government. For this purpose, Viet Nam could draw inspiration from the experience of Sweden's National Board of Housing, Building and Planning, which is a platform for greater collaboration, co-ordination, knowledge development, dissemination of knowledge and exchange of experience for sustainable urban development. This is an important link between practice and politics at the local, regional and national level, and it is a meeting place for local and regional initiatives. The platform is co-ordinated by the Swedish Energy Agency and the Swedish Agency for Economic and Regional Growth, as well as the Swedish Transport Administration.[2] Another option for Viet Nam is to establish a committee and inter-ministerial conferences as in Belgium where national and subnational level authorities discuss and agree on national urban priorities and strategies and, more importantly, assess the results of policy implementation. In Belgium the collaboration between the levels of government has been institutionalised by the creation of a Consultation Committee and Inter-ministerial Conferences. The first is composed of members from each government and treats ad hoc cases; the latter is used to for the preparation and development of joint policies for a certain policy field. There are also Collaboration Protocols for situations when competencies are shared and when the proper execution of competencies necessitates cross-government collaboration.[3]

Box 4.2. Viet Nam Urban Forum

The Viet Nam Urban Forum (VUF) was established in 2003 based on a consensus of government authorities and international and domestic organisations. Its leadership is held by the Ministry of Construction of Viet Nam, which is also in charge of urban development in the country. Its mission is "to promote dialogue for sharing of experiences and knowledge among government agencies, associations, unions, scientific/professional, social/political organisations and non-governmental organisations, entities and individuals of all economic sectors and the donor agencies, with the aim of actively contributing to the formulation and implementation of policies on urban development and management, and improving the effectiveness of urban development and management activities in Viet Nam". The VUF works as a network/platform of discussion between all these stakeholders, and is divided into seven member groups, as follows: multilateral donor organisations, bilateral donor organisations, government ministries (i.e. finance, natural resources and environment, and planning and investment) and agencies (i.e. Viet Nam Green Building Council, and the Association of Cities of Viet Nam), professional associations (i.e. Viet Nam Architects Associations) and academic institutions, cities, private sector corporations, and NGOs. Currently, the VUF counts 150 members and plans to reach 200 members by 2020.

The VUF is articulated around three types of events and activities: i) annual events, consisting of the Annual Conference (General Assembly) and the Viet Nam Urban Day; ii) conferences, workshops and seminars based on thematic discussions; and iii) the production of policy recommendations. In this regard, the VUF provides an interesting opportunity to bring around the table local governments, national government and international partners to foster urban development and green growth.

Source: Urban Development Agency, Ministry of Construction (2012), Viet Nam Urban Forum, Hanoi, www.geoviet.vn/FM/GetFile.aspx?ID=a2167cb2-8b36-4015-9af4-b68ca64d0db2 (accessed 20 June 2017).

…and strengthening accountability for urban development across ministries and agencies

Strengthening accountability for urban development is critical for designing incentives for collaboration and effective joint action. It is thus important to focus the conception and development of urban policy proposals on collective ministerial responsibility, to serve the broader public interest and to work across institutional lines to develop the best possible policy. There should be a balance in fulfilling individual accountabilities to their stakeholders and collective responsibilities to the broader public interest. To reinforce accountability, ministries should be clearly briefed on their areas of responsibility and how they are expected to contribute to cross-cutting issues such as urban development or green growth. The mandates and performance agreements of ministers and their deputies could explicitly reflect the need to work together and with central agencies. They could then manage urban related programmes and plans, in order to optimise the capacity of government to set, implement and monitor regional and urban policies. Ministries should be given the possibility to innovate by finding different ways to address policy issues in concert.

Paying for urbanisation

Overlaps in the distribution of expenditure responsibilities across levels of government

In Viet Nam governments' functions are centralised or are subject to strong central control and/or require follow up legislation. Some local responsibilities are still exercised by the central government and some others are not compensated with adequate financial resources. These problems are more evident in the main metropolitan areas of the country Hanoi and Ho Chi Minh City as functions are fragmented across separate jurisdictions (districts).

Viet Nam's 2015 State Budget Law (SBL) (No. 83/2015/QH13) is the only piece of legislation that attempts to clarify the roles of the National Assembly and the local authorities in deciding on revenue collection and expenditure policies, budget allocation norms, budget balances, targeted additions and percentages of allocations and delegation of powers to localities in areas of budget and organisation of personnel, thus ensuring consistency (see discussion below).[4] However, the unclear demarcation of the mandates of various agencies in charge of urban policies still exists to leave room for discretion in interpretation of responsibility and accountability where there are overlapping functions and duties. For example, articles 36 and 38 of the 2015 SBL, that set spending responsibilities for central and local governments respectively, are largely similar.

Article 38 of the 2015 SBL, for instance, states that the expenditures tasks of the local budgets include: i) investment of the construction of socio-economic infrastructure projects managed by localities; ii) investment in and support for enterprises, economic organisations and financial organisations of the State; iii) non-business economic activities in the fields of education and training, health care, social affairs, culture and information, art and literature, physical training and sports, science and technology, environment, and other non-business managed by the localities; iv) national defense, security and social order and safety in the portion allocated to the localities; v) the implementation of social policies for subjects managed by the localities; vi) the national programmes assigned by the Government to the localities for management; among others. These functions largely overlap with those assigned by Article 36 to the central government and most of the expenditures assignments are concurrent. Thus, service delivery gaps, redundancies, or inefficiencies are more likely to occur in detriment of policy effectiveness. Sectoral regulations have to be consulted for better clarity on expenditure responsibilities.

There are additional variety of expenditures specified for commune levels in Article 38, and over-detailed regulations on minimum allocation to certain areas (e.g. no less than 20% of total spending on education) which have a negative impact on the autonomy of local governments to decide on their particular priorities. Functions such as the "additions to the State reserve fund", and 'support for the social insurance fund' are exclusive responsibility of the central government.

The Law on the Organisation of Local Governments is rather generic when talking about the duties and powers of the People's Councils and People's Committees across "administrative units". The complexity of the administrative structure and the hierarchical organisation of the lower levels of government, under a system of control and command, make it difficult to provide clarity on responsibilities. This is because every level of government is responsible for the performance of the lower levels of government and sometimes the functions of district and communal levels are absorbed by upper level governments, for example in cases when the issue involves two or more local governments. Table 4.2 provides some examples of the duties and powers of the president of the people's committee of different administrative units (or levels of local government). It shows that there are still some overlapping responsibilities on issues such as housing, land use, and urban space management. The immediate consequences are the limited accountability for the execution of duties, the lower efficiency in the management of financial resources, and the reduction in the effectiveness of policies and programmes for urban development.

Table 4.2. Examples of duties and powers of the president of the People's Committee of different administrative units

Administrative unit	Sector				
	Housing	Land use-management	Infrastructure development	Transport	Administration
Provinces and centrally-governed cities	Manage urban houses; manage real estate business operations; use the reserve of state-owned houses to develop houses for city-dwellers	Manage urban land-reserve Implement measures to manage, protect urban space, architecture and landscape.	Mobilise funds for urban development. Implement the plan for urban infrastructure construction	Implement measures to manage traffic safety assurance and traffic jam alleviation.	Examine and supervise the organisation and operation of local governments within their territory
Urban districts	Manage urban residence in the district as decentralised and authorised by superior-level state organs.	Direct and organise the implementation of planning of urban infrastructure development, construction and urban space, architecture and landscape.	N/A	N/A	Lead and bear responsibility for the operations of the state administrative system from the district to the grassroots levels.
District-level towns, provincial city and municipality-controlled city	Manage urban houses, manage residential house business, use the reserve of state-owned houses for urban housing development, and inspect the compliance with the law during urban housing construction	Manage urban land reserve and use it for infrastructure construction	Direct and organise the implementation of the planning and proposals for urban infrastructure development, urban space management.	Direct and organise the implementation of duties to public order and traffic safety assurance, prevent and control traffic jams	Implement duties and powers delegated by superior-level state organs Examine and supervise the organisation and operation of local governments at the communal level.
Commune, wards and townships	Manage urban residence within the ward	Co-operate with the competent agencies and organisations in the implementation of the planning for urban infrastructure development, transport, urban environment protection, space and landscape			Implement duties and powers decentralised and delegated by superior-level State organs

Source: Government of Viet Nam (2015), Law on Organizing the Local Government, No. 77/2015/QH13, The National Assembly.

Viet Nam requires pursuing fiscal decentralisation and sharpening the distribution of responsibilities across levels of government

The experience of OECD countries shows that an absolute clear-cut allocation of responsibilities across levels of government is not possible and not appropriate, as many policy areas such as urban development, require shared interventions from different levels of government. In Viet Nam a clear cut is equally not possible due to the particularities of its political-administrative system. And an important point is that Vietnamese provinces assign local functions to lower levels of government and can themselves spend on responsibilities not reserved to the central level, while the norms are still set by the central government. In 2013, around 54.3% of public spending was carried out at the subnational level. Subnational governments were responsible of 73.92% of capital expenditures, and 89.8% of staff expenditures, while local staff are selected upon central government's approval. Ho Chi Minh City spends 44% of its budget on salaries and allowances. Nevertheless, Vietnamese authorities could consider the following recommendations to make public expenditure more efficient:

- *Sharpen the distinction between central and subnational governments' responsibilities*. To effectively implement urban-related policies, Viet Nam needs to set clear roles and responsibilities for all levels of government and stakeholders. A revision of the SBL in this respect would involve balancing responsibilities and access to resources to be able to put policies into practice. An analysis of the distribution of expenditure responsibilities across levels of government in OECD countries reveals a general pattern that may be considered by Vietnamese authorities (see Table 4.3). However, there is no best way for deciding which level of government should be responsible for what particular service. This has to be judged in terms of how well it achieves the goals or objectives set by government in its decentralisation strategy (McLure and Martinez-Vazquez, 2000).

Table 4.3. Breakdown of responsibilities across the subnational government levels: a general scheme

Municipal level (TL4)	Intermediary level (TL3)	Regional level (TL2)
A wide range of responsibilities: • General clause of competence • Eventually, additional allocations by the law Community services: • Education (nursery schools, pre-elementary and primary education) • Urban planning and management • Local utility networks (water, sewerage, waste, hygiene, etc.) • Local roads and city public transport • Social affairs (support for families and children, elderly, disabled, poverty, social benefits, etc.)	Specialised and more limited responsibilities of supra-municipal interest An important role of assistance towards small municipalities May exercise responsibilities delegated by the regions and central government Responsibilities determined by the functional level and the geographic area: • Secondary education or specialised education • Supra-municipal social youth welfare • Secondary hospitals • Waste collection and treatment • Secondary roads and public transport	Heterogeneous and more or less extensive responsibilities depending on countries (in particular federal vs unitary) Services of regional interest: • Secondary / higher education and professional training • Spatial planning • Regional economic development & innovation • Health (secondary care and hospitals) • Social affairs, e.g. employment services, training, inclusion, support to special groups, etc. • Regional roads and public transport

Table 4.3. Breakdown of responsibilities across the subnational government levels: a general scheme (*cont.*)

Municipal level (TL4)	Intermediary level (TL3)	Regional level (TL2)
• Primary and preventive healthcare • Recreation (sport) and culture • Public order and safety (municipal police, fire brigades) • Local economic development, tourism, trade fairs • Environment (green areas) • Social housing • Administrative and permit services	• Environment	• Culture, heritage and tourism • Environmental protection • Social housing • Public order and safety (e.g. regional police, civil protection) • Local government supervision (in federal countries)

Source: OECD (2016a), *OECD Regions at a Glance 2016*, OECD Publishing, Paris, http://dx.doi.org/10.1787/reg_glance-2016-en.

- *Promote fiscal decentralisation for a more dynamic urban management and more autonomy for public investment decisions.* Viet Nam is currently under pressure to reconsider the distribution of powers between central and subnational governments. Viet Nam could consider increasing the capacity for subnational governments to adjust revenue or spending (i.e. taxing autonomy, mandatory spending), and to increase borrowing (with or without central government oversight). In this sense, it is essential for Viet Nam to carefully phase in the decentralisation process so that local capacities match local responsibilities. An asymmetric decentralisation of responsibilities can be an interesting way forward in devolving expenditure responsibilities to subnational governments, as is the case in Colombia (OECD, 2016c). Asymmetric governance approaches involve risks, in terms of creating institutional complexity and preferential treatments, but at the same time, they are ways to better take into account various territorial, political or cultural situations, as in OECD countries like France, Italy, Spain, Sweden and the United Kingdom. Viet Nam may consider granting more autonomy to district and communal levels of government to make investment decisions on, for instance, local infrastructure projects. Although subnational governments depend on central government financial support, the central government also has a high degree of dependence on subnational governments' effectiveness in the delivery of public goods and services which are of high importance at the national level. Following the OECD Principles for Effective Public Investment across Levels of Government (Box 4.3), Viet Nam may wish to employ a fiscal framework adapted to the different investment policy objectives pursued.

Box 4.3. OECD Principles for Effective Public Investment across Levels of Government

Pillar I: Co-ordinate public investment across levels of government and policies

- Invest using an integrated strategy tailored to different places.
- Adopt effective co-ordination instruments across national and sub-national governments.
- Co-ordinate among sub-national governments to invest at the relevant scale.

Pillar II: Strengthen capacities for public investment and promote policy learning across levels of government

- Assess upfront long-term impacts and risks of public investment.
- Encourage stakeholder involvement throughout the investment cycle.
- Mobilise private actors and financing institutions to diversify sources of funding and strengthen capacities.
- Reinforce the expertise of public officials and institutions throughout the investment cycle.
- Focus on results and promote learning.

Pillar III: Ensure sound framework conditions for public investment at all levels of government

- Develop a fiscal framework adapted to the investment objectives pursued.
- Require sound, transparent financial management.
- Promote transparency and strategic use of public procurement at all levels of government.
- Strive for quality and consistency in regulatory systems across levels of government.

Source: OECD (2014), *Recommendation of the Council on Effective Public Investment Across Levels of Government*, Adopted on 12 March 2014, www.oecd.org/regional/regional-policy/Principles-Public-Investment.pdf and www.oecd.org/effective-public-investment-toolkit/.

- *Adopt a multi-level governance approach to fiscal decentralisation.* The experience of OECD countries shows that multi-level governance is always required for managing public policies in a decentralised context. Multi-level governance refers to the relationship between public actors situated at different administrative levels and the explicit or explicit sharing of policy-making authority, responsibility, development and implementation at different administrative and territorial levels. This is important for Viet Nam as the country continues to decentralise fiscal and administrative competences. The legal framework is under revision but it is expected more power to be delegated to local authorities. A multi-level governance mechanism is necessary to tailor expenditure and investment priorities to local needs (Charbit, 2011).

Subnational governments have limited sources of own revenue

The low capacity of subnational governments to finance their public investment is mainly due to an upward pressure on operating expenditures, which has not been accompanied by similar evolution in own revenues, or current and capital transfers received. Vietnamese subnational governments largely depend on central government for revenue, and the transfer system has tied central and subnational governments' fiscal policy closely together. Vietnamese SNGs have three main sources of revenue: i) revenues retained 100% by local authorities, such as taxes and fees related to land, local fees and charges; ii) revenue shared between local authorities and central government; and iii) transfers from upper levels of government. Figure 4.2 shows the share of subnational governments' revenue in Viet Nam compared to that of OECD countries. Vietnamese subnational governments' main source of income are taxes, followed by grants and subsidies. They collect more income from taxes than the average in OECD unitary countries.

Figure 4.2. Structure of subnational government revenue, 2014

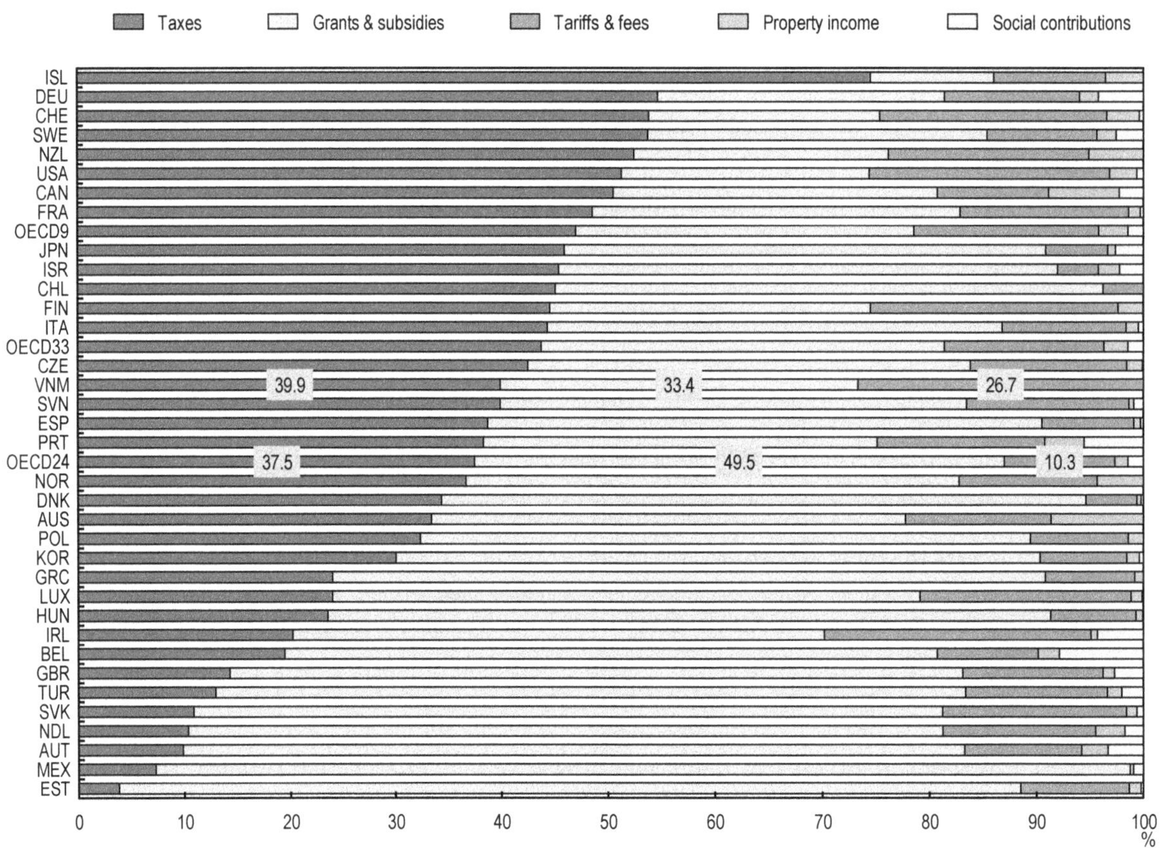

Note: OECD averages do not include Chile.

Source: OECD (2016a), *OECD Regions at a Glance 2016*, OECD Publishing, Paris. http://dx.doi.org/10.1787/reg_glance-2016-en.

According to the Constitution (Article 70. 4) tax rates and bases are determined by the National Assembly. Subnational governments only have limited independence on setting fees. Ceilings for fees are set in central level regulations and cities can adjust the fees relative to the central government standard to set them higher or lower. Article 37 of the SBL lays out the revenues that are retained 100% by subnational governments (Table 4.4). The Provincial People's Council decides revenues sources for each budgeting levels of the local governments.

Table 4.4. Central and local governments' revenues in Viet Nam

Sources of central government revenue	Sources of local budget revenues
Value added tax on import goods	Land house tax
Export tax	Natural source tax, excluding natural resource tax collected from oil and gas
Import tax	License tax
Special consumption tax on import goods	Land use right transfer tax
Enterprise income tax of the units applying the entire-branch accounting	Agricultural land use tax
Taxes and revenues from oil and gas	Land use levy
Retrieved money of central budget loans	Land rent
Non-refundable aids of the governments of other countries, international organisations and foreign individuals	Proceeds from the lease and/or sale of State-owned houses
	Registration fees
	Revenue from construction lottery
	Retrieval of local budget capital at economic organisations, revenue form the local financial funds
	Non-refundable aid of international organisations
	Charges, fees, revenues from non-business activities and other revenue payable into the local budgets
	Revenue from public land funds
	Voluntary contributions from organisations
Revenues divided in percentage between the central budget and the local budget	
Value added tax (excluding VAT on imported goods)	
Enterprise income tax excluding enterprise income tax of the units applying the entire-branch accounting (CIT)	
Special consumption tax on domestic goods and services	
Income tax on high-income earners	
Tax on transfers of profits abroad	
Petrol and oil charges	

Source: Government of Viet Nam (2015) State Budget Law.

Shared revenues constitute the bulk of revenues at all levels. Poorer provinces with a positive fiscal gap keep 100% of the shared taxes collected.[5] The richer provinces keep a lower portion of the shared taxes (between 15% and 60%). In the period 2011-2015, among all the 63 provinces, 13 kept only a portion of shared taxes, and 50 provinces retained 100% of the shared taxes collected within their jurisdiction. For example, the city of Da Lat has to send 67% of its income to the provincial government whereas Ho Chi Minh City remits 82%. In principle, revenue sharing is defined according to a 'sharing rate' set for a three to five years 'stability period'. However, the actual rates are reached by negotiation as there is no specific objective formula for determining them (World Bank, 2014). The central government, through the differential tax sharing ratios across provinces, is extracting additional transfers to the centre from relatively rich provinces, which subsidise poorer provinces. The World Bank (2014) noted that although relative income levels appear to be a major criterion for determining the non-identical tax sharing ratios for each province, this is not stated in the State Budget Law, which refers to fixing these ratios for 'stability periods' of 3-5 years.

Ho Chi Minh City, for instance, collects revenue from three sources: i) import and export taxes; ii) crude oil income, and iii) domestic revenues (i.e. land use, private income taxes). Income from the first two groups is transferred to the central government. Income from fees for housing and properties, certification, notary services etc. are kept 100% by the city. Districts in Ho Chi Minh City can collect taxes from state firms' income, FDI for the city and keep the VAT on non-state firms for their own budget which pays for small investments such as local alleys, health care centres etc. In 2014, in OECD unitary countries, local government expenditure represents on average 13% of GDP and 29% of public expenditure (Figure 4.3), whereas in Viet Nam local expenditure represents 20% of GDP and 54.3% of public expenditure. For the whole OECD area, subnational government expenditure accounts for 17% of GDP and 40% of total public expenditure. Although Viet Nam's level of subnational expenditure is almost comparable to the OECD average, it must be interpreted with care. It does not mean that Vietnamese subnational governments have considerable spending autonomy; in fact most of their spending is mandatory as they act as the paying agents of the central government. This is a similar situation in some OECD unitary countries such as Chile, Greece, Ireland and Turkey (OECD, 2016b).

Figure 4.3. Subnational government expenditure as a percentage of GDP and total public expenditure, 2014

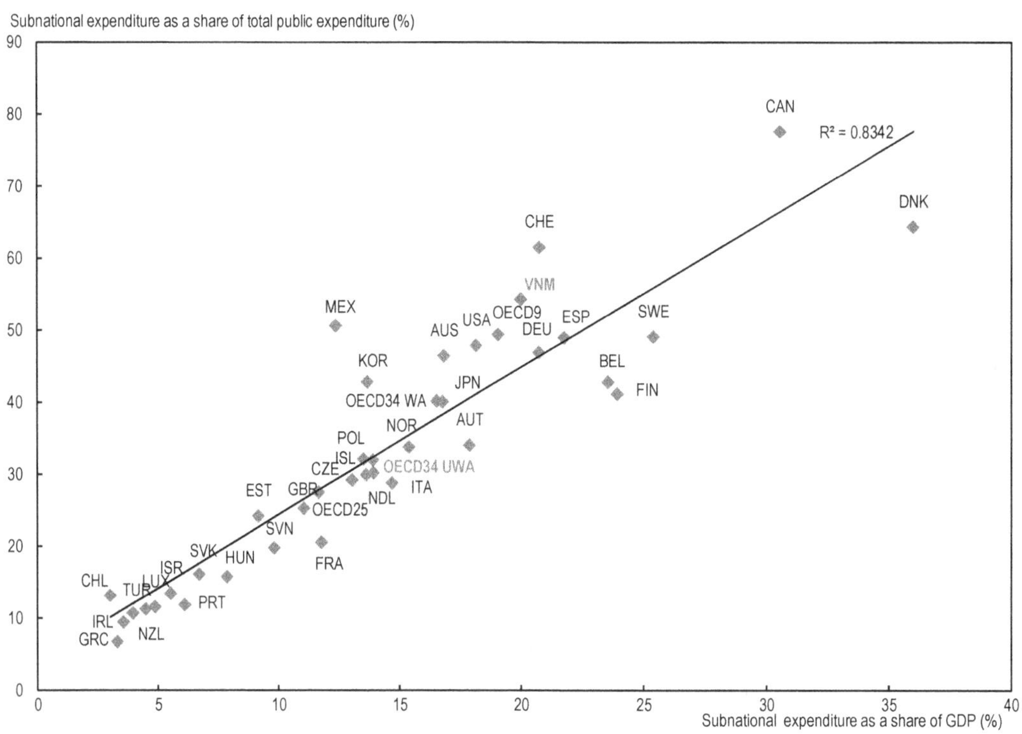

Note: Data for Viet Nam are for 2013.

Source: OECD (2016a), *OECD Regions at a Glance 2016*, OECD Publishing, Paris. http://dx.doi.org/10.1787/reg_glance-2016-en.

Article 38 of the SBL gives the provincial-level People's Councils the authority to decide on the concrete decentralisation of the revenue sources and expenditures tasks to the local administration's budgets of each level based on defined principles. For instance, it states that the commune and district township budgets should receive at least 70% of the revenue from tax on land use right transfer; land and house tax, license tax collected from business, individuals and households; agricultural land tax collected from family households; and land and house registration fees. Moreover, it instructs that the provincial capitals' and towns' budgets should receive at least 50% of the registration fees, excluding the house and land registration fees. Article 39 of the SBL gives commune, district-townships, provincial capitals and towns' administrations the opportunity to mobilise contributions from organisations and individuals for investment in the construction of infrastructure projects on the principle of voluntariness. The SBL states that the mobilisation, the management and use of these contributions should be public, inspected and controlled to ensure that they are used for the right purposes. It is worth noting that this faculty of revenue-raising powers was not given to provincial governments. To improve the fiscal system, Vietnamese authorities may consider the following recommendations:

- *Establish identical tax sharing ratios for all governments*. Vietnamese authorities may wish to follow the World Bank (2014) recommendation on establishing identical tax sharing ratios for all provinces and use the direct transfer mechanism exclusively for determining the size of the central budget transfers to provinces. This would be a simpler and more transparent system, provided the basis for determining the size of equalising transfers is transparent. This would put an end to the implicit system of interprovincial positive and negative transfers by which relatively rich provinces subsidise relatively poor provinces.
- *Grant more flexibility to subnational governments to set fees and charges for services delivered at the local level.* Allowing local governments to set tax fees and user charge rates so that the costs of local services are more nearly covered is an efficient strategy that increases the resources available to invest in better services or some basic infrastructure. Local authorities should be able to increase or decrease these rates but national authorities may wish to set a cap. These powers could be defined by law and should not depend on the decision of the provincial level government in order to guarantee certainty. For example, in Brazil municipalities are allowed to collect tax on services, urban property tax and set fines and public utilities fees; they collect 20% of their revenue form own-sources, larger Brazilian cities tend to collect more (Smoke, 2013).
- *Raise the efficiency of financing grants*. If Viet Nam's central government wants to control sub-national taxation, it has the possibility to limit the subnational tax base and provide grants to finance imposed programmes or minimum standards and basic subnational services. Non-earmarked general purpose and block grants are the most efficient instruments to finance subnational services (Bergvall, et.al., 2006). However, earmarked discretionary grants are a good instrument for the co-funding of temporary projects or programmes if the commitment of subnational authorities to performance targets is sought. Earmarked transfer can be used to foster metropolitan co-ordination for certain projects such as infrastructure as it is done in India. South Africa makes use of earmarked transfers to improve services in poor neighbourhoods and 24% of the allocations go to metropolitan-area local governments (Bahl, et.al. 2013). In Viet Nam, earmarked transfers at metropolitan-wide level could be used to boost rural-urban linkages by financing public services (i.e. public transport in Prague in the Czech Republic) and social cohesion projects (i.e. re-organisation of social services).

Subnational governments have a strong dependency on central government transfers

Another aspect to analyse is the mechanisms for direct or indirect intergovernmental transfers. These are critical points that affect the capacity of cities for service delivery and manage the process of urbanisation. Like in many other countries, in Viet Nam intergovernmental transfers do not just fill the gap between expenditure assignments and revenue-raising powers; they actually represent a sizable amount of subnational governments' income. For example, the province of Lam Dong receives 60% of its income from transfers. There are two types of intergovernmental transfers: balancing transfers (48% of total transfers in 2012), and targeted transfers (52%) to implement specific national priorities. Balancing transfers are kept during the 5-year stability period without taking into account inflation. On the other hand, targeted transfers lack predictability and are only loosely linked with local needs of funding. They have specific and time-bound objectives usually around poverty reduction or social outcomes. Article 40 (3) of the SBL states that a superior budget or upper-level budget can provide targeted additional allocations to support the subordinate or lower-level budgets upon the appearance of necessary important tasks which cannot be satisfied even after the rearrangements of budgets, the use of reserve funds and/or financial reserves. The problem is the ambiguity in determining what a 'necessary important task' is and according to whom. Four actions to improve the intergovernmental transfer system that Viet Nam may consider are:

- *Revise the intergovernmental transfer system* so that transfers can be determined as objectively as possible by introducing some formula and avoiding political negotiations. The formula should be transparent, based on credible factors and as simple as possible. Transfers could be decided by a quasi-independent experts body (i.e. a grants commission), or by some formal system of central-local committees. The transfers could be relatively stable from year to year to permit rational subnational budgeting but should also be flexible enough to avoid compromising national finances. Viet Nam may wish to set the total level of transfers as a fixed proportion of total central government revenues and periodically revised this level, for example every three years.
- *Clarify what 'necessary important tasks' mean.* Viet Nam could follow the World Bank's (2014) recommendation to redraft or eliminate Article 36 (3) of the 2002 SBL (that is, Articule 40 (3) in the 2015 SBL) as it gives room to interpretation and provides no obligation for the higher level budget to provide funds for the "necessary important tasks". As the World Bank (2014: 74) points out, this should take place in the context of a system of intergovernmental transfers, based on transparent formulae and criteria. Both levels of government should agree on what a 'necessary important task' is and what is needed to face it but this is not always the case. Viet Nam could establish some criteria to define it, lowering urban poverty levels, or bridging housing gaps. The SBL does not mention any special transfer to large urban or metropolitan areas.
- *Use equalisation or balancing transfers more efficiently*. Balancing grants aim to enable subnational governments to provide an average package of services at roughly the same tax effort. Balancing can be directed at compensation of low tax capacity or high service costs. Vietnamese authorities can achieve this in an efficient way via horizontal grants between subnational jurisdictions and additions or subtractions from general purpose grants that are given for financing purposes. However, Viet Nam should avoid full compensation of differences in tax or service capacity as it may compromise the incentive to expand the tax base. High tax-back rates should also be avoided (World Bank, 2014).[6]

- *Develop a metropolitan strategy while restructuring the intergovernmental transfer system.* This would mean taking special provisions for weaning its main metropolitan areas from transfers while ensuring that they have sufficient authority to tax and impose user charges. The idea is not to stop transfers completely as there will always be externalities to reckon with, but grants can be reduced dramatically. This would imply designing an asymmetric transfer system with metropolitan areas treated under a different regime than other local governments. The resulting revenue loss to metropolitan areas would be compensated by increasing taxing powers. This would allow central government to direct the grants to local governments that require more assistance (Bahl et. al., 2013).

Subnational governments need to make better use of borrowing

Local governments are legally allowed to mobilise capital from issuing local governments bonds and from other legal borrowing, but in practice this is very limited, depending upon central government approval and unclear regulations. Provinces are allowed to issue bonds for up to 30% of the value of the investment project. Local governments are allowed to borrow up to 30% of their capital budget but regulations on local deficits are not stated. Special provisions for borrowing by the two largest urban areas allow that Ho Chi Minh City and Hanoi can borrow up to 150% and 100% of their capital budget respectively (OECD/UCLG, 2016). Local governments cannot borrow to cover the debt service.

Viet Nam needs to make better use of borrowing and should facilitate its use by subnational governments under continuous monitoring of central government. Borrowing is arguably the most efficient way to pay for public assets that have a long life and generate revenue. By matching payment for infrastructure with the time pattern of benefits received, governments can capture the return from infrastructure investments while deferring the payment (Bahl et al., 2013: 21). Limiting the possibility of SNGs to borrow from capital markets prevents many local governments from accessing extra funding to finance infrastructure. Viet Nam may consider easing the limits for issuing bonds and borrowing for those subnational governments that have a strong base of own-source financing. A critical aspect for Viet Nam to consider is to impose a hard budget constraint on borrowers, to eliminate the possibility of a costly bailout by higher levels of government. A central-government-mandated borrowing framework would need to be issued with clear rules about who can borrow, how much, for what purpose, from whom, with what instruments and with what restrictions. The central government would have the task of monitoring compliance with the framework. Finally, providing loans to local governments for the renewal of urban infrastructure through central government programmes is a viable way to overcome the lack of funding. However, as Mexico's and Turkey's experiences suggest, it may require a specific institution providing technical and financial support to subnational governments. Such an institution could also help make project selection and prioritisation more transparent. Mexico's BANOBRAS (National Bank of Works and Public Services)[7] and Turkey's IlBank (Bank of Provinces)[8] are examples of development banks that provide financing to local governments for investment projects and that could be of inspiration to Viet Nam. These banks finance public investment in infrastructure and public services that contribute to social development and competitiveness.

Viet Nam finances infrastructure projects through ODA

Viet Nam's policies for Official Development Assistance (ODA) have been changing sharply. To date, an important proportion of the urban infrastructure in Viet Nam has been financed with ODA. The country is the biggest receptor of ODA in South East Asia, receiving since 2006 more than half of the total ODA for infrastructure in the region (almost 2% of Viet Nam's GDP) (Figure 4.4). Nevertheless, ODA resources have been decreasing in the last years as the country is reaching middle income levels. In 2015, ODA to infrastructure fell 9% annually while the average to the rest of Southeast Asian countries increased 26% (OECD, 2017). In the coming time, Vietnam has to switch to using mainly preferential loans and proceeding to borrow in full according to market conditions. Local budgets will also need to increase the rate of re-lending instead of being granted as before. In 2017, the central government issued a decree (No. 52/2017 / ND-CP) on relending the government's foreign loan capital to the People's Committees of provinces and cities and set conditions on provincial People's Committees to re-borrow from ODA and preferential loans. More than 50% of the ODA that Viet Nam receives goes to transport, followed by investments in energy production, and water (Figure 4.5). Given the fact that ODA resources are getting scarce, Viet Nam will need to develop ODA projects in policy areas that are more strategically urgent, such as in urban rail transport and flood protection (see Chapter 2 and 3).

Figure 4.4. ODA for infrastructure in Southeast Asia, percentage by countries, 2006-2015

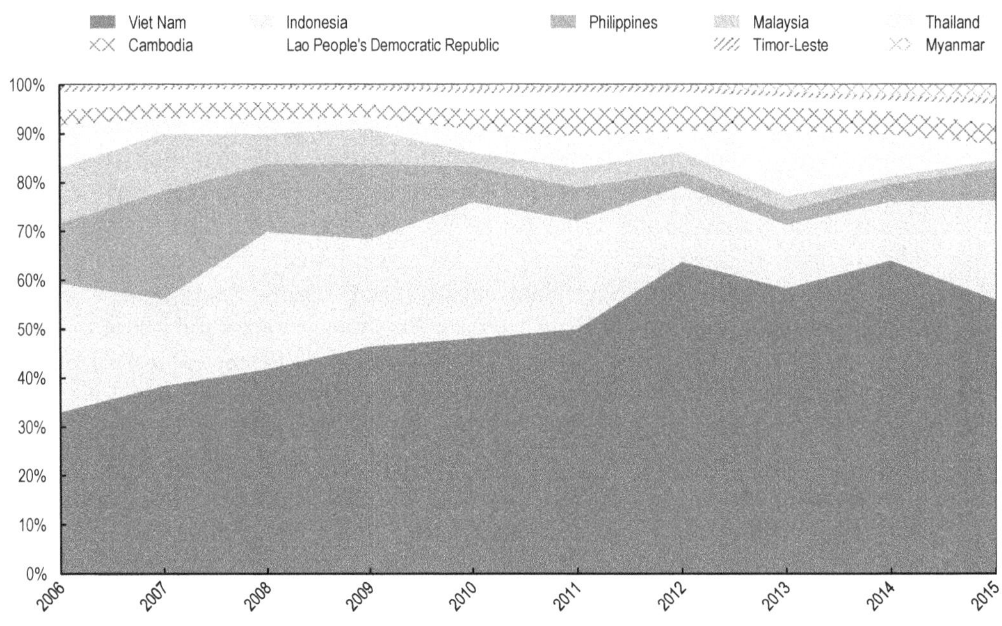

Source: OECD (2017), "Creditor Reporting System: Aid activities targeting Global Environmental Objectives", *OECD International Development Statistics* (database), http://dx.doi.org/10.1787/9c778247-en.

Another important consideration is that these international supports tend to have benefitted only large cities. An OECD study shows that capital cities concentrated 40.1% of environment-related official development finance (ODF) committed to cities in ASEAN-5 countries in 2002-14, although they concentrated only 15.9% of the total urban population (OECD, 2016d). In Viet Nam, Ha Noi and Ho Chi Minh City account for 46.1% of environment-related ODF committed to Vietnamese cities. In comparison, secondary cities are "left behind", or are not the object of major targeted projects supported by international aid. For example, Hai Phong received only 2% (OECD, 2016d). Given the growing inequality in the levels of urban infrastructure across cities, The Vietnamese government may wish to work together with subnational governments and develop a strategy to channel ODA to cities that are rapidly growing and struggling for financing their public service infrastructure. In this respect, the Vietnamese government could also engage in Decentralised Development Cooperation (DDC), which is increasingly considered a key tool to promote ODA and non-ODA collaboration among cities of various size, and in particular it allows developing peer to peer learning activities, transfer of technology and know-how, knowledge and good practice exchange (OECD, 2018 forthcoming).

Figure 4.5. ODA for infrastructure in Viet Nam, percentage by sector, 2006-2015

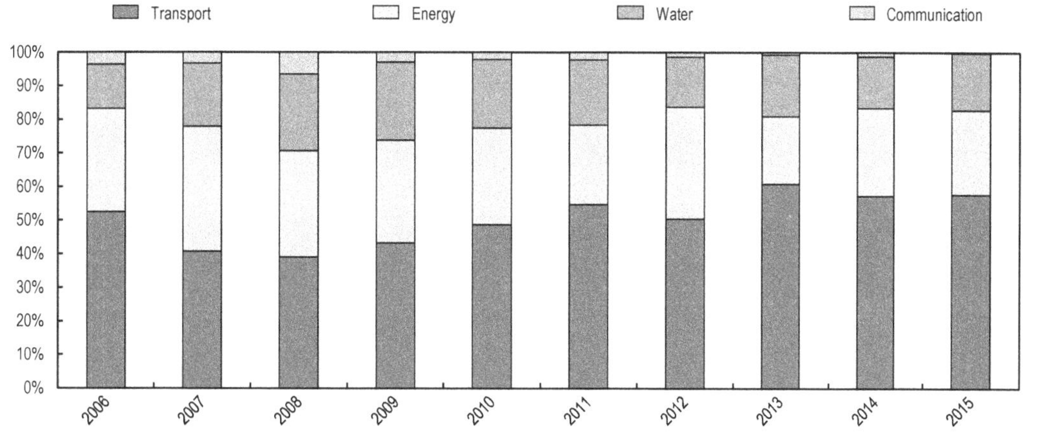

Source: OECD (2017), "Creditor Reporting System: Aid activities targeting Global Environmental Objectives", *OECD International Development Statistics* (database), http://dx.doi.org/10.1787/9c778247-en.

Improving capacity

National and subnational governments experience critical capacity gaps

Vietnamese public service faces a fundamental challenge: how to attract, retain and motivate high performing people into the civil service at national and subnational levels of government. Many attractive opportunities outside the public service may lure qualified and talented people away from the public administration. This situation creates the risks of leaving the civil service, particularly at subnational levels, under-qualified, and under-motivated. One consequence has been the impossibility of Vietnamese government to use and reflect the policy advice offered by international agencies on urban development strategies in laws, decrees and ordinances. For cities, this situation is of particular relevance because the lack of technical knowledge and experience of public servants to implement urban policies undermines the level of quality and coverage of public services and the effective and efficient use of resources. Some factors that may explain this situation are: the existence of a lean management policy, the inadequacy of the recruitment process, the low levels of remuneration, adequate training, and the little opportunities for local governments to adapt their workforce to their own needs.

As a whole, the public service seems to be understaffed and there is a lean management policy

The OECD team working for this review could not have access to data on public employment levels at national and subnational levels. However, interviews for this review highlighted that the public service as a whole is understaffed, and the problem becomes more acute at subnational levels. For example, the Urban Development Agency operates with only 20 specialists that work on the whole country and is reportedly underfinanced and lacks enough data and information to check the projects submitted by local governments. Subnational governments, in particular cities at provincial and intermediate level, reported the lack of budget to hire new people and their difficulties in getting the personnel with the right profile. It is possible to assume that cities at commune level have the same problems. It is surprising that, as Figure 4.6 shows, subnational government staff expenditure represents almost 90% of expenditure in public employees in general government.[9] This suggests that most of the public workforce is located in subnational governments, which are the main public employers in the country.

Figure 4.6. Subnational government staff expenditure as a percentage of total public staff expenditure and GDP

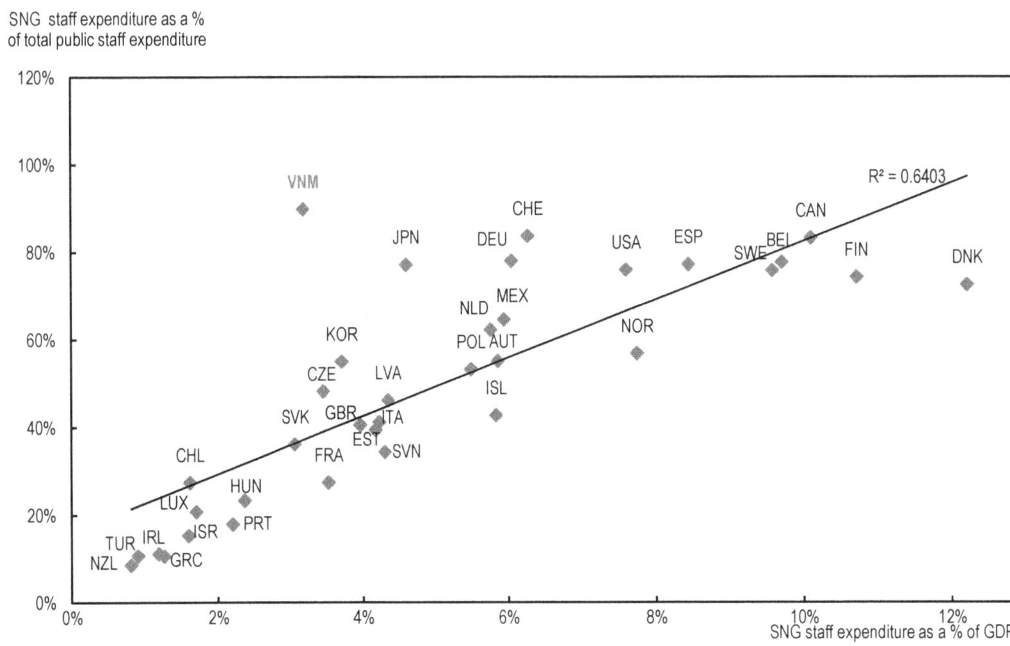

Source: OECD elaboration.

The national government has adopted a lean management policy. This is understandable in terms of reduced budgets, but Vietnamese authorities would be well-advised to consider some messages from the experience of OECD countries. First, shrinking staffs imperil the mission of national and city governments if there is a lack of strategy. If a lean public service policy is not accompanied by changes on how the public administration (and its agencies) operates, then public services will be affected as staff will be overworked and the ability of public organisations to achieve their organisational missions such as the effective delivery of public services is generally affected. Experience suggests that arbitrary staff cuts are generally restored within five to ten years if the public's demand for services is not reduced or if no change in the operational delivery modes is undertaken (OECD, 2011). Second, the moral of staff will be negatively impacted due to high levels of anxiety. For example, in Canada and Australia in the 1990s, the human resource aspects of cutbacks were not given sufficient attention and significant efforts were needed to restore morale and capacity. Third, downsizing may also reduce the capacity for organisational learning and knowledge management as it happened in the United States during the 2000s. Finally, in such conditions, the best staff tends to leave first, and the public sector ends up with the least productive people. In addition, when the government starts hiring again, it has to train people and devote scare resources to hiring procedures. Without a clear strategy that considers the government as a whole, the negative impact of downsizing will outweigh any possible benefit that the lean management policy may bring.

The understaffing problem is exacerbated due to fixed headcount/personnel quotation. And this is applied across the board in the Vietnamese public sector at all levels of government. While this provision may be of use to stabilise and control the level of public employment, it does not facilitate the active restructuring of the public services as national government and cities may not have the possibility to recruit much needed skilled staff.

Cities have serious management and technical knowledge deficit

Across the Vietnamese cities, the process of organising, assigning jobs and promoting civil servants could be refined. In several city organisations, many good staff have not been encouraged to and assigned appropriate tasks, many unqualified staff have not been replaced, leading to understaffing of competent personnel. In some cases, staff allocation is not tailored to the structure of administrative departments. Interviews for this review revealed that people with expertise are not in management positions and that the capacity of urban management staff is limited. Cities like Ha Noi, Da Lat, Hai Phong, Can Tho, Tan An, and Tam Ky reported the lack of management experience, lack of vocational training, and the limited capacity for consistent urban planning which is leading to ineffective policy-making and advisory processes. The city of Tan An lacks civil engineers and architects. Cities also need to improve their capacity to manage investments. It is worth noting that several cities like Tam Ky and Hai Phong are looking for ways to improve their capacity to design and implement green growth strategies and projects on ecological preservation. Large cities like Ha Noi also lack staff with updated knowledge in public finances and with experience in the management of investment projects. Graduates from local universities do not always have the necessary skills and knowledge.

Public sector salaries, in general, need to be more competitive to attract and retain highly trained staff

Information provided for this review suggests that there is a lack of high-quality and well remunerated jobs in both national and sub-national levels of government. The salary structure for civil servants includes a range of allowances, bonuses and additional income beyond the basic survey, the basic salary accounting for only 30% of total remuneration (World Bank, 2010). There is a perceived mismatch between salaries in the public and private sectors; private sector salaries in average are higher and this does not give public employees the incentives to do their best (Koh, *et. al*. 2009). Central government decides on the salary levels, the basic salary is the same everywhere in the government but the benefits are different. Salaries in the private sector could be three times higher than in the public sector. A professional urban planner or economist could earn USD 200 per month in the public sector. This could have important implications for the civil service in cities such as brain drain and increasing the temptation for civil servants to enrich themselves outside the rules. A salary step increase is too small to have an impact on motivation. Vietnamese authorities may wish to consider four actions in this respect.

- First, allowing higher salaries for vulnerable or highly specialised positions, and making salaries commensurate with risks and with market alternatives, can mitigate one factor that contributes to corruption and may be an incentive to attract qualified candidates.

- Second, cities, with the support of the central government, could make the salary scales simpler, by targeting increases on the skills profiles for which salaries are most out of line, or by matching salary increases with reduction in the number of state employees. This measure could be piloted in large cities and eventually transferred to intermediate and commune level cities.
- Third, making salary increases selective, and matching them to improved qualifications, skills or responsibilities rather than length of service could have a more positive effect to improve motivation and recognition.
- And fourth, full delegation of pay settings to local governments to adapt them to their particular needs could also be explored by the central government as part of the decentralisation process. This process could begin with a pilot test in the provincial-level cities.

The recruitment process should be merit based and focus more on skills and competences

Entry-level recruitment suffers from untrained interviewers and opaque evaluation criteria and recruitment results, creating extra-legal opportunities for recruitment. The recruitment of non-entry level positions is based on grade promotion examinations, but the merit orientation is undermined by the lack of competition from external candidates, which is a common weakness in career-based system such as Viet Nam's (OECD, 2005). For non-entry positions in particular, greater competition and transparency, and more openness to external competition, could increase the pool of applicants and help to bring in fresh ideas from outside the public service (World Bank, 2010). According to Decree No. 24/2010/ND-CP, the recruitment of civil servants must be based on job requirements, positions and payroll quotas of civil servant-employing agencies. The process for recruitment comprises of three stages: i) recruiting agencies publicly announce the vacancies; ii) recruitment examination: general knowledge to test candidates' understanding of the political system, State's laws and policies in the relevant domain; professional knowledge and foreign language; iii) the final decision is based on the academic records and interview.

The Law on Cadres and Civil Servants has adopted the principle of meritocracy, but translating it into concrete recruitment and managerial processes is a challenge for city authorities as often people with the right skills and knowledge are not being recruited. Interviews for this review revealed that although entry level recruitment is based on competitive examinations and personal interviews, there is much emphasis on theory and knowledge, with relative little attention to experience, competencies, skills or appropriateness of those skills for the position. As the experience of Hai Phong in public employment suggests, the assessment of individuals' drive for results is weak (OECD, 2016e). Training and upgrading of the civil servants is only at an initial stage. Sometimes the content is not fully relevant to civil servants' job. The curricula are not practical and there is too much emphasis on theories and too little on the training of skills relevant to the job. The performance of staff improves only a little after training. The requirement to obtain all formal qualifications (foreign language, computer skills, political training etc) has led to a situation where staff, by all means, try to become eligible to take recruitment or promotion exams. However, they may be incompetent although they have all formal qualifications. Thus, recruitment and promotion should focus more on skills and competencies rather than formal qualifications. A certification of competencies could be a way forward to ensure that all experience acquired is being put into practice and acknowledged as it is done in Belgium (OECD, 2007).

To increase capacity, the public workforce needs to be restructured strategically

Viet Nam's public service, at central and subnational levels, has the challenge to increase capacity and improving productivity of the workforce while controlling staffing costs. This is not an easy balance to achieve. However, some actions that Vietnamese authorities could take in this respect are:

- *Invest in developing capacity for strategic workforce planning.* This remains an underused instrument in Viet Nam and one of the most needed in the face of tight budgets, lean management and caps on the civil service. Workforce planning is an essential tool for anticipating possible future developments and maintaining a well-structure workforce of an appropriate size, which is able to meet the changing needs of the public service in a cost efficient manner. One basic step for Viet Nam is to keep a record and a data base of the number of staff in all levels of government to know what it has. This is essential to track the number of employees, costs and competences. Workforce planning is not necessarily the same as central or top-down planning. Adequate workforce planning can be developed in any organisation, centralised or decentralised, and by any level of government. At the very least, the Ministry of Home Affairs should have the responsibility to: i) track numbers of employees, costs and competencies; and ii) develop a framework for holding ministries and agencies accountable for workforce planning and, at a later stage, to SNGs. If workforce planning is to be effective, flexibility is needed in managing the pool of workers. Workforce planning need not be overly sophisticated, particularly when there is little or no experience. However, the approach given to Viet Nam's workforce planning strategy will depend on its own particular priorities. In general, OECD countries are using one or a combination of the approaches presented in Box 4.4.

Box 4.4. Approaches to workforce planning

Workforce approach: examines the current workforce and occupations and projects the number and characteristics of jobs and the number of employees needed to fill them at a specific point in future. It looks at issues such as what jobs exist, the number of people performing each job, the reporting relationship of these jobs, how essential each job is, and the characteristics of anticipated jobs.

Workload approach: focuses on the amount and type of work the organisation anticipates handling at a specific point in the future, and uses this information to project the number of resources (people and skills) needed to perform that work.

Competency approach: identifies sets of competencies aligned with the organisation's mission, vision, and strategic goals. This approach assumes the organisation has already considered workforce and workload and can focus not only on the number of people, but the competencies employees must master for organisational success.

Source: International Personnel Management Association (2002), "Workforce Planning Resource Guide for Public Sector Human Resource Professionals", www.ipma-hr.org.

- *Increase managerial flexibility by delegating human resource management responsibilities to subnational governments.* To help subnational governments, in particular district and communal level cities, to adapt their workforce to better meet their needs, the central government could delegate to them responsibility for HRM, to increase managerial flexibility and improve their performance and responsiveness. The district and communal people's committees would be in a better position to meet their duties if they were given the possibility to adapt the public workforce to their business needs, adjusting working conditions and even levels of remuneration. A complete delegation of authority for HRM may not be needed, but subnational governments should at least be given the option to determine how many employees they need, and which mix of skills they have. Another function that could be delegated is not recruiting as such, but the specification of the required competencies and criteria, which is essential to complement workforce planning. Staff training and development could also be handed down, since these constitute normal management functions. The central government might, however, want to establish minimum standards for recruitment, selection criteria and competency frameworks. All subnational governments also need to be able to motivate their employees: to reward them for good performance and behaviour and to sanction misconduct and unsatisfactory behaviour. This can be achieved in many different ways, but some control over monetary rewards is probably indispensable.
- *Enhance the training and competence management of central and subnational civil servants.* Training courses for civil servants on issues such as municipal governance, local budgets, inter-budgetary relations, personnel management, tax collection and administration, management of urban infrastructure and interaction with citizens could help bridge the gap between existing skills and the competencies needed to implement urban policies and programmes. The training programmes should ensure that civil servants have the right mix of skills and expertise to deliver effective services and avoid providing training on issues unrelated to the job. Beyond accrediting the technical knowledge, the Ministry of Home Affairs and the corresponding departments at subnational levels should provide their staff with formal and informal training to develop their skills. The Ministry of Home Affairs has a training centre where it prepares training materials for the provinces which should be used for this purpose. The managerial capacity of cities could be supported by strengthening the use of ITC in local governments' activities for public service delivery. In particular, the Viet Nam Urban Planning and Development Association could assume a key role in the training of urban specialist from cities and even in the certification of competences for urban management (Box 4.5). Cities' public servants could receive training on administrative services to improve institutional capacity to provide reliable and better quality of information as well as procedural improvements to reach a better quality of services, for example on land use certificates delivery. Land use planning courses should have an initial focus on procedures and techniques for civil servants to involve citizens at the early planning stage before decisions on how to use the land have been taken, and improving site clearance planning and implementation. This would respond to cities demands for techniques to reduce conflicts and avoid force evictions. Training courses should focus on techniques and models developed and tested in Viet Nam.

- *Professionalise the human resource management function at all levels of government.* The management of the public workforce has to be entrusted to human resource management (HRM) professionals. The Ministry of Home Affairs and its counterparts in subnational levels need to be staffed with experts. So far, HRM departments are in the hands of personnel whose understanding of HRM is limited to the daily paper work. Most of these staff will need to be retrained to acquire the skills necessary to modernise the management of the public workforce. In some cases, they might be reallocated to areas where tasks are more in line with their skills. This could open the opportunity to bring in people with more modern skills to senior positions. Regional centres for training of HRM staff could be created to train staff from district and rural levels where there is limited capacity to implement HRM policy reforms.

Box 4.5. Viet Nam Urban Planning and Development Association

The Viet Nam Urban Planning and Development Association (VUPDA) is a professional organisation of experts on urban planning and development. It was established in 1996 and has over seven thousand members. It has its own legal status, account and press organ. VUPDA represents Viet Nam in international forums and associations working in the same field. VUPDA operates nationwide to assist subnational governments to comply with the rules prescribed by the laws related to sustainable urban development. It specialises in providing advice on the management of large cities.

VUPDA works on the areas of urban and rural planning, architecture design of urban landscape, urban management and environmental protection, among others. It provides consulting and advisory services to local governments to implement the tasks assigned by the State. It conducts scientific research in urban planning and development. The national government frequently ask for VUPDA's opinion on several infrastructure projects. One of its functions is to disseminate knowledge, experience and laws to improve people's knowledge and understanding of urban planning and development. It organises training courses in urban development and management, and organises exchanges and co-operation with international organisations and foreign experts.

Source: Vietnam Urban Planning and Development Association (VUPDA) (2014), The International Symposium on City Planning – Vietnam 2014, Main Theme: Prospect of Planning for Megacity Region, Hanoi, http://vupda.org/iscp2014/vupda/.

Transparency and corruption are major obstacles to effective urban governance

Participation of citizens in local political activities and decision-making is crucial for the improvement of public governance. The 2016 Provincial Governance and Public Administration Performance Index (PAPI) Report suggested that the citizen participation and oversight in Viet Nam are not only low in local elections but also in public investment project, design and implementations (Box 4.6 and Figure 4.7). Among the five centrally run cities, only Can Tho was in the top performing group, Ha Noi and Da Nang were in the low-average performing group whereas Hai Phong and Ho Chi Minh City were in the poorest performing group, lower than the average score of other provinces. This indicates a need for innovative approaches to engage citizens in city management and planning.

Box 4.6. Viet Nam Provincial Governance and Public Administration Performance Index (PAPI)

The Vietnam Provincial Governance and Public Administration Performance Index (PAPI) is a policy monitoring tool that reflects citizen experiences with central to local governments in performing their governance, public administration and public service delivery functions. PAPI helps create motivation for public officials, civil servants and public employees at different levels and in different sectors to perform better in public sector management and public service delivery. PAPI ranks the performance of Vietnamese cities based on people's answers to a survey. Cities are assessed in six areas: i) participation at local levels; ii) transparency; iii) vertical accountability; iv) control of corruption in the public sector; v) public administration procedures; and vi) public service delivery.

Source: CECODES, VFF-CRT and UNDP (2017), "The Viet Nam Governance and Public Administration Performance Index (PAPI) 2016: Measuring Citizens' Experiences", A Joint Policy Research Paper by CECODES, VFF-CRT and UNDP. Ha Noi.

Figure 4.7. Governance and public administration performance in Viet Nam's major cities and provinces

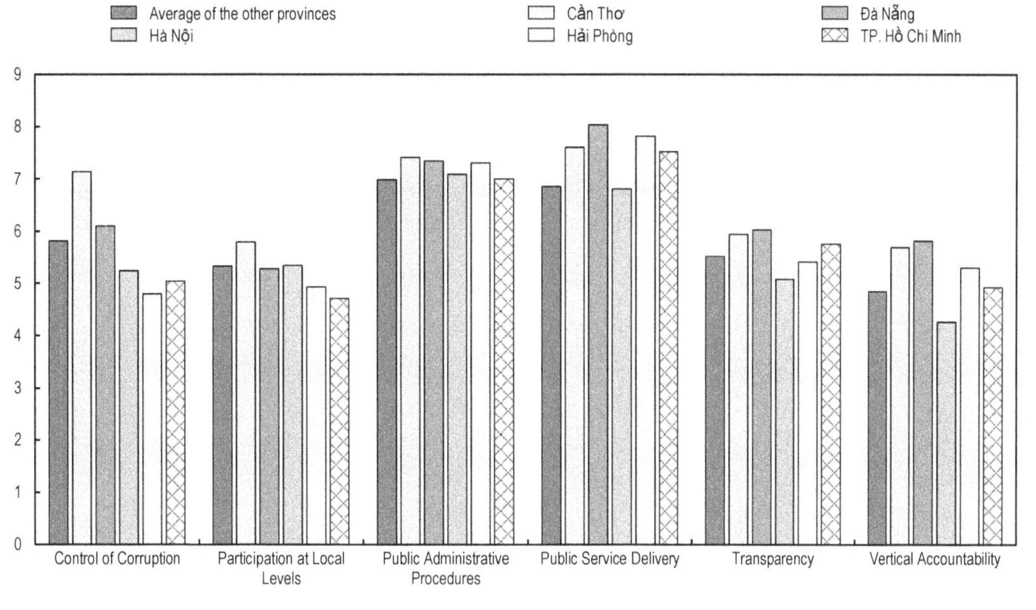

Source: CECODES, VFF-CRT and UNDP (2017), "The Viet Nam Governance and Public Administration Performance Index (PAPI) 2016: Measuring Citizens' Experiences", A Joint Policy Research Paper by CECODES, VFF-CRT and UNDP, Ha Noi.

Transparency remains the second biggest challenge in public governance in Vietnam, yet slightly improved in 2016. Part of the explanation for this improvement could be that citizens began to have more access to the land-use plans and government land compensation framework. While governments in other biggest cities are doing relatively well to improve its transparency, Hanoi has been performing poorer since 2012. With the problems of nepotism in state employment, bribery in the public sector and the lack of willingness to fight corruption persisting, the hope for a cleaner and more efficient state apparatus seems to be increasingly harder to achieve in Viet Nam. Three out of five centrally governed municipalities (i.e. Hanoi, Hai Phong and Ho Chi Minh City) performed weaker in control of corruption than the average of other provinces. Notably, Hanoi has stayed in the poorest performing groups in this governance aspect since 2011. The efforts of Vietnamese central and local governments in promoting better public administrative procedure scored positive result in 2016 such as streamlining the construction permits procedures. Although public service delivery has been improved overtime nationwide, the centrally governed cities still stay ahead of other provinces, except for the particular case of Ha Noi. A possible explanation would be that centrally governed cities have more autonomy in the management of their resources and deciding on investment projects. That is the reason why some cities aim to be upgraded to be under direct central government supervision.

Tackling corruption is an area that remains a challenge in Viet Nam. Corruption is the second most problematic factor in Viet Nam for doing business according to the World Economic Forum (2013c). Irregular payments and bribes, burden of government regulations and transparency of policy-making are areas where national and sub-national governments have large opportunities for improvement and by doing so improving competitiveness. Controlling petty corruption in provision of public healthcare and primary education services remains a challenge for city authorities. Citizens are more likely to be requested to pay bribes when applying for land use rights certificates, using public district hospital services and applying for jobs in the public sector (Huyen, 2014).

Tackling corruption in the public sector is important because if Vietnamese cities continue operating in a context of corruption and poor governance, it will limit cities abilities and opportunities to achieve their goals on poverty alleviation, economic and social development, social cohesion, environmental sustainability, among others. For that reason, it is important that for every urban development goal or aspiration Vietnamese urban practitioners, policy-makers and advocates require the challenge of corruption to be included and addressed.

Building trust in government is a must to enhance urban development

Citizens' participation, transparency and control of corruption are key challenges faced by the Vietnamese public administration according to the Public Administration Performance Index. This is damaging the trust in public institutions and public officials. Therefore, one way forward is to restore trust in government. For that purpose Viet Nam may wish to consider analysing in detail the following options:

- *Ensure sustained political commitment to ethical behaviour*. Its absence would make any efforts to encourage good behaviour be in vain. Across OECD countries, the attempts to improve public sector ethics have been sponsored at the highest political levels reflected in, for example, the OECD Council Recommendation on Public Integrity (2017c), the framework for assessing public sector integrity (OECD, 2005b), and the OECD guidelines for managing conflict of interest in the public service (OECD, 2004).
- *Establish workable codes of conduct*. They play a vital role in stating the expected standards of behaviour, particularly when countries adopt a more managerial style of public administration. Viet Nam may adopt a broad public service code of conduct from which individual agencies and levels of government design a purpose-built code to reflect their particular objectives and mission.

- *Set an ethics co-ordinating body.* These take various forms – parliamentary committees, central agencies, or specially created bodies – and assume various functions: "general promoter" of public sector ethics like in Norway; "counsellor and advisor" like in the United States and Canada; or "watchdog" like in France.
- *Install accountability mechanisms.* They should encourage behaviour by making unethical activities hard to commit and easy to detect. Accountability mechanisms should set guidelines for government activities, for checking that results have been achieved, and for checking that the due procedure has been observed.

Notes

1. Viet Nam has Construction Plans at the subnational scale, including for Ha Noi Capital Region, Ho Chi Minh City Region, Tay Nguyen (highland) Region, and for Northern Midlands and Mountains Region. Besides, Viet Nam has Masterplan for socio-economic development for the Red River Delta, Mekong River Delta, Central Coast and Southeast.
2. For further information see: www.government.se/government-agencies/swedish-national-board-of-housing-building-and-planning/.
3. See for example Belgium's Inter-ministerial Conference for the Environment www.health.belgium.be/en/interministerial-conference-environment-ice.
4. According to the 2015 SBL and its guiding documents, the policies, regimes and standards on state budget expenditures are all issued by the central government and implemented uniformly throughout the country. All state budget revenues are concentrated in the State Treasury and collected by the state budget collection agency. All State budget expenditures shall be made only when there are estimates already assigned by competent authorities and according to the spending regimes, criteria and norms prescribed by competent state agencies.
5. The fiscal gap is an estimate of how much the government's spending and debt obligations exceed its revenues over a specified period of time. It is calculated as a means of quantifying long-term fiscal debt sustainability. For further information see: www.pgpf.org/blog/2016/06/what-is-the-fiscal-gap
6. Taxpayers can often get a tax-back or tax refund, on their income tax if the tax they owe is less than the sum of the total amount of the withholding taxes and estimated taxes that they paid, plus the refundable tax credits that they claim. Tax refunds are money given back at the end of the year. https://en.wikipedia.org/wiki/Tax_refund
7. For further information on BANOBRAS, see: www.banobras.gob.mx/quienessomos/Paginas/Inicio.aspx.
8. For further information on IlBank, see: www.ilbank.gov.tr/.
9. General government includes four sectors: central/federal government and related sectors; federated government (states) and related public entities; local government, i.e. regional and local governments, and related public entities; and social security funds. Subnational government is defined as the sum of state governments and local/regional governments.

References

Bahl, R., J. Linn, D. Wetzel (2013) (eds.), "Governing and financing metropolitan areas in the developing world", in *Financing Metropolitan Governments in Developing Countries*, Lincoln Institute of Land Policy, Cambridge, Massachusetts.

Bergvall, D. et al. (2006), "Intergovernmental Transfers and Decentralised Public Spending", *OECD Working Papers on Fiscal Federalism,* No. 3, OECD Publishing. http://dx.doi.org/10.1787/5k97b11z2hxw-en.

Centre for Community Support and Development Studies (CECODES), Centre for Research and Training of the Viet Nam Fatherland Front (VFF-CRT), and United Nations Development Programme (UNDP) (2017), "The Viet Nam Governance and Public Administration Performance Index (PAPI) 2016: Measuring Citizens' Experiences", Joint Policy Research Paper by CECODES, VFF-CRT and UNDP, Ha Noi.

Charbit, C. (2011), "Governance of Public Policies in Decentralised Contexts: The Multi-level Approach", *OECD Regional Development Working Papers*, 2011/04, OECD Publishing, Paris, http://dx.doi.org/10.1787/5kg883pkxkhc-en.

Charbit, C. and M. Michalun (2009), "Mind the Gaps: Managing Mutual Dependence in Relations among Levels of Government", *OECD Working Papers on Public Governance*, No. 14, OECD Publishing, Paris, http://dx.doi.org/10.1787/221253707200.

CEMR (2013), "Urban-rural partnership – CEMR survey on integrated territorial development", Council of European Municipalities and Regions, www.ccre.org/docs/cemr_survey_urban_rural_relationship_en.pdf.

Dudek, C.M. (2005), "Coordinating regional policy in the EU", Department of Political Science, Hofstra University, http://aei.pitt.edu/3170/1/Regional_Policy_Paper-Dudek1-1.pdf.

Federal Ministry of Transport, Building and Urban Development (2012), Urban-Rural Partnerships. Growth and innovation through cooperation, Berlin.

Finding, S. (2015), "Who governs Britain – democracy in action? Directly elected mayors in England", *Cahiers du MIMMOC*, http://mimmoc.revues.org/2288.

Fritzen, S. (2006), "Probing system limits: Decentralisation and local political accountability in Viet Nam", *Asia-Pacific Journal of Public Administration*, Vol. 28(1), pp.1-24.

Government of the Czech Republic (2010), "Principles of Urban Policy", Ministry for Regional Development, www.mmr.cz/getmedia/f333120b-88d5-4bd8-bec9-dd58a26f9812/principles_of_urban_policy.pdf?ext=.pdf.

Government of Viet Nam (2015), Law on Organizing the Local Government, No. 77/2015/QH13, The National Assembly.

Government of Viet Nam (2015), State Budget Law No. 83/2015/QH13, The National Assembly.

Huyen, Do (2014), "A Tale of Five Cities: How centrally governed municipalities fair in citizens' assessment of governance performance", *Vietnam Law and Legal Forum*, UNDP Vietnam, July-August, pp. 9-14, 47, www.academia.edu/8039106/a_tale_of_five_cities_how_centrally_governed_municipalities_fair_in_citizens_assessment_of_governance_performance.

International Personnel Management Association (2002), "Workforce Planning Resource Guide for Public Sector Human Resource Professionals", www.ipma-hr.org.

Koh, D., D. Du Dam, and T.K.C. Nguyen (2009), "Government organization structure and excellent public services: the case of Ciet Nam and some recommendations for change" in UNDP (2009), *Reforming Public Administration in Vietnam, Current situation and Recommendations*, The National Political Publishing House, http://www.vn.undp.org/content/vietnam/en/home/library/democratic_governance/reforming-public-administration-in-viet-nam--current-situation-a.html.

Konrad-Adenauer Foundation and The Association of Cities of Vietnam (ACVN) (2009), "People's Participation and Local Governance – challenges and opportunities for municipalities", www.kas.de/wf/doc/kas_17873-1522-2-30.pdf?091019054634.

Laegrid, P., A. Dyrnes Nordo and L.H. Rykkja (2013), "The quality of coordination in the Norwegian central government: the importance of coordination arrangements and structural, cultural and demographic factors", *COCOPS Working Paper No. 14*, European Commission, European Research Area, www.cocops.eu/wp-content/uploads/2013/12/Working-Paper-no.-14.pdf.

McLure, C., and J. Martínez-Vazquez (2000), "The assignment of revenues and expenditures in intergovernmental fiscal relations", The World Bank, Washington DC, http://www1.worldbank.org/publicsector/pe/PEAMMarch2005/AssignmentRevenues.pdf.

OECD/UCLG (2016), "Subnational governments around the world: Structure and Finance", OECD, Paris, www.oecd.org/regional/regional-policy/sngs-around-the-world.htm.

OECD (2018, forthcoming), *Decentralised Development Co-operation: Financial Flows, Emerging Trends, and Innovative Paradigms*, OECD Publishing, Paris.

OECD (2017a), *Multi-level Governance Reforms: Overview of OECD Country Experiences*, OECD Multi-level Governance Studies, OECD Publishing, Paris, http://dx.doi.org/10.1787/9789264272866-en.

OECD (2017b), *OECD Urban Policy Reviews: Kazakhstan*, OECD Publishing, Paris, http://dx.doi.org/10.1787/9789264268852-en.

OECD (2017c), *OECD Recommendation of the Council on Public Integrity*, www.oecd.org/gov/ethics/recommendation-public-integrity.pdf.

OECD (2017), "Creditor Reporting System: Aid activities targeting Global Environmental Objectives", *OECD International Development Statistics* (database), http://dx.doi.org/10.1787/9c778247-en.

OECD (2016a), *OECD Regions at a Glance 2016*, OECD Publishing, Paris, http://dx.doi.org/10.1787/reg_glance-2016-en.

OECD (2016b), *OECD Regional Outlook 2016: Productive Regions for Inclusive Societies*, OECD Publishing, Paris, http://dx.doi.org/10.1787/9789264260245-en.

OECD (2016c), *Making the Most of Public Investment in Colombia: Working Effectively across Levels of Government*, OECD Multi-level Governance Studies, OECD Publishing, Paris. http://dx.doi.org/10.1787/9789264265288-en.

OECD (2016d), *Urban Green Growth in Dynamic Asia*, OECD Green Growth Studies, OECD Publishing, Paris, http://dx.doi.org/10.1787/9789264266360-en.

OECD (2016e), *Green Growth in Hai Phong, Viet Nam*, OECD Green Growth Studies, OECD Publishing, Paris, http://dx.doi.org/10.1787/9789264260207-en.

OECD (2015a), *Governing the City*, OECD Publishing, Paris, http://dx.doi.org/10.1787/9789264226500-en.

OECD (2015b), *The Metropolitan Century: Understanding Urbanisation and its Consequences*, OECD Publishing, Paris, http://dx.doi.org/10.1787/9789264228733-en.

OECD (2015c), *OECD Urban Policy Reviews: Mexico 2015: Transforming Urban Policy and Housing Finance*; OECD Publishing, Paris, http://dx.doi.org/10.1787/9789264227293-en.

OECD (2014), *Recommendation of the Council on Effective Public Investment Across Levels of Government*, Adopted on 12 March 2014, www.oecd.org/regional/regional-policy/Principles-Public-Investment.pdf and www.oecd.org/effective-public-investment-toolkit/.

OECD (2012), *Value for Money in Government: Denmark 2011*, OECD Publishing, Paris, http://dx.doi.org/10.1787/9789264130746-en.

OECD (2011), *Public Servants as Partners for Growth: Toward a Stronger, Leaner and More Equitable Workforce*, OECD Publishing, Paris, http://dx.doi.org/10.1787/9789264166707-en.

OECD (2007), *OECD Reviews of Human Resource Management in Government: Belgium 2007: Brussels-Capital Region, Federal Government, Flemish Government, French Community, Walloon Region*, OECD Publishing, Paris, http://dx.doi.org/10.1787/9789264038202-en.

OECD (2005a), *Modernising Government: The Way Forward*, OECD Publishing, Paris, http://dx.doi.org/10.1787/9789264010505-en.

OECD (2005b), "Public sector integrity – a framework for assessment", Paris.

OECD (2004), "OECD Guidelines for Managing Conflict of Interest in the Public Service", in *Managing Conflict of Interest in the Public Service: OECD Guidelines and Country Experiences*, OECD Publishing, Paris, http://dx.doi.org/10.1787/9789264104938-2-en.

Smoke, P. (2013), "Metropolitan Cities in the National Fiscal and Institutional Structure", in Bahl, R. Linn, J. and Wetzel, D. (eds) (2013), *Financing Metropolitan Governments in Developing Countries*, The Lincoln Institute of Land Policy, Massachusetts, pp. 57-84

Urban Development Agency, Ministry of Construction (2012), Viet Nam Urban Forum, Hanoi, www.geoviet.vn/FM/GetFile.aspx?ID=a2167cb2-8b36-4015-9af4-b68ca64d0db2 (accessed 20 June 2017).

Vietnam Urban Planning and Development Association (VUPDA) (2014), The International Symposium on City Planning – Vietnam 2014, Main Theme: Prospect of Planning for Megacity Region, Hanoi, http://vupda.org/iscp2014/vupda/.

Von Braun, J. (2014), "Urbanization and Decentralization: The changing urban-rural linkages and opportunities of decentralization of services", Paper for the 54th European Regional Science Association Congress (ERSA), St. Petersburg, August 26-29. https://ideas.repec.org/p/wiw/wiwrsa/ersa14p841.html .

Work, R. (2002), "Overview of Decentralisation Worldwide: a stepping stone to improve governance and human development". UNDP, second International Conference on "Decentralisation: Federalism: The Future of Decentralizing States?" 25-27 July, Manila, Philippines, www.cities-localgovernments.org/committees/dal/Upload/library/overviewofdecentralisationworldwide_work_2002.pdf.

World Bank (2014), "Revising Viet Nam's State Budget Law (2002): Proposals Drawing on International Experience. Policy Note", http://documents.worldbank.org/curated/en/236951468176957875/pdf/918820wp0p12870sept020140final0eng0.pdf.

World Bank (2010), "3Vietnam Development Report 2010 – Modern Institutions", The World Bank, www-wds.worldbank.org/external/default/wdscontentserver/wdsp/ib/2010/03/19/000333037_20100319004055/rendered/pdf/535730wp0p11221ng0reduced0file0size.pdf.

World Economic Forum, (2013c), "Vietnam country profile", www3.weforum.org/docs/GCR2014-15/Vietnam.pdf (accessed December 2017).

ORGANISATION FOR ECONOMIC CO-OPERATION AND DEVELOPMENT

The OECD is a unique forum where governments work together to address the economic, social and environmental challenges of globalisation. The OECD is also at the forefront of efforts to understand and to help governments respond to new developments and concerns, such as corporate governance, the information economy and the challenges of an ageing population. The Organisation provides a setting where governments can compare policy experiences, seek answers to common problems, identify good practice and work to co-ordinate domestic and international policies.

The OECD member countries are: Australia, Austria, Belgium, Canada, Chile, the Czech Republic, Denmark, Estonia, Finland, France, Germany, Greece, Hungary, Iceland, Ireland, Israel, Italy, Japan, Korea, Latvia, Luxembourg, Mexico, the Netherlands, New Zealand, Norway, Poland, Portugal, the Slovak Republic, Slovenia, Spain, Sweden, Switzerland, Turkey, the United Kingdom and the United States. The European Union takes part in the work of the OECD.

OECD Publishing disseminates widely the results of the Organisation's statistics gathering and research on economic, social and environmental issues, as well as the conventions, guidelines and standards agreed by its members.

OECD PUBLISHING, 2, rue André-Pascal, 75775 PARIS CEDEX 16
(04 2017 13 1 P) ISBN 978-92-64-28609-2 – 2018

www.ingramcontent.com/pod-product-compliance
Lightning Source LLC
Chambersburg PA
CBHW061212240926
51846CB00006B/1198
* 9 7 8 9 2 6 4 2 8 6 0 9 2 *